ON BEING
A MUSLIM

Oᴛʜᴇʀ ʙᴏᴏᴋs ᴏɴ Iꜱʟᴀᴍɪᴄ Sᴛᴜᴅɪᴇꜱ ᴘᴜʙʟɪꜱʜᴇᴅ ʙʏ Oɴᴇᴡᴏʀʟᴅ

The Qur'an: A Beginner's Guide, Farid Esack, ISBN 978–1–85168–624–7
Qur'an, Liberation and Pluralism, Farid Esack, ISBN 978–1–85168–121–1
Speaking in God's Name, Khaled Abou El Fadl, ISBN 978–1–85168–262–1
Sexual Ethics and Islam, Kecia Ali, ISBN 978–1–85168–456–4
Progressive Muslims, Omid Safi, ISBN 978–1–85168–316–1
Shari'ah Law, Mohammad Hashim Kamali, ISBN 978–1–85168–565–3
Hadith, Jonathan A.C. Brown, ISBN 978–1–85168–663–6
Inside the Gender Jihad, Amina Wadud, ISBN 978–1–85168–463–2

ON BEING
A MUSLIM

finding a religious path in the world today

FARID ESACK

ONEWORLD
OXFORD

ON BEING A MUSLIM

First published by Oneworld Publications, 1999
Reprinted 2002, 2005
First published in trade paperback, 2009
Reprinted 2010

Copyright © Farid Esack 1999

ISBN 978–1–85168–691–9

Cover design by James Nunn
Printed and bound by Thomson-Shore, Inc. USA

Oneworld Publications
UK: 185 Banbury Road, Oxford, OX2 7AR, England
USA: 38 Greene Street, 4th Floor, New York, NY 10013, USA
www.oneworld-publications.com

For Tasmia and Moosa,
Muhammed, Tahirah
and Ayesha

CONTENTS

ACKNOWLEDGEMENTS

On Being a Muslim has a long history and numerous people have had a hand in it. I offer my sincere gratitude to the following:

To Brother Norman Wray who gave me the support to dig up stories from early Islam and to make them come alive for the kids at St Patrick's Technical High School in Karachi.

To Yusuf Patel who first encouraged the idea of putting all my *Al Qalam* columns together.

To Rabi‘ah Terri Harris and Sohail Nakhooda who, in their work to have many of these essays published in *As-Salamu Alaikum* (New York) and *Islamica* (London), first led me to believe that someone outside South Africa may want to read what I have to say.

To Tahir Sitoto, Wiedaad Dollie, Nasiema Cassiem, Faizel Ismail, Kim Eliot, Nader Hashemi and Firdawsa Wahi for their useful and critical comments on the manuscript. While copies of manuscripts which they returned to me with their scribblings eventually ended up in the bin, I did consider their comments carefully and believe that it has substantially improved the quality of this work.

To my dear friend Ruwayda Hendrickse, who was initially going to be the only reader of the manuscript. Her raw honesty ('Farid, this is not a book that I want to see your name on; it's so bad, I don't know where to begin making suggestions for improvements') compelled me to send the manuscript off to all these other folk. (Ruwayda, blame it on all of the folks above, if you still think so after reading through it.)

To Juliet Mabey and Helen Coward of Oneworld Publications, for their editorial comments and for the gracious way they put up with my interminable delays.

To Sisa Maboza, my wonderful research assistant, for invaluable back-up in just about everything and for feeding my fish.

To the *Mail & Guardian*, *Cape Times* and *Sunday Independent* (South Africa) for permission to use previously published articles.

To all the people who have walked into – and occasionally over – my life and whose stories I tell in this book. (And I'm praying that my royalties will cover the defamation suits.)

And finally, to Allah, also for always being there (with 'always' meaning 'always', without it always feeling like that).

*If the last hour strikes
and finds you carrying a sapling
to the grove for planting,
go ahead and plant it.*

Prophet Muhammad (Peace be upon him)

INTRODUCTION

why were you not Zusya?

A rabbi disappears from his synagogue for a few hours every Day of Atonement. One of his followers suspects that he is secretly meeting the Almighty, and follows him. He watches as the rabbi puts on coarse peasant clothes and cares for an invalid woman in a cottage, cleaning her room and preparing food for her. The follower goes back to the synagogue. When he is asked, 'Did the rabbi ascend to heaven?' he replies, 'If not higher.'

Isaac Loeb Peretz, *If Not Higher*

WHAT'S THE BOTTOM LINE IN THIS BOOK?

There is an exciting and challenging wind of relevance blowing through the world of Islam. Numerous Muslims, especially among the young, are keen to know how Islam relates to our here and now. Many responses have been forthcoming as a part of this wind of relevance: these are often vague, repetitive, superficial and, at times, even alarming. Some of these responses are alarming not only to those who desire to be unfettered in their march to entrench their control over the global economy but also to many Muslims who value social justice and personal freedom. Alhamdulillah (Praise be to Allah), of the latter breed there is a growing band.

The more strident, angry and fanatical[1] displays of this revival receive a great deal of attention. This should not, however, detract from the genuineness of the 'new Muslim'. This Muslim is new in the sense that she is adamant that a stagnant and fossilized Islam confined to a set of rituals that are mere motions must make way for a personally meaningful and socially relevant Islam. Those of us who are deeply committed to a human and compassionate expression of our faith cannot allow ourselves to be swamped by the noise of religious obscurantism and the equally destructive caricaturing in some sections of the media of the whole of Islam as a threat to civilized values.

Much of the emphasis in contemporary works on Islam by committed Muslims has hitherto been on the more obviously ideological aspects of Islam. These works usually cater for those who simply see Islam as an alternative to the universal colonization of consciousness through a process of relentless McDonaldization, the accompanying destruction of local cultures and economic exploitation. Two other factors have contributed to the sharp, rather angry and often dehumanizing image of Islam. These are the suffering endured by Muslims in several parts of the world such as in Palestine, Chechnya, the Balkans and Kashmir, and a simplistic recourse to our religious heritage as both our safe haven and the mother of all weapons.

I believe that there is a path between dehumanizing fundamentalism and fossilized traditionalism. This is a path of a radical Islam committed to social justice, to individual liberty and the quest for the Transcendent who is beyond all institutional religious and dogmatic constructions; an Islam that challenges us to examine our faith in personally and socially relevant terms. This Islam, I believe, provides a set of personal responses in an increasingly materialistic society where most people are living, and very many dying, lives of quiet desperation with a frightening sense of alienation from themselves, others and Allah. Muslims *can* make an effective contribution alongside those of other religious convictions to the creation of a world wherein it is safe to be human.

One of the things that often distinguishes religious groups from other ideological groups is our commitment to personal introspection. We struggle not only to examine the socio-economic structures that create and entrench oppression but also to examine our personal roles in, as well as reactions to, them. We ask questions such as 'How do we relate to our faith in concrete terms?', 'How do we become "witness bearers for Allah" in an unjust society?', 'How do we strengthen ourselves in a common commitment to establish a just order on earth?' and 'How do we commit ourselves to others in an atmosphere of honesty and acceptance?' Our personal responses to these questions are, in the final analysis, the only barometer of our commitment to a holistic Islam.

It must, however, be emphasized that this re-examination or reviewing of our faith in personal terms cannot be done in isolation from the struggle to work against unjust socio-economic systems. Islam was never nurtured in a protective hothouse; the history of early Islam was a continuous struggle of socio-political engagement, introspection, revelation and more engagement.

And so the bottom line in this book is a comprehensive commitment to personal growth through involvement alongside others in a struggle to create a more humane and just world where people are truly free to make Allah the centre of their lives.

WHERE DOES THIS BOOK COME FROM?

On Being a Muslim has a long history, and this is reflected in the seeming unevenness of this work. During the seventies I started writing little essays to form position papers for workshops and retreats with adolescents in Pakistan, where I was a student of Islamic theology. Much later, I developed these into a manual on personal growth, *The Review of Faith*, in the Call of Islam, a South African organization committed to the struggle for a non-racial, non-sexist and democratic society.[2] The material therein formed the basis of many ideas elaborated upon in my regular column in *Al Qalam*, a South African Muslim monthly.

In the mid-1970s, Brother Norman Wray, a La Salle brother who was the Principal of St Patrick's Technical High School in Karachi, invited me to take charge of Islamic Studies at the school and to transform it into a programme of discussions, camps and excursions. It was in those groups that I first became acquainted with the struggle to relate Islam to, initially, our day-to-day realities and, later on, the struggle for a more humane society in Pakistan. Those were difficult days without a similar programme known to us, at a time when I was just emerging from a long night of spiritual anguish and emotional trauma. Two elements saw me and our core group through it all: the support and encouragement of a dear friend and brother, Moosa Desai, along with some Pakistani students of mine, and the support from Breakthrough, a group of young Christians in Karachi.

It wasn't that Moosa knew anything about group dynamics. In fact, his only involvement with any group was with the Tablighi Jama'ah, a conservative Muslim revivalist movement.[3] It was his ability to accept others as they were and his personal warmth that would allow the most clammed-up ones to venture into sharing themselves. I remember how the most difficult students would be assigned to his group for reflections and sharing. While I was 'Sir Farid' to the students, he was 'Moosa Bhai' (Brother Moosa). This was, of course, quite valuable even though it had its awkward moments. On one occasion I had to leave the group midway through a weekend programme and left them in what I thought were Moosa's responsible hands. Upon my return, Jan Blom, the Father Guardian of the Franciscan Seminary where we conducted our retreats, complained bitterly about how 'your people were caught busy with the coconut trees'. I explained with embarassment that the person whom I had left in charge of the group must have slipped off for a brief while, leaving the students free for their mischief. 'No,' Jan Blom replied, 'he was the one with the long stick trying to get the coconuts down!' Moosa's ability to blend with those with whom he worked was respon- sible for gaining the trust of many a young person; some of whom, like myself, had never trusted anyone until then.

Along with Moosa, I found the active support of some senior students deeply meaningful in developing a programme for critical and personal engagement with Islam and society. Sohail Salimuddin, Zulfiqar Selanie, Adil Khan, Najam Zahir Khan and the late Sayed Junaid Baghdadi were tremendous in the way they supported their fellow students and those who came after them in the numerous pro- grammes which we organized.

As I said, the other element that encouraged our search for a mean- ingful Islam was the presence of young Christians in a group called Breakthrough. Norman Wray, Bernadette Menezes, Derrick Dean, Lucia Gomes, Kenny Fernandes and others were engaged in their own struggle with their faith, seeking expression in the Pakistani battle for justice. Although I was very active in the Tablighi Jama'ah at that stage, I found the very existence of this group a source of much strength and encouragement and I shared many wonderful years of reflection with them. The companionship which they offered me did much to enable me to retain my faith as a Muslim. This was, after all, a time when I was studying at an institution that was to produce some of the leading figures in a group which later made a rather embarrassing appearance on the stage of political Islam, the Afghan Taliban.

My Pakistan experience affected my approach to Islam in several significant ways.

First, my own keeping the faith was in large measure due to being touched by the humanity of the religious other. This means that I am determined to find a space in my own theology for those who are not Muslim, yet are deeply committed to seeing the grace and compassion of an All-Loving Creator expressed in the righteous and caring works of ordinary men and women.

Second, the struggle of so many young Christians to relate their faith to concrete issues of justice and the involvement of the clergy in liberation movements in South Africa, Latin America, the Philippines and elsewhere forced me to re-examine the social relevance of my faith. 'Wisdom', as the hadith says, 'is the lost property of the believer, we retrieve it from wherever it comes.' If this wisdom is the product of involvement with the *mustad'afun fi'l-ard* (the downtrodden in the earth), in this case, Christians in Pakistan, then it is far more valuable than that produced by the enthralling theological gymnastics of the 'ulama (clerics) of the court. (Regrettably, we do not have a shortage of the latter in Islam.)

Third, my involvement with 'the Islamic Movement' through another group wherein I was active, Ittihad al-Tulaba al-Muslimin (Muslim Students' Union), in Pakistan made me realize how one can be totally committed to Islam and yet not have it touch one's inner being. This involvement also made me realize how one can be involved with others on a training programme for days and yet not be touched by any of them in a deeply personal and human way. The brothers in the movement were terribly excited when I introduced them to the more personable aspects of religious reflections that I developed in my work at school and incorporated into their programme. However, I never felt free to tell them about my gallivanting with the Christians in Breakthrough; they seemed too anti-everyone-other-than-ourselves.

Upon my return to South Africa, the Muslim Youth Movement, with which I was involved for a brief while, encouraged me to put some of these ideas on paper. The ideas, however, came alive when a few close

friends and I formed an *usrah* (literally family), a small group committed to reflection and to each other's personal and spiritual growth. The
involvement of that group in the South African struggle for justice
through a movement that we formed, the Call of Islam, afforded us a
new perspective of the vision and responsibility of the compassionate
Muslim in a racist and sexist society. Adli Jacobs, Ebrahim Rasool and
Shamil Manie were the other members of that group and though we
have each long since gone our own ways, their footprints lie all over
this work as they lie indelibly over my growth. I lived and grew with
them; wrote down the living and the growing; had it discussed with
prayers, laughter and tears.

After I parted company with the Call of Islam in 1989 and spent a
few years in England and Germany, I found the time to rethink many
of those ideas. I subsequently had a number of essays published in *Al
Qalam*, as well as in *As-Salamu Alaikum* and *Islamica*, regular publications produced in Johannesburg, New York and London
respectively. Various friends encouraged me to rework them in a collection
for wider dissemination.

WHAT DOES THIS BOOK DEAL WITH?

Sometimes, when one of my more unpleasant sides steps to the front,
my friends wonder if I'm really the guy who wrote this stuff. I too
wonder sometimes. I too am struggling to live alongside the ideas
expressed herein. I offer them to you as a co-struggler who has experienced, and who still is experiencing, all the joys and pain of trying to
actualize the will of Allah in personal and socio-political terms. My
consolation is that Allah will not question us about whether we
succeeded or not, but only as to how hard we tried.

There is a Hasidic legend that Rabbi Zusya said shortly before his
death, 'In the world to come I shall not be asked: "Why were you not
Moses?" I shall be asked: "Why were you not Zusya?"'

While all creative work is autobiographical, this work is unashamedly
so; it deals with the struggle to be a Muslim in this day and age, but it
essentially reflects my struggle and those with whom I have interacted.
I have been inspired by the primary sources of Muslim religious life,
the Qur'an and the example of the Prophet Muhammad (Peace and

blessings be upon him). I have simultaneously, and again unashamedly, utilized these to justify deeply cherished beliefs. And it is impossible to say whether the justification came before the inspiration or the other way around. This refusal to place the one before the other and the inter-connectedness of doing and thinking, in other words praxis as the basis for theory, characterize every page.

While each chapter has a neat heading trying to force different themes into respectable square blocks, little else is neat about my cate-gories, for there is nothing which is purely spiritual or purely political, purely this-worldly or purely other-worldly, purely self or purely other.

As my understanding of the enormous suffering of our people under apartheid South Africa grew, I became increasingly aware that there was a close relationship between those who emphasized 'spirituality' and collaboration in the system of oppression on the one hand, and those who did not make a big fuss about spirituality and participation in the struggle for liberation, on the other. How many were there who insisted that their path was one of 'spiritual reformation' and that they had nothing to do with 'politics' but who, in private, and occasionally not so privately, actively supported the apartheid regime? Spirituality without politics, I increasingly understood, was far from being neutral; quite the contrary, it was, and is, invariably supportive of oppressive socio-economic systems.

And so this work is, in many ways, about a South African engaged in the struggle for justice and trying to relate that struggle to his Islam. I am, however, also a post-apartheid South African, struggling to remain true to my religious heritage and invoking the best in it for the attainment of a truly non-racial and non-sexist South Africa. The strug-gle to live as a child of the times in a liberated society and to be committed to Islam is incredibly difficult if you take your theological heritage seriously. Every answer seems to be accompanied by a multi-tude of questions. I believe that the questions and perspectives experienced here can be useful for Muslims elsewhere, even if only in opening up the possibilities for critical questioning within the context of remaining faithful.

My own experience in the South African struggle has alerted me to the many dimensions of the endeavour to create a better world. I have experienced the way in which it is possible to address every struggle while ignoring the many struggles within oneself, the battles between oneself and others, and the wars between what one really believes and what one actually does. Few in our community are willing and able to deal with these battles in a sensitive and creative manner, yet they ravage numerous souls. Unlike the physical scars that a police baton or quirt leaves one with, our emotional scars are largely unattended and we have enormous difficulty talking about them. And so I commit some of my own insights into all of these issues into your trust.

ONE

on being with Allah

> And if My servants ask you about Me – behold, I am near; I
> respond to the call of the one who calls whenever he calls unto
> Me; let them then respond unto me and believe in Me; so that they
> may be guided.
>
> Qur'an 2:186

Belief in the existence and unity of Allah, the Transcendent, is central
to the life of a Muslim and the Qur'an places much emphasis on cultivating a relationship with Allah as a living and caring God to whom all
humankind will return and to whom we are all accountable. The presence of Allah in the world and ultimate accountability to Him[1] are
absolute assumptions for virtually all Muslims. I say, 'virtually all'
because, notwithstanding theological definitions of a 'muslim',[2] the
ummah (universal community of Muslims) is not without its children
who have, unannounced, walked away from their faith in Allah while
holding on to many of the cultural trappings of the religious community
of Muslims.

Most Muslims experience and give expression to this faith in Allah
through a range of religious practices and verbal utterances, and in the
way in which they seek refuge in the ultimate when personal, natural or
social calamities strike. Others, equally sincere, are desperate actually
to make sense of the presence of Allah in a world where, seemingly,
evil so often triumphs over good. While a religious life filled only with
rituals may be meaningful for some, many others whose faith is in
search of integrity cannot avoid the questions thrown up by being alive
to the world and all its challenges.

The Sufi tradition in Islam, acknowledging the limitations of religious life confined to ideology, laws and rituals, is one that has made a vibrant relationship with Allah and leading a God-conscious life the centre of its quest. Despite the seeming preponderance of the somewhat colder face of Islam, the vast majority of ordinary believers throughout the world still revere much of the Sufi tradition. At the most widely practised level, though, this has regrettably been reduced to a new set of folk rituals, with a focus on saints and other holy men as the primary means of reaching closeness to the Prophet (Peace be upon him), who is expected to intercede with Allah.

Our lives as Muslims are largely devoid of an ongoing and living connection with Allah. We confine this relationship to moments of personal difficulty, have it mediated through a professional class of religious figures – the managers of the sacred – or to the formal rituals of the five daily prayers, the pilgrimage to Mecca and fasting in the month of Ramadan. Absent is the warmth evident from the following *hadith qudsi* (a saying of Allah, in the words of the Prophet):

> When a servant of Mine seeks to approach Me through that which I like out of what I have made obligatory upon him [her] and continues to advance towards Me through voluntary effort beyond the prescribed, then I begin to love him [her]. When I Love him [her] I become the ears by which [s]he hears, the eyes by which [s]he sees, and the hands by which [s]he grasps, and the feet with which [s]he walks. When [s]he asks Me I bestow upon him [her] and when [s]he seeks My protection, I Protect him [her].[3]

Given the emphasis on this relationship in the Qur'an, and the insistence that Allah is the focus of a believer's life, most of this chapter deals with this relationship rather than the rituals which serve as the means to cultivate and express it.

The chapter starts with a rather personal account of wrestling with the presence of Allah during a visit to Mecca, and then deals with the way we often project our 'selves' on to Allah, and how we end up really seeing mirror images of our often ugly selves. The struggle for an authentic spirituality accompanied by righteous works and the need to avoid simplistic answers is then discussed.

Besides the pilgrimage to Mecca, the other two acts of devotion that virtually every Muslim is obliged to fulfil are the five daily prayers and the fast of the month of Ramadan. The last part of this chapter considers some of the challenges presented by these and suggests ways in which they can become more meaningful.

The relationship with Allah dealt with in this chapter is often uncomfortable, and I discuss it in the full awareness that many of us prefer to bury this discomfort. Despite the occasional funny or even flippant twist to my narratives, I do not regard this discomfort or wrestling with Allah lightly. I do, however, believe that in my own uttering of it I develop a deeper insight into it. In so doing, others may also understand their struggles a bit better. Hopefully, we can all respond in ways that take us closer to Allah.

CAN ALLAH BE SUPREMELY INDIFFERENT?

'Is Allah?', 'Is Allah a He?', 'Is He all powerful?', 'If He is all powerful can He make a stone so heavy that He is unable to move it?', 'Where is Allah?', 'Is He omnipresent?', 'If one takes everything that exists in the heaven and the earth and calls it "the whole", then that would also include Allah, wouldn't it?' 'Well, if that is the case, then is He smaller than "the whole"?', 'If He is, then will He still be Allah?' These are the kinds of questions that have dabbled with me since I was a kid.

They're OK, possibly even funny to some. If, however, you look at a three-year-old child dying of Aids and you also believe in an All-Powerful God, then the questions take a more serious turn. 'If He is, then why the silence in the face of suffering?' If Allah is a He then what does it say at the end of the day about the worth of the theological gymnastics that gender-sensitive Muslims engage in to make their Islam more palatable?

Many years ago a friend, Ashiek, who regularly questioned me on matters of faith, told me: 'Farid, I often feel that you answer me well, but that that answer is meant for me and that you yourself are far from satisfied with it.' I've come a little further in my quest for honesty since then and, mercifully, have stopped viewing myself as an answering machine.

Many of us who do take Allah seriously have been desperate for answers to questions that tear at our selves, and do not understand why

He watches us being destroyed by the absence of answers. How often have I not screamed at Allah: 'Do something!' (And as Nader, citing an anonymous source, tells me: 'I once heard a young man screaming at God for letting young children starve until he realized the starving children were God screaming at him for letting it happen.')

You have said: 'These are the days that we interspersed in between (the lives) of humankind that Allah may know those who [truly] believe and those among you who take witnesses [besides Him]' (Q. 3:140). OK, so now you have caught me out as 'one who takes witnesses besides you'. Oh no, I never bowed in front of an idol but there are many other gods – academic ladders, sex, power, prestige. 'So, here I am in front of you, I, a lousy hypocrite; so do something! Don't just leave me like this!' How often have I not stood in Medina at the grave of Muhammad, our shepherd and, like a lost sheep, begged to be found and returned to the flock?

Here follows my narration of one such encounter with Allah, who, at that time, appeared to be the Supremely Indifferent. It was in Mecca, the 'Mother of Cities' and the place that houses the Ka'bah, the small black cloth-covered cube-shaped construction referred to in the Qur'an as the 'first house determined for humankind' (Q. 3:96). For Muslims, a visit to Mecca is often the fulfilment of a lifelong dream. For some, as my story shows, the rewarding consequences and fulfilment coming from such a visit are often obscured and delayed.

Pepsi Shows the Way [4]

Mecca is referred to in the Qur'an as the *ma'ad*, the place of return (Q. 28:85). I had undertaken my first journey there some years ago and it was meant to be a journey 'home' before the ultimate journey 'home' (the Qur'an also describes all of life as part of this return to Allah, e.g., Q. 2:285; 3:38). For Muslims, a journey to Mecca is also an encounter with our roots; genealogical, religious and spiritual. It is in some ways a return to our genealogical roots because Adam and Eve (Peace be upon them) dwelt on the plains of the Mountain of 'Arafah, located there, after their departure from Paradise. It is a return to our religious roots because the Cave of Hira', where the Prophet Muhammad (Peace be upon him) encountered his first revelation, is the physical point of the beginning of Islam as a religion. Lastly, it is a return to our spiritual roots, because the Ka'bah is the symbol of the presence of Allah, the House of Allah.

I approached Mecca with a mixture of feelings. Social conditioning: the many tales of experiences of 'hearts overflowing' told by returning pilgrims compelling me to just 'feel the greatness of the moment'; my secular disposition militating against this and beckoning me to be calm; the *nafs al-lawwamah* (berating self) mockingly chiding: 'Are you not ashamed of defiling the sacred soil of Mecca with your footprints?' Anyway, the journey had cost a good few hundred dollars and no taunts from a berating self were going to make me turn back.

One actually descends into the *haram* (sacred area) from the barren surrounding hills. And here the Ka'bah rose in its full majesty and glory. If only I, too, I thought, could descend into a seemingly barren self and cause a new being to come forth from a desolate soul. As Muhammad Iqbal, the Pakistani poet, said: 'Re-chisel then your ancient frame and build up a new being – such being, being real being, or else your ego is a mere ring of smoke.' I hoped again for the first time in many years. If this land in its barrenness can become the spring where so much of humankind come to be nourished, then there must be hope. A spring can yet flow from my existence of seeming nothingness and allow me to drink from it, so that I may become fully human and fully Muslim.

Clad in *ihram*, the simple two-piece cotton wrapping worn by all pilgrims, a money bag tied to my waist, my soul tied to the travellers' cheques and my physical body to my passport therein, I joined the multitude in approaching the *bait al-atiq* (ancient house). I became lost in the crowd. Is there then just no limit to the times that one can get lost? Getting lost to intellectual jargon, hobbies, organizations, causes, one's family, even to one's self? Will I ever be found and returned to 'its rightful owner'? Just this once – answer me! I won't ask any more questions after this! (Silence.)

Clinging to my booklet of *du'as* (prayers) I hurriedly completed the seven *tawafs* (circumambulations) around the Ka'bah, dutifully reciting the prescribed *du'a* for each particular round. However desperately needed, there was still no self-expression or erratic, even frenzied, crying from a mutilated self. Was my soul the victim of a conspiracy between the 'ulama (clergy) and that book vendor who sold me this collection of prescribed litanies? Was the written word again going to be the separating wall between me and my Sustainer? Was the eternal alliance between religion and capitalism being replayed here, destroying the innocent and vulnerable?

I was desperate to get the preliminaries over before reaching the Hajar-al-Aswad (Black Stone), a stone reportedly from heaven and placed in that spot by Muhammad, and then ultimately the *multazam*, the door of the Ka'bah. Before I knew it, my first set of circumambu-lations around the Ka'bah was complete – the first part of an emptying process, a burning out while rotating around the candle before being consumed by the flame. (Was I also following the advice of Jalal al-Din Rumi, who said: 'die before you die', even as I was returning to my place of return, Mecca, before my ultimate return to my Lord?)

I elbowed my way to the Black Stone, fervently hoping that it might absorb my blackness (this was long before I wondered about the equa-tion of sin with blackness), my burdensome title, power games, politico-religious position, eloquence and mess-ups. And then, still clinging to my book of litanies, money bag and passport, I reached the door. Somewhere, something arose from deep within me to destroy the conspiracy between the book vendor and the clergy which demanded that I respond from a prescribed text, and between the modernists and capitalists which demanded that I 'control my emotions'. Temporarily liberated, I lowered my small book and my orderly litanies gave way to uncontrolled weeping. And I remembered the anecdotes of return-ing South African pilgrims: 'Oh, you should have seen how the poor Pakistanis clung to the cloth of the Ka'bah; it was a sight for sore eyes.' I sobbed and only remember choking in a single expression: 'humiliated in Your presence'. For once, I was happy to be a 'poor Pakistani'.

There were others, too, who sobbed, but this was one time when a person wrapped up in him or herself didn't make a nasty little bundle; I was at His door. I wept bitterly, for my past, present and future, I wept for what I believed was an existence in mud and actually hoped that someone would come from inside the door. For a Muslim, there is no physical point, 'defiled' as he or she may be, beyond that door and there I had reached. The burden of that moment was shattering.

As if that wasn't enough . . . The silence that greeted me was deaf-ening in its loudness. There was no glimmer of the emergence of a new being after being consumed by the flame. I sat there, drained and fright-ened, after what appeared to be hours of choking in 'humiliated in Your presence'. With my emptiness and nothingness complete, I stumbled away, repeating to myself: 'What did He have in mind to subject me to this apparently divine indifference?'

Much later, a body returned to complete the obligatory two *raka'at* (prayer units) at the Maqam al-Mahmud, the place where Abraham (Peace be upon him) is said to have prayed (Q. 2:125). A body went to drink from the sacred Zam Zam well, a body went to run between the hills of Saffa and Marwah in imitation of Hagar (Peace be upon her), the Black wife of Abraham, a body went to the hotel, a body returned to the *haram* five times a day for three days and a body got on to a bus which dropped it at the foot of the Mount of Light.

It was on this mountain that the Prophet Muhammad's anguished heart found solace through revelation, after being shattered. And who knows? I can always take a try. Anyway, I had nothing to lose. Being in the heart of summer, and midday at that, there were no other bodies or souls around. Seven-year-old Musa looked at me quizzically for a few seconds before venturing to ask: 'Are you sure you don't want to wait till it is cooler?' 'Musa! Unlike your namesake in the Qur'an, I am not looking for a match or wood or fire. There is no flock awaiting me. I am alone and this journey is a matter of life and death for me. I want the mountain to be abandoned when I make my discovery. Musa, surely you understand all about these mountain trips?' The poor kid looked at me as if I was potty. (Not that he was very far off the mark, mind you.) I paid him for my bottle of spring water and started the ascent to the Cave of Hira'.

The Saudi regime, being very 'puritanical' and vehemently opposed to any form of 'unorthodox' veneration, does not encourage visits to any of the traditional sacred places. There are, thus, no official signs showing the path to the Cave of Hirah. You've got to follow the peo-ple. And if there are none around? Follow the Pepsi cans! Thousands and thousands of them, all along the route right up to the mouth of the cave, a few even littering its interior. What a sad spectacle! Along comes this 'follower' of Muhammad, his soul tied to Cook's American

Dollar travellers' cheques, following a Pepsi-littered path and he says
he is searching for Truth! Why don't you try another one, 'follower' of
Muhammad?

Let me not be unfair to attempts by Muslims to outline the path for
themselves. There were a few shoddily painted arrows pointing in the
same direction as the Pepsi cans. Whatever little use these attempts to
'outline the path' may have been, was neutralized by the fact that there,
in the same paint, in the same shoddy manner, were arrows pointing to
exactly opposite directions! As if my agony at having to exorcize a
thousand devils was not enough! As if having sheets of plastic ripped
off the heads of our people at five o'clock on a cold winter morning in
apartheid South Africa was not enough! As if having to mix sand with
flour and feeding our children with it was not enough![5] As if two
billion people going to bed on the floor or straw or dust at night, on
empty stomachs, was not enough! As if . . . And now, arrows pointing
in opposite directions!

I continued following the Pepsi cans.

The path was steep and the journey agonizing. Along the way I
noticed another guy with a Palestinian scarf next to him, fast asleep.
He, too, I said to myself, is a searcher. Let him also be. ('Also be'? And
since when did it dawn upon you to be?) I eventually reached the cave,
where I offered a lame two prayer units and studied the graffiti; the
many 'Galiema and Fatima was here – 1967' and the numerous public
declarations of love. I chuckled at the banality of it all and felt that perhaps there was nothing more to life than this.

So I have arrived and, well, if this is 'it' then so be it. Why not call
it quits? The one side of the Mount of Light is rather steep and I looked
down contemplating the time duration of my 'calling it quits'. In those
few seconds my existence flashed in front of me. Just before doing
what I wanted to do, I heard the voice of my fellow searcher, whom I
thought I had long since left behind. *'Bhai jan! Ap ki; taswir khenchi?
Sirf bis riyal hai?'* (My brother, can I take your photo? It will cost you
only twenty riyals) – as he smilingly uncovered his Kodak Instamatic
from the Palestinian scarf. He was in search of suckers.

I died my second death in as many days.

Some Sufis refer to 'the night of the spirit'. This was the culmina-
tion of my darkest night. I had been desperate to make sense of Islam

and my relationship with Allah and now, for the first time, everything seemed so perfectly pointless. Upon my return to South Africa a curious even if seemingly unremarkable thing happened. The extent of my spiritual crisis was so severe that I simply had to reach out to others, even if only to ensure my physical survival. I met on a regular basis with three other close friends, Adli, Shamil and Ebrahim, to discuss the question of our own spiritual emptiness and struggles to lead lives of submission to the will of Allah in a racially divided and economically exploited society. From that support and discussion group grew the Call of Islam, a movement that was to play a very significant role in ensuring that Muslims were an integral, even if often unwilling, part of the struggle for non-racialism and non-sexism in South Africa. For a number of years I found this movement and, more specifically, the founding group, deeply supportive in my wrestling with Allah and self. Through them I developed a new appreciation of the verse in the Qur'an: 'Those who struggle in Us [Our path], unto them We shall show them Our ways' (Q. 29:69).

And so it appears as if Allah does have ideas for us, but that He does not panic when we do . . . and that His ways are often so roundabout as to drive one around the bend . . . and sometimes nearly over the cliff.

BETWEEN ALLAH AND A NEUROTIC SELF

Like most writers and speakers, I usually discuss those issues wherein I am reasonably competent; in so doing, I do not run the risk of being hypocritical. For me, this means that I sincerely believe in the ideas that I espouse and that I am actually engaged in a serious attempt to live alongside them. This is perhaps why I tend to avoid what are commonly regarded as 'more spiritual matters' in my talks and writing. For someone who is also concerned about a comprehensive Islam this is not something that can be avoided indefinitely, however. Much of the Qur'an talks about the quest for the pleasure of Allah, the remembrance of Allah, the importance of the formal prayers (*salah*), self-purification, the journeying unto Allah, and a host of 'spiritual' matters which cannot be reduced to appendages of socio-religious activism.

Why, then, my reluctance to deal with these themes?

During my early childhood and well into my youth, I was regarded as 'deeply spiritual'; I was a mere ten years old when I commenced my formal religious commitment in the Tablighi Jama'ah. This path, on which I persisted rather stubbornly for eleven years, saw all my school holidays and most weekends being spent 'in the path of Allah', i.e., participating in the group's programmes. Nevertheless, I remained deeply unhappy and unfulfilled as a person. Looking back, I now know that spirituality for me was an escape from facing raw and unpleasant truths about myself. It took me years of desperation and a nervous breakdown to realize the truth of two sayings of the Prophet Muhammad (Peace be upon him): first, that 'actions are judged by their motivations' and second, that 'he who knows his self has come to know his Lord'.

In this context, the first hadith quite simply means that one cannot use Islam or its spirituality to run away from one's self; one needs to re-examine continuously the factors that truly drive one, and to do so with a substantial dose of honesty. While spirituality is for many a religiously sanctioned form of neurosis, it also has the potential to assist us as we confront our selves and our neurosis. Uncovering our motives will enable us to confront the truth about who we really are, and in this truth we will also come to know our Lord.

The second hadith has a number of very interesting readings. Besides suggesting that an authentic relationship with one's self will lead one to an authentic relationship with Allah, it also suggests that people construct images of Allah. I have always wondered about the way some Muslims from the Indo-Pak subcontinent seem to think that Allah is an Urdu-speaking Indian or Pakistani. Other examples of this projection include Pakistani cricketers falling on their knees in prostration, in gratitude to Allah after victory on the field; Diego Maradonna making the sign of the cross after having scored or George Bush praying with Billy Graham on the eve of his attack on Baghdad.

In truth, those of us committed to justice and pluralism seek an Allah who is just and inclusive and those committed to chauvinism and to narrow nationalism seek and, sadly, find a God who is a male – despite protestations of dogma to the contrary – Indian, Pakistani, American or Argentinian. This lends a bit of an unusual twist to the hadith that if you know your self then you know your Lord; in other words, you do not necessarily come to know Allah, but an entity who reflects who you are and your values. There is also another hadith that is even more explicit on the question of projection: 'Allah says: I am towards every servant as he conceives me to be'.

A number of thinkers have, of course, long argued that religion is essentially projection. While I have no doubt that it also, and mostly, functions as such, I do not believe that Allah or religion is only projection and that there is nothing beyond us and our material world. Given the little that we know of ourselves and our world, the inescapably marvellous in nature and the miracle of our existences, it would be rather foolish to claim definitively that whatever is out there is merely a reflection of what is in here.

The Qur'an has an interesting refrain to the question of projection: 'Allah is free from what they ascribe unto Him' (Q. 37:159; 43:82). In other words, all our doctrinal formulations and perceptions of Allah are just those; as for Allah, He is the eternally 'greater'. The *adhan* (call to prayer) commences with the statement *Allahu Akbar*, as does every change in the movements of the formal prayer. Allah is not the greatest, as this statement is often mistakenly translated, but simply 'greater' . . . greater than the prisons of any historical or religious community, greater than any soccer team or cricket club, greater than any of the sides in any war and greater than all of our projections. The invitation to Allah is thus one to transcendence, to go beyond ourselves.

Much of the Qur'an is devoted to drawing humankind's attention to Allah, the worshipping of Him, His omnipresence in the world, His care and concern for humankind, His characteristics and accountability to Him. The Qur'an emphasizes the idea of life as a continuous journey towards Allah and insists that Allah is above whatever people ascribe unto Him. The vast majority of Muslims, though, experience Allah only via the trappings of reified Islam and often as an afterthought; an all-powerful being to be invoked in appendages to everyday speech: *insha Allah* (God willing), *masha Allah* (as God pleased) or when disaster strikes.

So, Allah is, and Allah is greater. I do not know what all of this means, nor do I wish to justify it, but this is my first certainty. This presence of Allah in the world and in my life, whatever else it may be, is real enough for me to believe in. This belief, although it has not always sat comfortably with me, has served me well. Somehow, having had my face dragged through the bitter cold sleet in my night of the spirit, an ordeal which I recounted above, I never regained complete 'spiritual consciousness', the intensity of concentration in my prayers and the earnestness in my quest for Allah. I have never, furthermore, yearned for a return to those days. In my personal experience spirituality has always been conflated with being emotionally messed up. I simply had to find a more authentic way of living out my yearning for nearness to Allah. Wherever that would lead me, I would not be going along the path of those who felt that being with Allah was a safe alternative to being consciously and actively with Allah's family, the people.

I first met Amir Behram Izadyar in Tehran where he was a student of Islamic theology, trustworthy enough to be appointed as a guide for guests of the late Ayatollah Ruhullah Khomeini. Amir mouthed all the 'proper' responses to my many queries about the revolution and its slide into fascism. Underneath the well-rehearsed responses I sensed a real person wanting to break free and just be. Subsequently, in Washington DC where he became a student of international relations, I wanted to know how far he had come and where he was then. 'I don't know,' he said. 'What I do know is that human beings are a treasure from Allah and that we have to walk very carefully with this treasure.' This is my second certainty.

The Prophet Muhammad emphasized this sanctity of people when he asked his Companions if they knew who a pauper was. They replied that among them a pauper was one who had nothing, neither cash nor property. The Prophet then said: 'A pauper among my people is one who faces the Day of Judgement with a record of *salah*, fasts and *zakah* (wealth tax), but who will have abused this one, slandered that one, stole from a third, shed the blood of the fourth and physically assaulted the fifth' (Muslim).

ALLAH: MORE THAN AN IDEOLOGICAL APPENDAGE

I know of several really fine people who left Muslim groups that are committed to living out their Islam in the sphere of social activism because they felt that the programmes of these groups were 'not spiritual enough'. Some scholars, such as Dr Israr Ahmed from Pakistan, have even argued that the very basis of Muslim social activist organizations necessarily implies that Allah will forever be a marginal factor in their conscious organizational lives and programmes.

Most friends lamenting the lack of spirituality in these groups are hard pressed to define what exactly they mean by 'spiritual'. For most, though, it seems to imply some sort of living connection with Allah that enables one to feel an inner calm. This connection, it is usually suggested, can come from greater emphasis on the formal prayers, invocations, communal liturgical gatherings, etc. Others though, counter that our spirituality does not operate in a vacuum and that, for them, participating in a funeral for a victim of a racial murder or sharing a deeply fulfiling relationship were by themselves spiritually enriching.

I am more inclined to the latter view. There is, however, more to the story, even if it discomforts. In the words of the Qur'an, 'It is possible that you like something and yet it is not good for you' (Q. 2:216). How is it possible for a person who lives an integrated and balanced life to worship Allah as Allah and not merely as an extension of ideological systems? Is it possible to speak to Allah as Allah and not only in terms of where He fits into our perception of the world? (Is the very fact of my referring to Allah as 'He' not already indicative of the problem?) Can I be truly aware of Allah as 'the Light of the Heavens and Earth' (Q. 24:35) rather than the entity to be hurriedly approached – 'mumbled to' may be more appropriate – at the end of meetings or religious study circles? Can the committed Muslim return to that model of the Companions of the Prophet (May Allah be pleased with them) as committed warriors on horseback during the day and ascetics on prayer mats in intense communication with their Lord at night?

I recently heard Seyyed Hossein Nasr making a very interesting point. He said that he had yet to come across a villager who was an atheist; disbelief in the existence of the Transcendent, he observed, is essentially an urban phenomenon. Now, one is not suggesting that we all go back to the village; toothpaste cannot go back into the tube, after all. However, if we are to avoid the clumsy responses to the problem of our alienation from Allah then we have to reflect seriously on the context within which we want to do this.

Some years ago I came across an article that left an abiding impression on me: 'Modern Science and the Dehumanization of Man', by

Phillip Sherrard (*Studies in Comparative Religion*, 1976). There are
many who will argue, not without some validity, that scientific endeav-
ours can also be 'spiritual'; that such activity can, in fact, take one
closer to Allah. The point which Sherrard argues, though, is that essentially spiritual activity and activity relating to the Transcendent will
remain a marginal activity in a world which is moulded by science and
technology. The attempts to put communication with Allah at the centre
of our lives and our organizational programmes must, therefore, be
accompanied by a struggle to remould the world and 're-sanctify' it.

Sherrard compares our world with the medieval one and says that
'the highest type of activity in that world had nothing to do with what
is "practical", "productive" or "efficient"; it was contemplation'. This
contemplative activity, which the Qur'an refers to variously as 'pon-
dering' or 'meditating', led to a deep sense of humankind's status as a
creature of the earth, shaped out of it and returning to it. He points out
that earlier generations felt their 'whole inner being nourished and
enriched by their organic contact with nature' and with the 'breath of
Spirit that had fashioned them as nature's masterwork' (p.76). It is not
so much that one wants to return to that world; rather the issue is to
address the complexity of the task awaiting those who are concerned
about the centrality of the Transcendent in our lives.

Our world, Sherrard argues, is one that reflects the desire of the
human mind to cut its links with the divine and with the earth. In so far
as this world has any ideals, these are purely temporal and finite and
concern only the terrestrial welfare of its members.

We have, however, paid a terrible price for fabricating around us a
society which is as artificial and as mechanized as our own. The
inorganic technological world that we have invented lays hold on
our interior being and seeks to reduce that to a blind inorganic
mechanical thing. It seeks to eliminate whole emotional areas of
our life, as it has been understood in both the religious and the
humanist ages – one that has no heart, no affections, no spon-
taneity, and is as impersonal as the metals and processes of
calculation in which it is involved. And it is not only our emotional world that is deadened. The world of our creative
imagination and intelligence is also impoverished (p. 77).

One may not agree with all that he has said. He does, however, raise some profound and challenging issues upon which any committed Muslim must seriously reflect. Arguments such as these prevent one from mouthing all the clichés about shortcuts to spiritual contentment that we hear all the time from pulpits and 'religious' friends. We have to actually suffer the pain of avoiding hollow answers because it is clear that there is a definite relationship between so-called 'private spirituality' and socio-technological structures.

One can therefore see the problem that many of us have: we are not willing to undertake the radical questioning of our lives and lifestyles to ensure a reordering wherein the Transcendent occupies a central place in it; we merely want to tinker around the edges, carry on 'normally' and feel good about that normality. We seem to want a bit of meditation or prayer, a diet only slightly flavoured with the presence of Allah, somewhat like the 'add some mint leaves for an attractive presentation' that one comes across in some recipes.

Have we thought of how our careers interfere with the spiritual quest? Does our isolation from nature work against genuine contemplative activity? Do the kinds of homes that we live in and the transport that we use play a role in shaping our relationship with Allah? How much of our organizational activity, even if 'Islamic', our neat sticking to schedules and ticking off 'tasks completed' at the end of each day, are actually part of our flight away from ourselves and of our attempts to go it alone without Allah?

We want things to go better with Coke but do not want to take a critical look at the 'things' that are supposed to go better, i.e. our basic daily diet. The problem, though, is that Coke has little or no nutritional value by itself and is little more than sugar, water and gas. Is it a small wonder that we feel so flat just a few minutes after our 'spiritual' exercises?

WORDS AND WORKS FOR A WINDOW

There is a commonly quoted text from the second chapter in the Qur'an that I have always found disturbing and, paradoxically, strengthening:

> And when My servants question you concerning Me, then surely
> I am near. I respond to the prayer of the caller when he [she] cries

unto Me. So let them hear My call and let them trust in Me, in
order that they may be led right. (Q. 2:186)

The idea of Allah being close to people is certainly very common in the
Qur'an; that Allah is caring is seen in the qur'anic description of
Himself as *rabb*, the 'being which brings forth from non-existence,
nourishes, cares and sustains until completion or perfection is reached'.
Anas (May Allah be pleased with him), a Companion, reports that he
heard the Prophet Muhammad (Peace be upon him) saying

Allah says: 'When a servant of Mine advances to me by a foot, I
advance to him [her] by a yard, and when [s]he advances towards
Me a yard, I advance towards him [her] the length of his [her]
arms' spread. When [s]he comes to me walking, I go to him [her]
running.'

In looking at this text, I want to reflect on how one can get to see Allah
as approachable; I want to share a window that has enabled me to view
and experience the possible in a relationship with Allah. This has
allowed my many question marks to exist in harmony with Allah's
durability.

Most Christians have made great play about the idea of the
Transcendent being a personal God of boundless love. Some of them
have, at times, tried to contrast this with the notion that the 'God of
Islam' is a cold entity who is merely interested in exacting punishment
from his offending slaves in the name of justice. In part, their arguments against the Muslim understanding of Allah were facilitated by an
Islam that has been overwhelmingly dominated by a narrow legalism,
where jurisprudence has become synonymous with Islam. I, for one,
have no memories of being taught about a loving God that cares for me,
not at any stage of my long trek from *alif* with my stern and unsmiling
great-grandfather, Tata, to studying Hadith in Pakistan with the very
loving Mawlana Nasrullah Khan.

The idea of an Allah who is compassionate and merciful is one that
we need to retrieve in order to recapture Islam from those who insist
that our faith and Allah are only about anger and vengeance. 'Umar ibn
Khattab (May Allah be pleased with him) relates that some prisoners of

war were brought to the Prophet. Among them was a woman who ran all over the place. When she found a child, apparently hers, she lifted it, drew it close towards her and suckled it. The Prophet then said: 'Can you imagine this women throwing her child into the fire?' When they said 'No', he said: 'Allah is much more compassionate towards His servants than she is towards the child.'

Equally significant though, is the point that much of this talk of a 'God of love' has become little more than Western conservative Christianity avoiding fundamental issues of structural social injustice and poverty in a society that prevents the love of Allah from being experienced in concrete terms in the daily lives of ordinary people. In this rather sophisticated political love that condones social suffering, they certainly have a lot of fellow travellers among some Muslim groups.

Here I want to reflect on how the use of words and works can enable one to edge slightly closer to Allah and to walk a path between the apolitical, fuzzy love of God and the relentless coldness of a distant Transcendent Being who only cares via retribution.

There are, of course, set formulae that we learn to use in our daily prayers and the other rituals of Islam. These are important for they bind us to our historical tradition and to the community. We are, after all, not only individuals but also part of a universal community. The fixed *du'as* (invocations) are, of course, helpful in giving one a sense of connection and stability. It is, nevertheless, great to let go of one's head occasionally and chant along unthinkingly while being touched by the sounds of the sacred. There are indeed times when one can be imprisoned by the predetermined words of prayers. It is very difficult to picture the first Muslims just using memorized formulae; why should one allow words to be a barrier between oneself and Allah?

Skilful use of the tongue can work in two ways: it can eloquently articulate the stirring of our souls or it can be used to mask them while giving the impression of earnest communication with Allah. While words are one of the ways in which we reach out to each other, however ineffectively, with Allah it seems as if a greater requirement is a heart filled with earnestness and awe rather than a tongue filled with words.

One of the most meaningful ways in which some of us in the Call of Islam have experienced communication with Allah has been in a small group of close friends. Fairly common in Christian circles – in fact I first picked up the idea from a group of Christians in Pakistan – this way of praying to Allah was also practised by the earliest Muslims. The late Mawlana Zakariyyah Kandhlawi, in his *Stories of the Sahaba*, tells an interesting story of two Companions of the Prophet who prayed on the eve of the Battle of Uhud: 'Come and let us pray together', the one told the other. 'Let each pray to Allah for the fulfilment of his desires, and the other would say "*amin*" to it. This way of praying would be more likely to be answered by Allah.' The next day, both saw their prayers granted as they had asked.

Today the idea of praying together is strange to most Muslims. One of the reasons is that we have imprisoned words such as *du'a* (invocation) and *salah* (prayer) into very fixed notions. In this incident we have two friends getting together and asking Allah to fulfil their aspirations. They share their hopes and fears with their partners and assist each other with the knocking at Allah's door by saying *amin*. In this way, too, do our brothers and sisters become carriers of our burdens or joys. Initially, you'll probably feel quite embarrassed about having to talk to Allah in the presence of others, but do give it a try: it's worth it.

Words, of course, only work if accompanied by works. While Allah is the Cause of Causes and the Originator of all the natural laws and, therefore, at liberty to suspend all or any of His laws and respond to us without our intervention, this is not His divine pattern. We turn to Him before we experience His nearness. To invoke a text that seems to have worked well for me during my own Meccan crucible – a story told at the beginning of this chapter – 'To those who strive towards us, to them we shall show the way' (Q. 29:69).

Neither is it a question of trusting in Allah *but* tying up your camel; it's one of trusting in Allah *and* tying up your camel. He desires that we strive and call upon Him; not call upon Him but strive. These two actions are not mutually exclusive, as if our striving is our side of the deal and our calling Him a reminder that He must complete His side of the deal; the very ability to strive comes from Him. To call upon Him without having exhausted what He had already given us is a rejection of His grace.

What if all of these words and works fail to open windows, let alone doors? One can be desperate for Allah to respond to one's calls and seemingly fulfil all that is possible for a young person in this day and age. As I recounted above, I have often felt that I was met with a deafening silence. Alas, rather belatedly I have discovered that I do not control the agenda.

Timing, my sister, timing. We do what we must do; the timing is Allah's.

MORE TO THE RITUALS THAN MOTIONS?

Someone once asked 'Ali ibn Abi Talib (May Allah be pleased with him), a cousin of the Prophet (Peace be upon him), about his turning pale at the time of prayers. 'Ali replied that it was 'the time to discharge that trust which Allah offered to the heavens, the earth and the mountains, but they have declined and I have assumed it'. What a sense of responsibility, of the awesomeness of the role of prayer in one's life!

Where do the formal prayers fit into the Islamic scheme of things that they should be seen as synonymous with the trust assumed by humankind? Prayers, being the second of the five pillars of Islam, cannot be viewed apart from the rest of the structure for they do not have an intrinsic value of their own. All the acts of ritual service (*'ibadat*) and all of life that we seek to make dimensions of service, must be viewed in terms of the 'whole', which is the oneness of Allah (*tawhid*) and the struggle to actualize it on earth. Prayer is, or rather, ought to be, a key element in our quest for what the late Mawlana Fazlur Rahman Ansari described as an 'integrated or *tawhidi* existence'; a support in our personal and communal lives as persons struggling to become Muslims.

Prayer in Islam is truly an institution of *tawhid*, the oneness of Allah, reflecting it and directed towards it. The body is involved in the physical acts of the ritual; the heart reflects on the greatness of Allah, and the mind adheres to the legalities governing the prayers; all of these struggle to reach out to the One. At times, we do this entirely on our own and at other times we stand 'shoulder to shoulder' with others as a symbol of the unity of the community and a reaffirmation of the commitment to its realization. We stand on the earth and rest our heads on it, remembering the saying of the Prophet that the entire earth is a place of worship (i.e. sacred). We become at one with the earth from

which we come and to which we have to return. We are reminded of
our being a part of the ecosystem and our responsibility to the earth as
a trust from Allah. Is this, the worshipper's direct involvement with
tawhid in all its manifestations, perhaps the reason why the formal
prayers are referred to as the highest form of (ritual) service and 'the
ascension (*mi'raj*) of the believer unto Allah'?

The concept of achieving communion with Allah as an end in itself,
the 'vertical quest', while avoiding direct involvement with the seemingly this-worldly, the 'horizontal quest', is unfounded in Islam. The
emphasis on performing the formal prayers in congregation is one such
example. Similarly, in what is often seen as a purely spiritual quest, the
pilgrimage to Mecca, one finds in the Prophet's first such pilgrimage a
distinctly political content: he was permitted to perform the minor
pilgrimage by the Meccans even while he was still in exile in Medina.
When they entered Mecca, he instructed his companions to circumam-
bulate the Ka'bah in a very brisk fashion in order to demonstrate an
image of a physically fit force to the Meccans who were observing the
Muslims from the surrounding hills. Here one sees the example of
Muslims, deeply engrossed in a seemingly purely spiritual matter,
simultaneously transmitting political messages to their adversaries.

This relationship between the supposedly sacred and the supposedly
profane is also seen on the occasion of his ascension (*mi'raj*), when the
Prophet reached the highest peak in his quest for Allah.[6] If being in the
presence of Allah had been 'the It' in life, he would have stayed there.
Instead, he returned to earth because it was where he was planted,
where he had to bloom and where, among *al-nas*, the family of Allah,
he had to discover the 'face' of Allah.

These ideas, however, cannot become the conscience rags to wipe
away guilt feelings about a lack of an authentic spirituality in our lives.
Spirituality is also visiting a person imprisoned for his or her commitment to justice or witnessing for Allah's justice by protesting against
the persecution of Tibetans by the Chinese, of Muslims in Kashmir by
the occupying Indian army, of the people of East Timor by the
Indonesian army or of Baha'is by a fanatical regime in Iran.
Spirituality, however, is not only in these acts of witness. The importance of direct communication with Allah, such as reaching out to Him,
acquiring His pleasure, offering your 'self' to Him permeates the entire

Qur'an. While we must find personally meaningful and socially
relevant avenues to actualize this quest, for Muslims, the centrality
of the formal prayers in the struggle to reach closeness to Allah
is inescapable.

It is, nonetheless, possible to complete all one's legal obligations in
respect of the prayers and bypass Allah completely. When reading
personal accounts of prayers in the lives of the early Muslims one is
struck by their obsession with a spirit of devotion and humility in the
full knowledge that they were in the presence of Allah. This 'in the
presence of Allah' is a vital element in prayer that many of us seem to
have sacrificed at the altar of legality. We are able to rush through the
'whole thing' in a few minutes flat to get it over with.

When I was studying in Pakistan, our imam (prayer leader) in the
Binnuri Town mosque in Karachi had the habit of reciting very
lengthy chapters for the early morning prayers, which, incidentally,
was the Prophet's practice. A number of us, theology students, would
not join the prayers at their commencement. Instead, we would remain
in a sitting position, pretending to be in the last prayer unit of our optional
prayers which preceded the congregational one. We sat near the back
row and as soon as the imam had said '*Allahu Akbar*' (God is greater)
to commence the next posture, a bow (*ruku'*), we would pretend to conclude our optional prayers and rush into the bowing mode so as to
'catch' the first prayer unit. (If one manages to be in the bowing position for a few seconds before the imam rises, then one has 'caught' the
unit.) This enabled us to complete the two units of the early morning
prayers without subjecting ourselves to the inconvenience of standing
throughout the lengthy reading of the first unit. Now, if these are the
games of full-time students of Islam who understand Arabic, then . . .
(Or is it because we are professional theologians?)

For Muslims, the externals or legality of Islam have been laid down
by Allah and exemplified by the Prophet as the way of achieving the
morality of Islam. While the means may not be totally divorced from
the end, we cannot hold on to them to dodge the end. When we
become all wrapped up in the details of prayer and obsessed with its
finer points then prayer can even become our means of avoiding communion with Allah. Referring to the ritual of animal sacrifice, the
Qur'an says that 'their flesh and blood reach not Allah, but the

devotion from you reaches Him' (Q. 22:37). A saying of the Prophet further underlines this: 'It is not a sixth, nor a tenth of a person's devotion which is acceptable to Allah, but only such portion thereof as he [she] offers with understanding and a truly devotional spirit.'

DON'T FORGET TO MARINATE THE MEAT!

The Qur'an contains several references to formal prayers and the problem of absentmindedness; the sayings of the Prophet Muhammad (Peace be upon him), even more. For Muslims, these sources remain the anchor from which we derive our support and inspiration. The problem is one of invoking these sources in a world where, by and large, they fall on deaf ears. I do believe though, that virtually all Muslims genuinely want to become more committed to Islam and that those who pray sincerely desire greater constancy and regularity in doing so as well as more fulfilment from it.

Many of us have relegated *salah* to the activity sphere of the 'pious' or legalists, the ones who love laws and all their nitty-gritties. For most of us, it does not seem to be a natural part of our lives. It is an effort that can be avoided if I'm not wearing 'clean clothes' (and by 'clean' we do not mean 'pure' in the juristic sense), can't find a cap or don't work near a mosque. In many ways, this escapism is only incidentally about the formal prayers; it is actually about Allah and Allah's presence or absence in our lives. The problem is thus not one of the moment when the call to prayer (*adhan*) is being sounded and our temporary deafness, but one relating to a general numbness to this 'presence', a numbness that only gets disturbed when disaster strikes and we become desperate for Allah's support.

Prayer in the lives of the Prophet's Companions was an extension of their lives, lives which were part of their journey to Allah. They prayed wherever the occasion found them and removing their footwear wasn't even a part of the ritual. Prayer was as natural as breathing and eating. The intrinsic part that the formal prayers played in their lives is seen in the fact that their days and activities were organized around the times of prayer. Where, for example, we speak about 'nine to five' as a time reference, they spoke about '*fajr* to *zuhr*' (i.e. 'daybreak to noon' and, simultaneously, the descriptions of the prayers corresponding to these times). This, besides indicating their prayer consciousness, also reflects their relationship with their natural surroundings. We therefore need to reflect on the improbability of prayer ever becoming a natural outflow of life if that life has to be lived as a cog in a modern industrial state. Perhaps living in a modern industrial state is unavoidable; being a cog in it is not. There are numerous individuals all over the world who are exploring alternative ways of living and it is only within these that we can reclaim spaces for our selves and reaffirm the centrality of Allah in them.

What about those among us who do actually stop five times a day but never get filled up, and find that the next prayer time finds us exactly where the last one left us? What about we who have been queuing up for petrol for years and our tanks are still empty? In part, the answer is related to what I said in the beginning. Prayer does not only influence our lives, it is also influenced by it. The act itself is important but the idea that prayer takes just a few minutes is rather foolish. One does not pour a jug of water into a pot along with the food ingredients and boil it to produce a great meal. What preceded it? Do you have all the ingredients or do you think that you can skip the onions? How fresh are your ingredients? How tender the meat? Did it require marinating? There is no reason to suppose that our spiritual sustenance requires any less effort and energy than our material sustenance.

Whatever momentary value prayer may have in the life of a believer, its real efficacy is judged by the impact that it has on our daily lives. The qur'anic statement 'prayer prevents lewdness and evil' (Q. 29:45) is significant in this regard. Besides dealing with the relationship between one of the pillars of Islam and the moral–ethical system to be built on it, the verse also instructs the believer to make sure that his or her prayer does, in fact, prevent him or her from lewdness and evil. Prayer is like a petrol station that enables the believer to fill up five times a day for a pleasant and smooth journey to Allah.

The act in and by itself, as well as what comes from, it is important. As much as the outcome depends on what we bring into it, so does it depend on how we go about it. 'Do not attempt to pray while you are drunk; until you know what you are saying,' says the Qur'an (Q. 4:43). I may not consume alcohol but how often are the consequences just about the same for me, so that I do not remember whether or not I read the *Surah Fatihah* (the opening chapter), or, immediately, after my prayers I cannot recall which short sections I read at all? And how often am I not 'drunk' during prayers with some new idea that I picked up in some book or with the potential of the Commission on Gender Equality securing funds from that donor agency in the afternoon?

'And know that Allah does not answer the prayers of a wandering heart,' said the Prophet. Perhaps that is not really the problem, for we make jolly well sure that we concentrate on the prayers we want to have answered.

So much for cursing the darkness; now to strike a match: some years ago I came across a valuable article, 'Absentmindedness in Prayer', in a Muslim Youth Movement publication. The following ideas, some of which I found helpful, are culled from it.

- Do not repeat the same short chapters. Breaking the entrenched habit of frequently repeated short chapters can help overcome absent-mindedness. This will expose us to more of Allah's words and require us to ponder their meanings.
- We do not have to repeat the same formulae (*tasbih*) in bowing (*ruku'*) and prostration (*sujud*). The Prophet used several different ones.
- Create mental checkpoints during your prayers and adhere to them before proceeding. For instance, before going into the bowing position check on the state of your standing position (*qiyam*): did everything go OK? Was I conscious? If we force ourselves to start again every time we wander, our minds will eventually anticipate the checkpoint and concentrate before we get to it.
- We must know what we are praying. We should gradually increase our knowledge of the meaning of the words and verses for at least the texts which we use in the Qur'an and the other prayers, and then try to relate these to our lives.

If, after this, you still find your tank leaking, do not panic. 'Some of you perform prayers in full,' said the Prophet, 'while others perform one-half, one-third, one-quarter, one-fifth and up to one-tenth of them.' If I truly believe that prayers are like petrol stations then I'm going to continue hanging around. If my praying is offered without devotion and concentration then I'm going to continue because it is only within it that these qualities can grow. If I continue praying then there's a chance that

I'll develop it and that my tank may be filled up, but if I stop, then there's a guarantee that I'll never acquire it and my tank will remain empty.

(PS Don't forget to check on the roadworthiness of the car before you set out!)

RAMADAN: WHEN BOATS ARE SAFE IN THE HARBOUR

I have lived abroad for much of my life and travel extensively. Much as I love my geographical home, South Africa, and much as I am committed to my religious home, Islam, I enjoy being abroad. I feel quite comfortable with other cultures and with followers of other religious persuasions as well as with those who have none. I am, in fact, desperate to understand others, to be enriched by them, and sincerely believe that the only meaningful life is one lived with one's spiritual doors and windows wide open to strangers. I do not yearn for the future, nor do I long for the past. Both of these options, I believe, are escapes from the challenge and sometimes the pain of living in the present. I thus believe in blooming wherever I am planted or, more appropriately, regularly replanted. And so I joyfully try to make do with wherever and whosoever I am.

One time of year, though, wherever I may find myself, I yearn for home and, indeed, make my way home. It is a time when I want to touch base with my own, want to be strengthened by them and unashamedly rejoice in being a part of it all. It is a time when I recognize that living with open doors and windows actually implies that there is a place called 'home'! When the month of fasting, Ramadan, approaches, I head for Cape Town.

The month of Ramadan was a period when the Prophet Muhammad (Peace be upon him) regularly sought refuge in the mountains of Mecca from the social evils and injustices of Arab society before Islam. It was during one such sojourn in the Cave of Hira' that he received the first of the qur'anic revelations. Later on, as Islam unfolded, the practice of *i'tikaf*, retreating into the mosque for either the entire month or the latter third thereof, became a common practice among the more devout Muslims. The month concludes with the dispensing of the *sadqah al-fitrah*, a form of charity given to the indigent to 'validate' your fast and to ensure that they also have some means to celebrate.

Here I want to reflect on some of the difficulties and joys presented by the month of Ramadan: the 'problem' of the marginalized (the poor and women), the difficulty of sustaining the spiritual high and, finally, the relevance of fasting in our daily lives.

The Problem of the Marginalized

Sometimes, when I reflect on the misery around us – all wrought by our own hands – I wonder why Allah still keeps the world intact. I often conclude that it is because of the sincerity and devotion of a few that things still move, the few who feel called to withdraw for periods from the world just to pray and contemplate. Even in this consolation though there is a dark cloud. While in many parts of the world women also frequent the mosque, this retreat of the last ten days of Ramadan is confined to men. Then again, I reflect on the injustice towards women aided and abetted by religion.

The last few days of Ramadan also see every person who has fasted contributing to what may be called the 'celebration costs' of the less privileged. The minimum amount is fixed and has to be dispensed before one heads for prayers on the morning of the festival that marks the end of Ramadan. Thus we are reminded that our duty of fasting – while it may have been for our own self-discipline and to incur the pleasure of Allah – was also about our responsibility to those around us.

I love this part of Ramadan. For a long time though, I have believed that the major reason many people die because they do not eat enough is that a few people are dying because they eat too much. I also have to reflect on the nature of charity and kindness, therefore. So often this seems to imply that the poor will always be with us and that we need the poor for our own purification. Connected to this is another curious fact. Many scholars, and certainly many socially aware Muslims, often say that one of the reasons we fast is to empathize with the poor and the hungry. Does it mean that we think of Muslims as wealthy or, at least, self-sufficient? Who shapes this discourse whereby the wealthy are the subjects of religion and poor its objects and we, even if unwittingly, suggest that they do not fast or do not have to fast?

The Difficulty of Sustaining the Spiritual High

What is so significant about this period? 'Why can't we be like this all the time?' one may ask. Quite simply, the human condition. We are unable to sustain the same level of heightened Allah-consciousness throughout the year. If we were, then Ramadan would no longer be Ramadan. If summer existed without winter then it would just be known as 'time', not as 'summer'. Let us not ask why it can't be summer all the time. Rather, ask 'What do I need to do in the summer to enjoy it thoroughly, yet always keep an eye on preparing for the winter?'

Boats are safe in the harbour, and it's tempting to want to hang around there permanently, but that's not exactly what boats are made for. The month of Ramadan is the period in which we return to our harbours to repair our weather-beaten souls and prepare for the next lap of our struggle to reach closer union with Allah, with our higher selves, with nature and with other human beings.

Just a few days into the post-Ramadan journey, though, it becomes clear that things are not nearly as smooth as they were when we were in the harbour. Indeed, for many the sojourn in the harbour itself becomes a bit of a bore when, midway, we can no longer get ourselves to go for the optional night prayers (*tarawih*) and the intense spirituality of the month seems to collapse entirely under the weight of all the preparations for the *'Id al-Fitr*, the day of celebration.

So what's the point of going in the beginning when you will not keep it up? What's the point of fasting when you do not pray five times a day? Our struggle is to make sure that the next port of call finds our ship in a better shape than the previous one, that the next Ramadan finds me in a better state than the previous one, for as John Powell, a Jesuit scholar, says in *Fully Human, Fully Alive*: 'In the garden of humanity, whatever is not growing is busy dying.'

The fact that we will not or cannot do all is not a legitimate reason for refusing to do a bit. It is not completeness that we are out to achieve, it is progress. My goal is not to become a perfect Muslim (at least not this Ramadan); it is only to ensure that the next Ramadan finds me a bit closer to Allah and a somewhat more pleasant person than this one did. To have completed the fast of Ramadan, as Seyyed Hossein Nasr says, 'is to have undergone a rejuvenation and rebirth which prepares each Muslim to face another year with determination to live according to the Divine Will'.

The Personal Significance of the Month of Ramadan

While for some the most significant element in spiritual growth is letting go and placing oneself entirely at the ever-unfolding will of Allah,
for me it comes with a sense of being anchored, a sense of rootedness.
As Ahmad Engar told me years ago, 'For as long as the leaf is attached
to the tree, it is alive.' When the leaf exists apart from the tree then
death is inevitable and it can no longer be a part of that reaching out to
provide shade to others. For me, this rootedness is both in my community, the Muslims of Cape Town, and in the month of Ramadan; a time
that personifies the peak of a Muslim's attempts to be a committed servant of Allah and personifies Allah's grace upon us.

'We have revealed the Qur'an in the month of Ramadan' says Allah
in the Qur'an, 'a guidance for humankind. Thus let those who witness
the month fast. As for others who may be ill or travelling, let them complete it some other time. Allah desires ease for you and not difficulty or
discomfort' (Q. 2:185). Elsewhere the Qur'an explains that fasting has
been prescribed in order that we 'may attain unto piety' (Q. 2:183).

Ramadan is thus a month of heightened awareness of Allah, of a
more intense struggle to reach closeness with Allah. During this month
abstinence from food, drink and sexual activity from dawn to sunset, on
the one hand, and increased spiritual devotions, on the other, are an
intrinsic part of this struggle. However, there is more to Ramadan than
the formal burdens on the flesh! 'Many a person', said the Prophet
Muhammad, 'fasts yet gains little thereby except hunger, prays, yet
gains little thereby except fatigue.'

Fasting is one of the pillars of Islam and pillars, attractive as they
may be from time to time, are meant to accommodate structures: we
build upon them. Thus we are to learn discipline, patience, forbearance
and sacrifice during this month. 'When someone seeks to pick an argument with you, say: "I am fasting,"' said the Prophet. While we fast in
order to attain the pleasure of Allah, how we conduct ourselves during
this month is pretty much about other people and how we relate to
them. Piety requires moments of quiet reflection and withdrawal, but is
not essentially about these; it is about testing one's faith in the real
world, in the world of personal hurts and hopes, of laughter and tears
and, as we South Africans know only too well, on the battlefield
between justice and injustice.

Now all this sounds rather earnest, and it is. However, is it only about this? Is the search for oneness with Allah really without any fun? Piety is also about rejoicing and I know of few communities who know as much about this as the Muslims of Cape Town. The month of Ramadan is a month of great joy, of togetherness, of vibrancy and sharing. Just before sunset children are seen criss-crossing the neighbourhoods with small plates of cakes or biscuits for their neighbours. The mosques are filled with men and women – all of us sincerely believing that prayerful activity earns us bonus points in this month. Yet we also gather to reconnect with each other, to meet friends.

It's not with empty pietism that one hears people voicing sadness when the month eventually comes to an end. They're serious; it's really like seeing the departure of a warm and enriching friend, someone whose company gave you great pleasure and strengthened you. This is why the Ramadan messages in newspapers from non-Muslim businesses 'wishing all their Muslim clients and customers well over the fast' always confused me when I was a child. Wishing us well? What do you mean? The struggle for piety can be fun. 'God desires ease for us and does not wish us discomfort' (Q. 2:185).

To return to a theme with which I started: reaching out to others requires a sense of belonging somewhere. In the yearly cycle Ramadan is the spiritual home for the Muslim. Much as I continue to see one of the reasons for my own existence as having to reach out to people of other religious persuasions and even of no such persuasions, I must return to a place called home, to my own to check on the state of my own barometer and my compass, to be sustained by the great warmth and excitement among our people that accompanies the religious quest in this month. Soon thereafter I may hit the road again. Yet I am aware that all rituals and religious practices can become so social and cultural that they can be stripped entirely of the true awareness of Allah that is meant to accompany them and towards which we are supposed to move, and so there is something beyond all the rituals, religious practices and sense of community. Thus as I set out on my travels again I must be guided not only by my compass but also by the ever present stars above, the Spirit of Allah blown into all of us at the time of the creation of humankind. 'And when my servants ask you about me,' says Allah in the Qur'an, 'indeed, I am near. I respond to the one who calls unto me. Let them then call unto me, and believe in me, so that they might be guided' (Q. 2:186).

TWO

on being with myself

Had I not learnt lately that death is not something that happens at the end of our life? It is imprisonment in one moment of time, confinement in one sharp uncompromising deed or aspect of our selves . . . Hell is time arrested within and refusing to join the movement of mind and stars. Heaven is the boulder unrolled to let new life out.

Laurens van der Post

This chapter is about self-renewal and some of the conditions that I have found helpful in the struggle for it, not that the outcome has always been as new as I, or those whom I deal with on an ongoing basis, would have wanted. The struggle for renewal is an infinitely difficult one. While there are times when one marvels at how far one has come, at other times one feels that after years of chiselling away at one's unpleasant self, the only thing that has changed is the colour of the fossil.

I am becoming increasingly aware that if one is in a position of responsibility over others then one has a particular responsibility to renew oneself in order that one may not inflict upon them the negative fallout from one's own inadequacies and power games. The responsibility to renewal though is essentially to one's self. In the words of an unknown author:

Just go the mirror and look at yourself
And see what the person has to say:
For it isn't your father, or mother, or wife
Who judgement upon you must pass.
The fellow whose verdict counts most in your life
Is the one staring back from the glass.

The very idea of self-renewal, *islah*, implies the freedom to choose to renew one's life. The debate about freedom of choice and predetermination is an old one in Islam and the positions of the main protagonists, the Ash'arites with their notions of predetermination and the Mu'tazilites with their support for freedom of choice, are well documented. I do not wish to revisit any of these, for I find most of this argumentation rather confusing, even bewildering.

I start with the assumption of our freedom to remould our personal and social lives, because this is the only assumption that makes my own life worth living and allows for the belief in a God who is just. The awareness of this freedom and the awesome responsibility that it places on us to lead conscious lives is the first condition of becoming unstuck and growing.

The second condition that I have found helpful is a critical and honest awareness of oneself and the games that one plays with oneself and with others. Games, at a very basic level, are those interactions that serve to mask the real interaction taking place, whether with oneself or with others. (Telling oneself 'I'll get down to my studies as soon as this TV programme is over' or telling one's partner 'I love you' while really crying out 'Please tell me that you love me!')

The third condition is the promise of respecting oneself. Life is tough; the great perversity of our age is our desperation to make it even tougher on ourselves. There are sufficient numbers of people around who will refuse to recognize us and our worth. There is no great need for us to add to their numbers. The promise of self-esteem is not a protection blanket against change but a prerequisite for change. It is the acknowledgement that, while we have many inadequacies and may have committed numerous blunders, we need to be our own best friends in the journey of self-renewal. In the same way that Allah never abandons us despite our failings, we too should stick around for ourselves.

Sticking around is the fourth condition for growth. To remain committed to a relationship based on self-renewal, honesty, a self-critical attitude and self-esteem is not the same as a stubbornness to hold on to outdated positions, discredited theories or false evaluations of one's own worth; that is the path of stagnation and death. Consistency means making comebacks in our lives, never ignoring all the possible lessons from our previous falls, however difficult it may be to live alongside all the implications of these lessons.

FREEDOM ISN'T FREE

Karl van Holdt is a wise friend who has taught me much. In his teens he was a prominent surfer who was permanently and severely physically disabled in a surfing accident. He introduced me to the work of one of today's most significant thinkers, Victor Frankl, the late author of *Man's Search for Meaning*. Frankl, a Jewish survivor of the Nazi concentration camps at Auschwitz, was the founder of what is known as the Third Viennese School of psychotherapy. Karl wrote to me about how

> from that hell in Auschwitz he [Frankl] devises a philosophy of hope and strength. He says our frail and last freedom which can never be torn away and towards which it behoves us to take responsibility, is the freedom of our attitude to our suffering. And he says something which struck me through and through. I must cease asking what more can I expect from life and ask instead, what might life be expecting from me?

This going beyond one's self and one's own plight, the freedom to be free, is epitomized in something that happened in the ninth year after the Prophet (Peace be upon him) was called to prophethood. After the deaths of his first wife Khadijah al-Kubra (May Allah be pleased with her) and his uncle, Abu Talib, in 619, the Prophet was convinced that he could no longer stay in Mecca. There simply was no hope of security against the persecution to which he and his followers were subjected in Mecca. Before things became too critical, he had to act vigorously to secure an alternative, and he set out for Taif, a city to the north of Mecca.

Once there, he went to the three chiefs and tried to explain his message to them. After a series of negative responses, he tried approaching some of the ordinary people, but nobody would listen to him. When he realized that further efforts were in vain, he decided to leave the town. The leaders, however, urged some of the town's rough elements to pursue him with abuse and stones. It is said that the Prophet was pelted with stones to the extent that much of his body was covered with blood with his sandals clogged to his feet. When he was free from the mob, the following prayer filled with pathos, yearning, hope and absolute dependence on Allah, came from his troubled heart:

> O Lord! Unto you do I complain of my frailty, lack of resources
> and my insignificance before these people. O Most Merciful of
> the Merciful, You are the Lord of the oppressed and You are my
> Lord. To whom will You abandon me? To one afar who looks
> askance at me or to an enemy to whom You have given mastery
> over me? If Your indignation is not against me, I have no worry
> for Your security encompasses everything. I seek refuge in the
> light of Your Presence, which illuminates the darkness and the
> light by which the affairs of this life and the Hereafter have been
> rightly ordered, lest Your wrath descends on me, or Your indig-
> nation descends upon me . . . There is no other resource nor power,
> but in You. (Bukhari)

Hadith records that the heavens were moved by the prayer and the
Angel Gabriel appeared before him, greeted the Prophet and said: 'O
Prophet of Allah! I am at your service; if you wish, I can cause the
mountains overlooking this town on both sides to collide with each
other, so that all the people therein would be crushed to death, or you
may suggest any other punishment for them.' The Prophet is reported
to have replied that 'even if these people do not accept the path of sub-
mitting to the will of Allah, I do hope that there will be persons from
among their progeny who would worship Allah and serve His cause.'
Years afterwards, when the Prophet was asked what the most frightening moment in his life was, he is reported to have answered that this
was when he saw some angels hovering over the city of Taif, ready to
destroy it. Here was the Messenger of Allah, safe in the protection of
his Lord, saying that the threat to the lives of a community that had just
insulted and injured him was, in fact, a threat to his own life!

The Prophet refused to allow the people of Taif to determine his
behaviour; instead, he decided on the nature of his own responses. He
did not say that their antagonism led to bitterness on his part; instead,
he assumed personal responsibility for his reaction. Even when com-
plaining to Allah, it is essentially what he perceived as his own
limitations that he lamented. I do not want to suggest that one must
accept responsibility for the wrongs of others. There is, however something really liberating in the idea that one can be in charge of one's own
responses; that one is not a helpless victim of an environment; that

while one may not be able to control events all the time, one is able to control one's response. In South Africa, I recently heard the Dalai Lama narrating a similar, deeply moving account of humankind's boundless possibilities of freedom. A senior Tibetan Buddhist lama who had been severely tortured by the Chinese was asked what was the greatest danger which he ever faced. He replied: 'The danger of losing compassion towards my torturers.'

The acceptance of the freedom to decide one's own course is not only liberating but also frightening, because it places an enormous responsibility on our shoulders. No longer can one say: 'I don't want to have anything to do with her because she never shows me a pleasant face' or 'I'm angry because the food is not ready.' One would have to say: 'She does what she does and I do what I do – and I alone, am responsible for what I do. I cannot any longer blame my mood, or attitude on her.'

The late Mawlana Idris was a venerable figure who taught Hadith at the *madrassah* where I studied in Pakistan. One day, after he came out of the mosque he found that his slippers had disappeared from the spot where he had left them earlier. After a month or so, his attendant spotted the slippers as he was accompanying Mawlana Idris out of the mosque. He picked the slippers up and offered to take them to Mawlana Idris's house. The latter cheerfully declined saying 'How do you expect the poor fellow to get home?'

To take responsibility for one's life and ownership of one's responses is enormously difficult. I remember being ditched for someone else by a woman whom I loved very deeply. While she felt deeply pained for me and did whatever she could to assuage my hurt, she stubbornly refused to own responsibility for my anger and hurt. I now know that her refusal to own my responses assisted me enormously in dealing creatively with my pain. Had she played the game of owning my reaction it might have momentarily deluded me into thinking that I had her back, and would have delayed my having to live up to the truth that the party was over.

Equally significant is the idea that the socio-economic system wherein we find ourselves – irredeemably capitalist, racist and patriarchal – does what it does but I am responsible for my reaction; I can decide to be a victim of this system or a part of a comprehensive struggle for freedom and justice; if the economic system causes a recession then I do have a choice: to organize or starve.

This is clearly not the same as the passive turning of the other cheek; it is saying that if you slap me on my cheek then I have the freedom to walk away or to slap you in return. This also confirms the qur'anic idea that no soul carries the burden of another, in other words a refusal to transfer responsibility for your reactions to the other person. At a personal level we may at times have to be firm and tell another person exactly where to get off. The point, though, is that our response is rooted in our understanding of ourselves as beings in a state of journeying towards Allah and is not a blind reaction to these forces.

The Qur'an gives an interesting example of what constitutes liberating discourse and behaviour on the one hand, and imprisoning discourse and behaviour on the other:

> See you not how Allah coins a similitude: A good saying, as a good tree, its root set firm, its branches reaching into heaven, giving its fruit at every season by permission of its Lord? Allah coins the similes for humankind in order that they may reflect. And the parable of an evil word is that of a bad tree uprooted from the surface of the earth having no stability. (Q. 14:24–6)

In a commentary on these verses, the Prophet is reported to have said that the good tree is an allusion to the date palm while the bad tree refers to the wild gourd. I'd like to use this analogy to look at the ways in which we encounter life and how we have the choice to make this encounter either liberating or imprisoning.

The first characteristic of truly liberating speech and behaviour is that these emerge from firm roots, rather than being informed by the vagaries of everyday weather which is, nonetheless, a product of a particular climate. For me, this means that I must listen to the voice deep within myself; the voice which is an echo of the Spirit of Allah blown into all humankind at the time of our creation. The Prophet Muhammad is reported to have said: 'Virtue is that which satisfies the soul and comforts the heart; and sin is that which perturbs the soul and troubles the heart, even if people should pronounce it lawful and should seek your views on such matters. Seek, therefore a fatwa (legal opinion) from your heart.' While I believe that this voice, which some may call the conscience, is also being refined by my commitment to the religion of Islam, others may have theirs refined by their own traditions or commitments.

This brings me to another dimension of rootedness: while the date palm is not subjected to the vagaries of everyday weather it is nonetheless a product of a particular climate and, while it may be nourished from deep subterranean water sources, it nevertheless grows in a particular direction, even as it grows vertically. However we grow, and grow we must, we invariably do so as children of our environments. For me, this seems to reflect the tension between us and our environments. I will not stand apart from my community but, at the same time, I will grow beyond the limitations of the given and the acceptable and into my dreams of what ought to be. The challenge to me as a Muslim is thus to avoid living a life of perpetual war with all that is around me but to live contemporaneously, fully alive to and responsive to all the impulses of modernity and postmodernity, even as I struggle to reach out to Allah.

The second characteristic of liberating speech and behaviour is that it transcends the muddiness of the ordinary and of knee-jerk responses to the challenges of life: in the words of the Qur'an, 'its branches reach towards the sky'. To me this means to have aspirations in life that reach beyond the desert sand of humdrum existence; to reach towards Allah who is the goal of a believer's life; to rise above the petty bickering, insults and put-downs that come from the ordinary course of life: while the winds can certainly determine much of the direction in which the tree leans, the sand dunes, no matter how vast, cannot suffocate the date palm.

I find much of this 'branches reaching out towards the sky' referred to in this verse reflected in the words of Rabindranath Tagore, the distinguished Bengali poet, in his work *Gitanjali*:

Where the mind is without fear and the head is held high
Where knowledge is free
Where the world had not been broken up into fragments by
    narrow domestic walls
Where words come from the depth of truth
Where tireless striving stretches its arms towards perfection
Where the clear stream of reason has not lost its way into
    the dreary desert sand of dead habit
Where the mind is led forward by thee into ever widening
    thought and action
Into that heaven of freedom, my Father, let my country awake!

The third characteristic of the date palm mentioned in this text is that 'it yields its fruit in all seasons'. How do I have a meaningful presence among people despite being subjected to the vagaries of ever-changing weather conditions around me – and the many times when I switch off for no apparent reason? Elizabeth Kubler Ross, in her book *Death and Dying*, speaks of stained glass radiating beauty when the sun shines upon it, its inability to do so on a cloudy day and the need for an internal lamp to ensure its glow during all seasons.

The following are some of the factors that enable us, as Muslims, to lead lives that are meaningful to others: a combination of firm roots in our beliefs and ethico-moral values, a clear vision of the kind of society that we seek to create as well as a vibrant Spirit of Allah that we recognize in those spiritual luminaries of our times.

In the qur'anic verse cited above, there is an acknowledgment of seasons; the assumption is that there are autumns in our lives when we may seemingly have little to offer and springs when we appear much more attractive and wholesome. For those struggling to be Muslim, though, it is not what has happened to them in life or on that day which determines whether their branches are going to be spread out. They attempt to spread out their branches throughout all seasons and they continue to touch others – even if only in the honest sharing of their own autumns and creative ways of dealing with nakedness.

DYING BY THE INCHES?

Someone once asked 'Has life become like a shoe that pinches? Is living a matter of dying by the inches?'

Some years ago when I was still a kid, we experienced a very rare phenomenon: tensions in the Tablighi Jama'ah between 'reformers' and 'conservatives'. The reformers described themselves as *verligt* (enlightened) and the others as *verkrampt* (backward). Tahir Levy, the leading light of the 'reformers', reminded us that it is 'good and healthy to be *verligt* and that even those who are *verkrampt* must be respected'. 'However, dear fellows,' he intoned, 'never, but never, become *verlépt* [wasted].'

Not to lead a wasted life, to view every day as a challenge, to take our lives afresh into our hands and to seize the day and use it for our own growth . . . The Prophet (Peace be upon him) is reported to have said that 'not a single dawn breaks out without two angels calling out: "O child of Adam, I am a new day and I witness your actions, so make the best of me because I will never return till the Day of Judgement."'

How many of us would not dread the idea of ending our lives with a single act and yet think nothing about ending it bit by bit, every day? It was Cardinal Newman who said 'Fear not that your life shall come to an end, but fear rather that it shall never have a beginning.' We have these irritating pebbles in our shoes. They are seemingly small but, nonetheless, prevent us from walking through life comfortably, and, for some, even to start walking.

The 'Wheel of Growth' reproduced from the *Life Line Trainees' Manual* below reflects some of the stages in our encounters with ourselves and the potential which they have for growth. The conditions necessary for moving onwards are for us to face realities, to accept responsibility for the next move and to have the willingness to come back into orbit after being flung out by our fears and illusions.

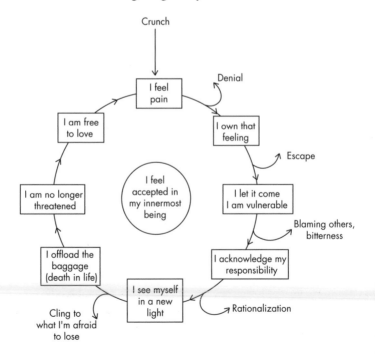

The Wheel of Growth

To illustrate the message of the Wheel of Growth, I narrate here the story of a friend of mine, with the details somewhat amended.

Ahmad was a forty-year-old married man with three sons. He appeared to be greying rather rapidly and seemed to be tired all the time. I caringly inquired about this and he confided that his marriage was becoming a bit of a hell. He was greying and tired. (I feel pain.) However, it 'didn't bother' him much 'since it's really her [his wife's] problem'. (Denial.) The problem, it appeared, centred around the education of two of their sons who had to enter high school. He, arguing that children should not be isolated from their community, insisted that they attend a local high school where standards were known to be dropping. She, arguing that only the best was good enough for the children, insisted that they attend a private school.

He argued that, being the male partner in the marriage, he should have the final say in the matter and that if she didn't toe the line then she could go back to her parents and take the kids with her. He later on admitted that the endless arguing, tears and accusations did hurt him. (I own that feeling.) However, unable to cope with all the tension, he went on long and frequent business trips and slept whenever he was at home. (Escape.)

Listening to him made it clear that, as the 'sultan of the household', he would not be able to cope with the loss of face and the loss of carefully nurtured awe, fear and respect that the children had for him. The very real prospect of these children siding with their mother now stared him in the face. (I am vulnerable.) He nevertheless insisted that his attitude was correct and that the children would have sided with him 'had she not made them turn against me.' (Bitterness and blaming others.)

After some discussion he finally accepted that he had not gone about things correctly. (I acknowledge my responsibility.) However, he argued that his only error had been in the way he had insisted that the children went to a government school. He maintained that his sexism and chauvinism, his living in a protective shell and his fragile ego had nothing to do with the problem. He was still right about the moral and political correctness of avoiding private schools and it was only a matter of time before his wife would come around to seeing things his way. (Rationalization.)

That was the end of the drama for the moment. The children went to a private school. It was a 'victory' for his wife. However, all his real problems remain buried and will probably emerge again some other time around a completely different issue. He could have gone on to put his whole life under the microscope. He could have genuinely recognized the incompatible values between himself and his wife as a problem and also, I believe, concluded that his values were, in fact, superior. That could have opened a tin of truth whose contents might have been difficult to swallow. He might even have started wondering whether he hadn't, in fact, been married to the wrong person for all those years. Furthermore, he might have recognized all his hang-ups and the macho image that hid them all. Had he done this, he would have seen himself and their marriage for what it really was. (I see myself in a new light.)

He could then have remained afraid of the loss of face despite knowing that he was vulnerable and weak, which is really just being human. (Clinging to what I am afraid to lose.) The alternative to this is to undertake a very painful struggle for authenticity. This would have involved dumping his cold self-assured image and the awe with which his family regarded him. (I offload my baggage.) However, he has learnt how to live behind walls and the openness could be terrifying. His wife could also, he feared, take undue advantage of him. The kids might take him for a ride. He felt that he wasn't able to deal with all this.

Major parts of his self would have had to die for him to have coped creatively. In the words of Jalal al-Din Rumi, the famous Persian poet: 'You must die before you die. You must be born while you're yet alive.' It is only when the walls are down and one lives openly that one truly lives. (I am no longer threatened.)

The great tragedy of our lives is often our inability to see that we can actually remould them. We do not have to be stuck for the rest of our lives with a bad temper, an image of strength, a bottomless need to be loved (and to manipulate others to fulfil that need), a passion for gossiping and a million other burdens. We don't have to journey through life dragging all this unwanted luggage with us until physical death catches up with us. The Prophet is reported to have said: 'The one whose two days are equal is a sure loser.' The alternative is reflected in the illustration opposite, in which every step and choice taken is a step further on the road to self-discovery, where one reaches one's core and comes face to face with Allah, fulfiling the meaning of the hadith that the person who knows him (her)self has come to know Allah.

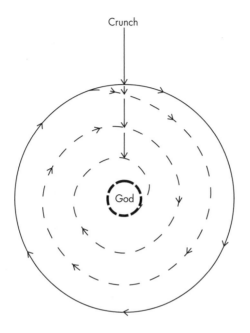

The Road to Self-Discovery

Having completed the full turn of the Wheel of Growth, I am more free to love, more able to give and more vulnerable. Then the next crunch comes and again the wheel turns, but this time the journey is shorter. I move faster and in a smaller circle. Each crunch that comes sends me spinning into another turn of the wheel, in ever-decreasing circles, forming a spiral which ends at the innermost centre, where God is, where I am no longer driven by my needs and desires and where I no longer feel pain. (*Life Line Trainees' Manual*)

The saying wherein the Prophet asks us to 'speak the truth, though it be bitter' is always seen as emphasizing the need to force others to see the truth about themselves. The truth, however, can only be conveyed to others when we have cultivated the habit of facing truths about ourselves. This is the invitation extended to us by Allah when he says: 'And into your selves do you not look?' (Q. 51:21). We, too, must discover our buried emotions, motivations and the games that we have developed over the years to dodge unpleasant truths about ourselves. If we don't do this then our keenness to point out unpleasant truths in others is not a love for the truth or a genuine desire to see the other person becoming more honest. It is only when we look at ourselves, warts and all, and remain aware of all our potential that we can start looking at the areas of stagnation and irritation, the pebbles.

I remember being awfully depressed in the early months of my theology studies in Karachi and often could not sleep for many nights on end. I spent much of the night in the post-midnight optional prayers (*tahajjud*) thereby earning the title 'Sufi'. When the call for the dawn prayers was sounded, more often than not I was still awake, and immediately after the call I would go around switching on all the lights in the hostel. My fellow students were, to put it mildly, rather annoyed, and understandably so. The prayers only commenced about forty-five minutes after the call and they had a good half an hour or more to sleep. They could not complain, however; they were, after all, students of Islamic studies! I, on the other hand, hoped to cash in on my sleeplessness and depression and earn a few bonus points in the Hereafter. The truth, however, was that I resented their ability to put out the lights, rest their heads on their pillows and go off to dreamland. Indeed, it was with a burning anger that I switched those lights on.

In our unwillingness or refusal to look at ourselves, it becomes possible for us to view those little pebbles as diamonds; they may make walking in those shoes miserable, but we hold on to them because we believe they are valuable. It's rather like some people whom one occasionally comes across on the Indo-Pak subcontinent. Known as *malams*, the 'blamed', they wear absolutely nothing save metres of metal chains of various kinds and sizes. Unwashed and unshaven for years, they nevertheless feel that their burdens of filth and metal lend them some air of superiority, even righteousness, over others.

In my own life, as well as in Islamic work that I have observed around me, I have seen how often it is possible for people to be moved by anger or egoism and yet believe that their actions are rooted in a desire to please Allah. We get wrapped up in a flurry of activity, even if 'Islamic', to avoid being with ourselves and confronting an empty soul; we push our negative emotions onto other people and defend our bitterness under the cloak of a hadith that encourages us to have both love and anger for the sake of Allah.

AND THE TRUTH SHALL SET YOU FREE

Like all good Muslim children, I was sent off to *madrassah* at an early age and, as is the habit in the Cape, moved from one *madrassah* to another, until, at the age of twelve, I came across Boeta Samoudien Frieslaar. My previous *madrassah* saw me 'ending off' somewhere in the Qur'an and I presumed that I would continue from there with Boeta Samoudien. When called to the front, I was asked to read one of the very short chapters at the back, and I did so with confidence until he asked me to move my finger along the exact spot where I was reading. The boys behind me started giggling. Boeta Samoudien then placed a primer, called a *soerat* or a *qaidah*, in front of me and asked me to start from the beginning. Despite my offended ego, I managed to 'read', believing that I would quickly disprove the mocking laughter behind me challenging my competence. I could not; the primer in front of me was a new one that I had never seen before, which had all the letters of the Arabic alphabet jumbled up. I had been conditioned to memorizing my lessons with the assistance of another student, without recognizing any of the letters.

I was now caught out: at twelve years old, having already started the short chapters at the back of the Qur'an, it was discovered that I couldn't recognize an *alif* from a *baa*! With humiliating discomfort I agreed to buy the new primer, but couldn't make myself return the next day. When asked why I was not keen on the new *madrassah*, I told my mother about the primer. She then consulted her cousin, Aunty Salamah, also a *madrassah* teacher, who concurred that this modern primer was 'bad'. In fact, they agreed, this was probably one of the ways in which the Ahmadis/Qadianis, a group viewed by most Muslims as heretical, wanted to subvert Islam. Phew! I was saved . . . to continue my dying in ignorance.

I had a 'known'; it was my way of learning the Qur'an. I knew how to wait for someone to make me rehearse my few lines. I knew how to parrot those lines without recognizing the letters of the alphabet, but it was a process that I had been conditioned to over the years. I was dying, but it was preferable to the agony of heading for the unknown and starting off all over again in a new primer. Victor Frankl writes in *Man's Search for Meaning* about his fellow prisoners in the Nazi concentration camp at Auschwitz. Some of those prisoners who yearned so desperately for their freedom had been held captive for so long that, when they were eventually released, they walked into the sunlight, blinked nervously and then silently walked back into the familiar darkness of the prisons to which they had been accustomed for such a long time.

Many of us die behind our masks, dragging slow and uncomfortable steps. Yet we nevertheless feel that we are moving – as I moved from *alif* to the opening chapter of the Qur'an and beyond – even if it is a meaningless motion deeper into ignorance of who we, and those around us, really are.

It is only the truth that will set us free.

There is an interesting story about 'Ali ibn Abi Talib (May Allah be pleased with him), a cousin of the Prophet (Peace be upon him) and the fourth caliph of the Muslims, which I find rather instructive for personal growth. He had apparently overpowered an opponent during armed jihad. The man lost his sword in the scuffle and 'Ali was about to smite him when, in a final act of defiance in the face of certain death, the man spat at him. 'Ali lifted his sword, replaced it in its sheath and withdrew from the man. When the startled, but grateful, opponent of Islam inquired about the sudden change of heart on the part of the Prophet's cousin, 'Ali replied: 'Had I killed you before you spat in my face, then my killing you would have been for a sacred cause. After you spat in my face, my anger blinded me to that cause and I wanted to kill you to express that anger.'

The significance of clarity in motivations also comes out in a hadith of the Prophet. He was asked which of three people truly strives in the cause of Allah: one who fights in order to display his bravery, one who fights out of a feeling of indignation, or one who fights in order to show off. The Prophet replied: 'He who fights so that the word of Allah be exalted is the one who strives in the cause of Allah.'

It is possible for us, as Paul tells us in the Gospels, 'to give ourselves to be burnt at the stake and for it not to be an act of love'; to promote ourselves and believe that we are promoting Islam. In some ways, we will probably always be driven by self-serving motives. The question is whether it is our higher or lower selves that are served by what we do, the extent to which we regard the sanctity of others as we proceed and the willingness to look our motivations in the face and to recognize them accurately for what they are. The hadith that 'actions are [to be judged] according to motivations' is interesting because it implies that only those deeds that are motivated by altruism or service of the higher self will be recognized by Allah.

While recognizing the true nature of our motives may not necessarily sanctify our deeds in the short term, doing so is vital if we want to grow into authentic human beings. The saying of the Prophet that 'he who recognizes his self has come to know his Lord', besides emphasizing the need to know oneself, also shows the new horizons to which this self knowledge will lead. It is in the recognition of who we truly are and what really drives us that we find the key to authenticity, to growth and to the possibility of encountering the presence of Allah.

During the month of Ramadan, the month of fasting, some years ago, I asked my class in Pakistan to list some of the problems and major irritants of everyday life. I heard a student whispering 'Ramzan' (Urdu for 'Ramadan') and added that to the other problems on the board. The entire class protested and appeared genuinely distressed at the idea of Ramadan being regarded as a problem. I refused to erase it, saying that that student, who by now could not be traced, was entitled to have his contribution on the board. After conducting an anonymous survey, I found that of eighteen students, all adults, three fasted regularly, five did so occasionally and the rest did not fast at all. To fifteen people then, the month Ramadan must have been at least a major irritant: the inability to eat in public, the unwillingness of parents to prepare lunch, having to go to the toilet to smoke, to a backyard canteen for coffee. They were simply unable, or refused, to see any problem at all. It is this inability to recognize the truth about ourselves that is often the greatest stumbling block in leading a full life.

There a few things that I have always found helpful when I am reflecting upon where I am, without it degenerating into a futile exercise in narcissistic navel-gazing or self-beration. First, we require moments of silence in our lives; not empty moments, but moments when we are with ourselves in intimacy, wherein we can look ourselves in the eye and in truth. Sometimes we may want to withdraw from others for a while for the extra space that we need from time to time. That's OK. We must, however, understand that the 'self' is not a concrete entity that one can actually know completely after having withdrawn from activity. I am not the same person today that I was yesterday, so there is no question of sorting myself out once and for all. We seize our moments of soul searching at all times and we remain on the path of self-discovery until we leave this world. Someone knocked on the door of Abu Yazid al-Bustami, a famous Sufi, and inquired where he would be able to find Abu Yazid. The latter replied: 'I have been looking for him for forty years and still haven't found him!'

Second, this opening of our bosoms and struggling to come to grips with who we are must be accompanied by a loving and compassionate gentleness. We need to promise ourselves kindness, irrespective of what is uncovered in our journey of self-discovery. I am like a gift unto myself from someone whom I hold in high regard. This gift may have become dirtied in a lot of muck and I shall struggle to cleanse it. I shall enjoy the struggle but I shall not be impatient and destroy it with self-hatred. I am I, inadequate and with lots of hang-ups, but there is only one me and so I must be gentle with myself.

Third, we need to remember that it costs little courage to face negative truths about ourselves and that we need to acknowledge the many fine qualities that Allah has endowed all of us with. Introspection is not synonymous with self-beration; it is a loving and honest reflection on who we are and the promise of self-esteem as we struggle to become.

WHO SAYS I'M NOT IMPORTANT?

It's always nice to see my name in print and, with this book, it's going to be nice again. I think that the thrill is in the knowledge that others will also see it. They will see 'it', they will see 'me'; and this is the point. I want to be seen and, hopefully, stamped with an 'approved of' label. I love the wave that I get from Brother Norman when he spots me in the crowds; Ruwaydah telling me: 'I think of you often and these thoughts strengthen me'; Moosa saying: 'Thanks for being what you are'; the joy in my new class's eyes when they hear that I'm going to be their teacher. In the words of Dale Baughman, 'Every person needs recognition. It is cogently expressed by the lad who says, "Mother, let's play darts. I'll throw the darts and you say 'Wonderful'."'

And yes, we feel empty when we do not see these signs of approval forthcoming. Here lies the snag; assurances and recognition of one's worth have to come all the time because they come from without and not from within. Most of us lack a deep appreciation of ourselves and need to believe that we are beautifully complicated and gifted gifts from Allah unto ourselves, gifts that remain worth loving because the Great Bestower Himself loves His gifts.

Although many of us are used to thinking that we actually have a religious duty to think of ourselves as pieces of you-know-what-I-mean, self-esteem is, in fact, a prerequisite for growth. The problem with most people is not that they think too much of themselves; it is that they think too little of themselves. There are many of us who actively dislike ourselves and spend days, even a lifetime, wishing we were someone else more likeable. How we destroy ourselves in our self-hatred! How we turn ourselves upside down, inside out, in desperate attempts to make ourselves OK to others! Nothing works except being OK to oneself and a conscious decision to become your own best friend. 'A'isha (May Allah be pleased with her) narrates that she heard the Prophet saying: 'Let none of you say "My soul is corrupted (*khabusat*)". But if [s]he must, [s]he might say: "My soul is in a bad shape (*laqasat*)."'

Allah 'distinguished the Children of Adam' (Q. 17:70) and did this despite knowing all about our inadequacies and that we will become immersed in corruption and bloodshed. The nobility of humankind is enshrined in our being chosen as the vicegerents of Allah on earth. The superior consciousness of Adam is seen in his knowledge of 'the names' and in his free will. This compelled the angels to bow to him (Q. 2:30–3). We, by virtue of these attributes given to us by Allah through Adam and above all, by the Spirit of Allah blown into us at the time of creation, became distinguished. So if Allah elevated the Children of Adam, I may not diminish my own worth, nor must I allow anyone to tear at my or anyone else's, skin.

This is, of course, also true at a broader socio-political level where we must struggle against all that works against the dignity of people – all people. Racism dehumanizes, so do poverty and sexism. Believing in the dignity of people means being a part of the struggle to eliminate these. You cannot 'trust' your own community and believe that all others are no good; nor your own gender and think the other to be inferior. That is not trust, but arrogance rooted in one's own insecurity. An injury to one segment of humankind is an injury to all. However, it is easy for us to acknowledge the need to protect human dignity at a socio-political level and yet deny it to ourselves at a personal level.

The great sin in the Qur'an is '*kufr*', ingratitude to the many gifts of Allah, and we are promised that His bounties unto us will be increased if we give thanks (Q. 14:07). There can be no question of gratitude if there is no acknowledgement and there can be no acknowledgement if there is no self-esteem. We have to be aware of the many fine qualities that we have been imbued with. A refusal to do so, even under the garb of humility or modesty, is tantamount to a denial of the blessings of Allah. How often have we not recognized what wonderful gifts others have and yet denied our own? How many times have we not praised others for small kindnesses shown to us and yet remained blind to those that we show to others? A recognition of all the small wonders in our lives, of the many unnoticed little miracles, is a precondition for giving thanks to Allah and that, in turn, is a precondition for our getting more.

The hadith wherein the Prophet says 'None of you truly believe until you love for your fellow what you love for yourself' (Bukhari), is nearly always seen as referring to others. What we ignore is that it presupposes that we already desire good for ourselves. If I am going to go around feeling that I'm a no-good or that I do not deserve your kindness or your gift of love, then there is no way that I can desire these for my brothers or sisters. It is then, as John Powell says in *Why Am I Afraid to Tell You Who I Am?* 'a package deal'; when you love your neighbour as yourself, it means that you love your neighbour and yourself.

But what about my head? Oh yes, we are terrified that our heads will swell and in our desire to hold on to the known and very comforting self-hatred we could even hold on to a hadith wherein the Prophet is reported to have said that no person with an iota of pride shall enter Paradise. If one is going to acknowledge that one gets on very well with people, or that one is a really fine teacher, or that one's handwriting is pleasant to look at . . . is this not pride that has been condemned by Allah? The late Mufti Muhammad Shafi in his commentary on the Qur'an, *Ma'arifal Qur'an*, tells of the Prophet's reply when his companions asked him a similar question: the Prophet said that self-esteem is the respect that we have for ourselves because of what we are, together with an acknowledgment that this is from Allah. He also said that arrogance is the idea that one is a somebody because one regards the other person to be a nobody.

All the hadith of the Prophet condemning pride make it clear that an arrogant attitude towards others is spoken about. Take the case of Hudhaifah (May Allah be pleased with him), a Companion of the Prophet, who told a congregation that he often led in prayers: 'Brothers, find another leader or pray alone because I am beginning to feel puffed up with your leadership.' Now, he didn't say that his leadership was not the most competent or deny he was the most learned. He only expressed his inability to handle that honour *vis-à-vis* the congregation, that is, he thought too much of himself because he considered them too 'little'.

Self-esteem is an affirmation of the self because 'I am' and not because 'you are not'. Indeed, 'you are not and therefore I am' is the opposite of self-esteem as Eric Fromm explains in *Escape from Freedom*:

> Selfishness is not identical with self-esteem, but its very opposite. Selfishness is a kind of greediness. Like all greediness, it contains an insatiability, as a bottomless pit which exhausts the person in an endless effort to satisfy the need without ever reaching satisfaction . . . This person is basically not fond of him[her]self at all, but deeply dislikes him[her]self. Selfishness rooted in this very lack of fondness of oneself.

I am chosen because I am chosen, not because you are frozen. There is only one me; no one else has ever come into this whole wide world or will ever come into it who is an exact replica of me. My fingerprints, the colour of my eyes and the sound of my voice are uniquely mine. This is truly a manifestation of the Glory of Allah. I am *farid* (unique) and so are you. (I hope that my book sells out before they start cloning human beings!)

We are an *amanah* (trust) from Allah unto ourselves. We must, therefore, try to look after this trust and not damage it too much since it has to be returned one day. If we damage it in moments of spiritual carelessness or if gets dirty along the journey of life then we should try to fix it or clean it. But we should never detest it, never look down upon it. We, our bodies and very existence, are witnesses to the power of Allah. We must, therefore, stand in front of ourselves in awe and amazement at the wonder of creation and the genius of the Creator and exclaim: 'Our Lord, You have not created this in vain! Glory be to You and save us from the fire' (Q. 3:191).

I have understood all this for a long while. Yet, it was only a few years ago that I started fulfilling my promise of self-esteem. There were long periods, especially after some show of overwhelming public support or appreciation for my articulateness, insight or contribution to the struggle for liberation, in which I experienced periods of deep self-hatred and berating myself. I have often felt, and still do, that the gap between others' perception of me and my real self was immense. And so I fully understand that it is possible to comprehend, accept and even write about certain concepts or values and yet be absolutely crippled when it comes to doing anything about it. Much of what is written here has been written over the last five years and I am sometimes surprised at the things that I write about. I am surprised because in practical terms some of these things look so alien and difficult to act upon, and I wonder about the morality of offering medicine to another person that you yourself have difficulty swallowing. Perhaps it's fine for as long as you still regard yourself, and not only the others, as having a need for the medicine.

Anyway, a conscious moving towards honesty with myself and those who love me has led to increased self-esteem and I feel OK with myself, more OK than ever before. As Thomas Harris says in *I'm OK, You're OK*: 'The feeling of being OK does not mean that I have over-come all my inadequacies. It only means that I refuse to be paralyzed by them'.

LIFE! LIFE! (OR IS IT 'WIFE! WIFE!'?)

Who says that it's easy being a Muslim today? Was it ever easy? To fly the flag in solidarity with Muslims suffering somewhere may well be; to wear the tag, even easier. To be a submitter to the will of Allah, the literal meaning of the word *muslim*, is an infinitely more difficult kettle of fish. Why, to even have the tenacity to engage in a lifelong struggle to understand what that 'will' is requires an enormous personal commitment. Small wonder that Abu Bakr al-Siddiq (May Allah be pleased with him), the successor of the Prophet (Peace be upon him), was reported to have said that he wished he were a blade of grass, from which no accountability would be required.

In Germany I lived just two tram stops outside the city boundary of Frankfurt am Main in a town called Offenbach. A number of factors made me carry my 'islam', my submission to Allah's will, in my hand just about every day, factors which regularly threatened to have it fall to the ground, melting into nothingness like snowflakes. At Stadtgrenze, the boundary, the fare doubled and alighting there meant an additional ten minutes' walking. In winter, when the weather is often below freezing point, this was no minor feat for someone from sunny South Africa. On the financial front, I lived on a student allowance and could well have done with saving the additional fare. Furthermore, there are no regular conductors on the trams in Germany and friends told me that, in their lifetimes, inspectors had never covered the distance beyond the city boundary. Add to all this the fact that in apartheid South Africa I was part of, and actively supported, a culture wherein it was a matter of honour and self-respect, even a matter of Islam, to subvert 'the system'. Get the drift?

Deep inside us is that call to submission which prevents us from looking at ourselves in the mirror whenever we have defied it. Many of us are often distant from that constant and sometimes unwelcome companion: the conscience, the call to islam. Often we even yearn for a divorce. Alas! we are inexorably tied to each other from that day known as *yawmi alast*; the day when our souls faced our Lord and we were asked: *'Alastu bi rabbikum?'* (Am I not your Lord?). We said: *'Bala!'* (Indeed).[1] We can smother it, ignore it and refuse to let it bother us, but it will not go away. And if it appears to have been conquered and eliminated, be assured that it will still resurface on 'the day when every person will flee from his/her companion, from his/her mother and father, from his/her partner and children' (Q. 80:34–7).

I, for one, find it infinitely difficult to co-exist in a reverential and obedient relationship with that voice; a voice I often hear in ways that are far from clear. Yet I know that my humanness and my islam depend on how hard I try to discern its message and to live alongside it.

Hanzlah (May Allah be pleased with him), one of the Companions of the Prophet, spoke of their hearts becoming soft and tears flowing from their eyes when they were in his company or when he advised them. 'We were clear about where we stood,' he said. However, when alone he felt that the effect of the Prophet's words had gone and he wondered if he was not actually a hypocrite. The Prophet assured him that the feeling of intense and uninterrupted devotion was extremely unusual: 'By Him who controls my life!', said the Prophet, 'If you could keep this up at all times, the angels would greet you in your walking and in your beds. But, O Hanzlah, this is rare, this is rare!'

The term hypocrite (*munafiq*) is, of course one of those 'heavy ones', a term that only the more careless among us fling at others and that the more sensitive are terrified of applying to themselves. Yet from the Qur'an, it is quite evident that hypocrisy can co-exist with faith. It may not be of the kind that causes one to betray one's islam to the enemy but it is certainly sufficient for it to be abandoned in the face of personal pressures such as a temperature of minus 6! The enemy is not always the external Other. Otherness can, and indeed does, exist within oneself. In fact, otherness is a condition of selfhood.

An Arabic proverb says that 'consistency is greater than greatness'. To do good, even in small measure, but to do it with regularity and gentle determination is, I believe, far more conducive to spiritual growth than sudden and earth-shattering changes. 'Upon no one', said the Prophet, 'has been bestowed a bounty better and more comprehensive than consistency.' Often we fail to assess accurately where we are in our personal struggles and decide to revolutionize our lives, to pray five times a day from now on, and so on. It may be less grand, but it is certainly far more realistic to resolve to offer prayers once or twice a day consistently, with the intention of moving beyond that at some point later on. We need to take ourselves, the real selves, from where we are and not from where we would like to be, the ideal selves.

Taking ourselves from the ideal self more often than not leads to what a friend described as the 'Eno's Fruit Salts syndrome' whereby we have spurts of enthusiasm and bursts of activity followed by unpleasant crash landings. Ever tried Eno's after the gas has left it? That is what our commitments must be feeling like after we have abandoned them. The Prophet said that the qur'anic chapter 'Hud' had given him grey hairs. Upon being asked if this was due to the fact that this particular chapter contained accounts of the destruction of peoples who flouted the laws of Allah, he said no, it was a single verse in that chapter that had caused his grey hairs: 'Be consistent, as you had been instructed' (Q. 11:113).

It would be fantastic (even if somewhat boring?) if we could all maintain the same tempo of islam; but that would be turning a blind eye to our essential humanness. Karl van Holdt, a dear friend mentioned at the beginning of this chapter, wrote to me in my spiritual desolation in Pakistan from the prison of his wheelchair: 'The young bird that learns how to fly has to fall many times. The only real fall, though, is the fall from which it doesn't get up again. It is then either dead or busy dying.' In the garden of humanity we are all permanent learners. Falling is an integral part of growing. Fluctuations in our will to live fully and to struggle determinedly are part and parcel of the human situation. Our falling, though, does not become the starting point of death. Falling must be used to teach us more about our weakness, to enable us to become more realistic in assessing our strength as persons or groups. The essential thing in life is that we insist on making comebacks.

In the Tablighi Jama'ah the lecture is invariably followed by a request for the names of those willing to participate in their pro-grammes. They also push pretty hard for a time commitment. Occasionally, after a really rousing talk, some guy with a bit of mis-placed enthusiasm will stand up and proclaim: 'Life, *insha Allah* (God willing)!', meaning thereby that he wants to spend his entire life in the group. It was on one such occasion that my adolescent guru, Abdurrahman Salie, quietly whispered to me: 'Let these brothers stand up now and proclaim "life!"; by the time that they go home to collect some money, clothes and their bedding, they'll be shouting "wife!"' While cynicism about one's companions does not come easily to the Tablighi Jama'ah crowd, he was only echoing the gap between ill-con-sidered but noble intentions and the real lives of people.[2] Consistency is premised on a careful combination on what we would like to do and what we are capable of doing.

'A'isha (May Allah be pleased with her) relates that the Prophet came in when there was a woman with her and when he enquired as to who she was, 'A'isha replied: 'She is the one whose *salah* [prayer] is much spoken about.' The Prophet then told 'A'isha, 'Now wait a moment; you are only required to do that much which you can carry out easily. Allah does not tire of you until you tire of Him. Allah likes that spiritual exercise best which a worshipper can carry out consistently.' Ibn Mas'ud (May Allah be pleased with him) also narrates that he heard the Prophet saying 'Ruined are those who insist on hardship in matters of faith' and that he repeated this three times.

In this struggle to remain true to the beckoning of the voice within our deepest selves, the call to *islam*, consistency and perseverance (*sabr*) are probably the most important qualities. The qur'anic use of *sabr* has little to with the word *saaba* that is often invoked in South Africa or the Urdu *sabr* as used in India and Pakistan. The latter denotes patience, endurance, self-restraint, resignation, submission or suffering. *Sabr* in Arabic, not necessarily in Arab society, is the active quality of exercising fortitude and perseverance in the midst of a struggle to heed the voice of one's *islam*. It is fortitude during the struggle to discern what is required from us in the various stages of our journey to Allah, the struggle to gradually narrow the gap between our beliefs and actions.

'O you who believe,' says the Qur'an, 'have *sabr*, outdo each other in *sabr* and be prepared so that you may attain unto success' (Q. 3:200). Surely we are not called upon to outdo each other in sitting back, suffering, or resignation? The challenge to the one who desires to be a muslim is to refuse to sit back; to hang in there despite falling many times, despite the uncertain hold on our faith, despite the hypocritical other that lurks within us, and despite the inconvenience of walking two extra stops in sub-zero temperatures.

As for me, I hang in there, however perilously, because of a single certainty. Dietrich Bonhoeffer, one of this century's great Christian theologians, beautifully articulated this from his cell on death row in Nazi Germany, where his opposition to Hitler had landed him:

> Who am I? This or the Other?
> Am I one person today and tomorrow another?
> Am I both at once? A hypocrite before others,
> and before myself a contemptible woebegone weakling?
> Or is something within me still like a beaten army
> Fleeing in disorder from victory already achieved?
>
> Who am I? They mock me, these lonely questions of mine.
> Whoever I am, Thou knowest, O God, I am thine.

(*The Cost of Discipleship*)

THREE

on being with you

Oh, the comfort, the inexpressible comfort,
Of feeling safe with a friend,
Having neither to weigh thoughts nor measure words
But pouring them out
Just as they are,
Grain and chaff together,
Certain that a faithful hand
Will take and sift them,
Keep what is worth keeping
And, with the breath of kindness,
Blow the rest away

George Eliot

The Qur'an, Hadith and Muslim literature on ethical conduct are filled with advice on the conduct of personal relationships, although these are often bracketed under the headings of marriage, family, friendship or neighbourliness. In this chapter an attempt is made to utilize these sources and to integrate them with my own experiences, as well as with contemporary insights. Given the more diverse and overlapping nature of personal relationships today, I have chosen to integrate my insights into all of them and have consciously opted for more open-ended categories.

The themes of honesty and esteem, first dealt with in the previous chapter, are extended here to the area of interpersonal relationships. Honesty and a commitment to non-judgemental listening are basic to any meaningful relationship. Honesty, however, is not only about communicating negative feelings or perceptions, it is also about affirming the other person and his or her value in our lives.

To accept the other despite his or her failings and to abandon agendas that you may have for his or her growth, ways of dressing or hairstyle are also central to growth. Instead, we need to work on a common agenda and explore ways of supporting each other, ways of bringing out the best of what is within our nature. *Nasihah* (counselling or advice) is an intrinsic part of our faith, yet the wrong advice, unsolicited, untimely or inappropriate can be disastrous. If you are really the object of my caring, then it is your growth that is at stake and not my agenda.

To my mind, the core of a meaningful relationship is to be there for the other. This implies a commitment to your needs and a willingness to hang in there for better or for worse. In dealing with the question of permanence in a commitment, I certainly do not wish to share the cynicism of the person who commented: 'While marriage is a wonderful institution, I cannot imagine why anyone would want to live in an institution all of his or her life.' However, there are times when, for whatever reason and however painful it may be, one decides to call it quits. When this happens there is an even greater need to hold the other person sacred. This need is also dealt with in the last section of this chapter, which deals with our relationship with those who for whatever reason, we generally dislike. The need to safeguard others from our tongues is one of those requirements of character that is dealt with in virtually every Islamic work on personal ethics. I have found a chapter of Ghazali's *Al-Ihya Ulum al-Din* dealing with fellowship, translated by Muhtar Holland under the title *The Duties of Brotherhood in Islam* (Leicester: Islamic Foundation, 1983) particularly inspirational in my own life and have made generous use of it in this chapter.

One should try to give each serious relationship one's best shot without trying too hard, for one's companions will bolt. There is an obvious need to sit down with each other from time to time and touch base. However, we need to be careful that this does not absorb too much of our time and energies, for many relationships are really there to be enjoyed rather than constantly analysed, discussed and scrutinized.

BEYOND THE MASKS

Ja'far al-Sadiq, the sixth Shi'ite Imam and a teacher of two of the great Sunni Imams, Malik ibn Anas Malik and Abu Hanifah (May Allah be pleased with them), is reported to have said: 'The heaviest of my brothers upon me is the one who discomforts me and with whom I must observe formality, while the lightest on my heart is the one with whom I can be as I would be on my own.'

Nice statement, isn't it?

We share little when we give of our possessions, for real sharing lies in giving of ourselves, entrusting the deepest parts of ourselves to those who love us and utilizing our energies in the service of those values that we cherish. In sharing ourselves we come to know who we really are. We therefore need those with whom we can be as on our own. Through this kind of openness, we discover ourselves and experience the totality of life. This is why I believe that relationships liberated from the burden of formality mean a continuous mutual discovery of oneself and those close to one, as layer after layer is revealed. The initial feeling when one embarks on such a relationship is always one of relief; as if one has, subconsciously at least, always had a deep-felt need for such a person with whom one can be as one is with oneself.

Such a relationship is certainly not painless; indeed, no meaningful relationship is. This pain, though, is either a part of growth within that relationship or, in a general sense, contributes to the process of becoming a more authentic human being. This is quite different from the seemingly meaningless jolts and hurts that we experience as a part of everyday existence. We all know what it is like to exist in relationships of masks, to engage in dialogues of the deaf, and we know that it's not comfortable. We just have this nagging feeling that somewhere along the line we're missing something. Yet we have grown accustomed to this sense of 'missing something'.

While all this talk about openness may sound quite nice, a number of us may also find it frightening. We have rarely got to know a person better and then liked that person less. Yet somehow we feel that it'll be different with us. Will you still care for me if you really know me? This is the question that troubles many of us. There is no guarantee that we are going to be loved when our masks come off. Some people can only exist within the prisons of superficial politeness: being exposed to our authentic selves can be threatening.

I know of an elderly man who remarried pretty soon after his wife had died. Everyone knew that his marriage with his deceased wife had been a living hell for the couple. No one ever referred to it or asked about it. This man, in his seventies, came to life upon his second marriage and became the personification of joy. His 'friends' reacted with anger and disgust at his refusal to put on a display of sorrowful mourning and they deeply resented his very obvious rebirth. They preferred the prison of a facade to authenticity.

The truth is that those people were never really his friends; acquaintances, yes. There may yet be a sense of loss or sorrow when these acquaintances turn their backs on those who have walked the path of openness. Yet that separation is vital in the road to self-discovery. I do not want to suggest that we do not need others. On the contrary, as John Powell says in *Why Am I Afraid to Tell You Who I Am?*, 'the freedom from being locked into an interior, painful and endless civil war' frees us for others. The more we accept ourselves, the more we are liberated from doubt about whether others will approve of and accept us. We are freed to be ourselves with confidence. But whether we are authentic or not, loving and living for oneself alone becomes a small and often imprisoning world. We must learn to go out of ourselves and into genuine loving relationships.

Living openly is not easy and this perhaps explains why many of us often feel that we are dying. It was 'Ali ibn Abi Talib (May Allah be pleased with him) who challenged us to break down our walls when he said: 'The worst of friends is one who discomforts you and obliges you to be polite and resort to making apologies.' I can, however, contribute to a climate of openness by gradually becoming more open myself, by listening carefully when others speak and by refraining from passing judgement.

When I was lived in England, I had a major achievement; in fact, Toby Howarth, a wonderful friend, suggested that Woodbrooke, the institution where I was then based, ought to proclaim a two-day holiday to celebrate it! After years of false starts, much perseverance and the gentle encouragement and skilful coaching of numerous friends, I now swim quite comfortably in deep water, although still only in heated pools. Until a week before my breakthrough, I did one lap at a time in the twenty-metre pool: I swam from the shallow end, paused at the deep end, removed my goggles as I recovered my breath and summoned the courage for the return lap. I then decided to abandon my pause and go back immediately – I did no less than twenty laps in this manner! Wow! The next day I did fifty laps uninterruptedly and after announcing my victory to all and sundry, did another twenty for good

measure! Alas! My excitement was not shared by all. A medical prac-
titioner friend from home told me that it was actually foolish to do what
I did and that, in fact, it's dangerous to escalate a particular activity in
this manner.

Go gently with yourself and with your partners in your quest for
openness. A valuable lesson that I learnt, even if somewhat belatedly,
is that none of one's partners, friends, spouses or lovers (and I am not
saying that one is not the other!) are willing to put up with anyone
wrapped up in him or herself and wanting to bare his or her soul at
every opportunity.

In England I was fortunate in that most pools are heated. Swimming
is so much more pleasurable; like being oneself in a relationship of
warmth and acceptance. Beginners such as myself usually need to test
the water by putting our feet into it before taking the plunge. (And in this
venture called 'life' who ever stops being a beginner?) Far too many of
us ask 'What kind of friend or partner will he or she make?', 'How
warm does he or she make the water for me?' The search for pleasant
swimming conditions starts with oneself: 'How warm do I make the
water for others and how do I warm it?' are the major questions.

During the early days of my battle to swim I found some of the most
unhelpful advice coming from those most keen to see me swimming:
'Don't worry, just jump in at the deep end; your body will float auto-
matically.' It doesn't work like that. Take me from where I am or leave
me alone! Before I got to the pool I just had one problem: how to swim.
Now I have two: how to swim and how to cope with the pressures coming from you!

WHY TWO EARS AND ONE MOUTH?

The late King Faisal al-Sa'ud of Saudi Arabia once said that he was given
two ears and one mouth so that he could listen twice as much as talk.

To listen and to affirm are the major tasks of anyone who wants to
enable others to swim. The ability to discern the moments that require
silence and those that require affirming – or critical – words is perhaps
the greatest gift that anyone can bring to a relationship. Listen carefully
to others, both to what they are saying and to what they are not saying.
The most important need of people when they test the water with us is
to have someone listening. When a friend says: 'You know, I perform

my prayers with the sole intention of finishing them', 'Most of the time, I feel that Allah doesn't care two hoots about the world' or whatever, she reveals her spiritual angst. Yet, more significant is her willingness to face the truth and to share it with us. Throwing a fatwa at her about how she is wasting her time because on the Day of Judgement her prayers will be flung at her like a dirty rag is far from helpful. Such a response will not facilitate her struggle to get closer to Allah. Our own hurried escapes into the certainties of clichés are more likely to reveal the shallowness of our own spirituality.

We do not have to approve of all that is shared with us. Abu al-Darda (May Allah be pleased with him) referred to this when he was asked: 'Do you dislike your brother when he tells you he has done such and such?' He replied: 'I only disapprove of what he has done. As for him, he is still my brother.' An opinion about the importance of concentration during prayers or the wickedness of sex outside marriage may be helpful at some other point in time, but at the moment the requirement may just be for someone to listen.

To recognize the other as a unique treasure from Allah is perhaps the finest gift that we can offer another person. To get to this point we need truly to listen and to allow that person to stand in front of us as he or she really is. To do this we need to recognize that, above everything, when we deal with others we deal with people. They may be awfully important, they may project an image of supreme self-confidence, they may come across as puffed up with a sense of self-importance or deeply religious, passionate revolutionaries or hardened right-wingers; they are still people. As someone said 'To "listen" to another soul as a condition of disclosure and discovery may be almost the greatest service that any human being ever performed for another.' Truly to listen to another person is an act of enabling, of empowering the other person to be whoever he or she truly is at that moment.

Listening has always been a significant criterion for me when I choose those whom I want to walk with in life. This is not so much because I talk a lot (which I do!) but because I believe that a friend capable of listening is one of the finest joys of life and that an inability to listen is really reflective of someone wrapped up in him or herself. A while ago I came across the following poem in the *Life Line Trainees' Manual*. The author is not known.

You are not listening to me when . . .
You do not care about me;
When you say you understand before you know me well enough;
or when you have an answer for my problem before I've finished
    telling you what my problem is;
When you cut me off before I've finished speaking;
Or when you finish my sentence for me.

You are not listening to me when . . .
You feel critical of my vocabulary, grammar or accent;
When you are dying to tell me something;
When you tell me about your experience,
making mine seem unimportant;
When you are communicating with someone else in the room;
When you refuse my thanks by saying you haven't really done
    anything.

You are listening to me when . . .
You come quietly into my private world and let me be me;
When you really try to understand me
even if I'm not making much sense;
When you grasp my point of view
even when it's against your own sincere convictions;
When you realize that the hour I took from you has left you a
    bit tired and drained;

You are listening to me when . . .
You allow me the dignity of making my own decisions
even though you think they might be wrong;
When you do not take my problem away from me,
but allow me to deal with it in my own way;
When you hold back your desire to give me good advice;
When you do not offer me religious solace
when you sense that I am not ready for it;
When you give me enough room to discover for myself what is
    really going on;
When you accept my gift of gratitude by telling me how good it
    makes you feel to know that you have been helpful.

An enabling and compassionate listening is but one dimension of affirming another person. There is another: to speak your belief in and care for the one in need of you or your listening. One of the more painful aspects of our lives today is our inability to communicate our feelings to others, especially our love for others and our need to be loved. We have never been as alienated from ourselves, from others and from Allah as in this age. Yet, we have never been as afraid of love, to receive love, to express our joy at receiving it or our pain at it being withheld from us.

Some years ago I asked my Pakistani students to write letters to their parents starting with 'Dear Mummy and Daddy, I have always wanted to tell you but I have never had the guts . . .' A number of them simply wrote something along the lines of 'I have always wanted to tell you that I love you but I have never had the guts.' It pained me to read through those letters. These kids were so young and already they were so locked in. On the other hand, there was a multitude of parents who would never hear these words from their kids. They slog away in kitchens, factories and offices wondering if any of the labour, emotional energy and financial resources they spend are even noticed by their kids. The Prophet (Peace be upon him) is reported to have said: 'If you love your brother, let him know it.' This, presumably, applies to partners in life, friends, parents and kids as well.

A friend in Pakistan experienced the death of her father while she was on a visit to Bangladesh and, upon her return, it fell to us to inform her of his death. She wept bitterly and people tried to console her by saying all the usual things about Allah's will, etc. She then blurted out: 'I'm not crying because he's dead; I'm crying that he's gone and that I never told him how much I love him. Surely, it is not Allah's will that he should die without knowing this!'

More recently, within a rather short space of time we in South Africa lost two of our most remarkable companions and comrades, Soraya Bosch and Shamima Shaikh. Commemoration gatherings were held for them at various parts of the country and the most moving tributes were paid to these two activists who had returned to their Lord. Alas, they were not able to hear them.

If it is with pleasure that you are viewing any work
   that I am doing,
If you like me, or you love me, tell me now.
Don't withhold your approbation till the priest makes his
   oration and I lie with snowy lilies o'er my brow.

For no matter how you shout it, I'll not care much about it
I won't see how many tears you've shed.

If you think some praise is due me, now's the time to slip it to me,
For I cannot read my tombstone when I'm dead.

(Anon)

The child who grows up well cared for by hardworking parents but has never been told that she is loved, remains a deprived child. At a head level she may later understand and accept that her parents were, in fact, loving and caring but, at a heart level, the scars of the absence of a direct confirmation of love remain. Similarly, parents who are served by caring children but who have never been told how much they are valued or loved remain deprived parents.

In brief, there is no substitute for the expression 'I love you', 'I care about you' or 'I enjoy being with you'. Anas (May Allah be pleased with him) relates that a man was with the Prophet when another man passed and the former said: 'I really love that man.' The Prophet said: 'Tell him so!' On another occasion, the Prophet was asked: 'What about a person who does some good deeds and people praise him for it?' He answered: 'This is an immediate appreciation of a believer's good deeds.' Imam Ghazali, in his usual wisdom, wrote:

Companionship requires the expression of pleasant sentiments. Indeed, this is a feature of [genuine] caring because anyone satisfied with silence alone may as well seek the fellowship of the people inhabiting the tombs. Use your tongue to express affection to your companion, your appreciation of his children, his family, his appearance, his handwriting, his poetry and communicate to him the praise of anyone who praises him, showing him your pleasure.

Here too we must walk carefully. Hurried and careless expressions of approval or affection can backfire as badly as reckless plunges into the deep end or swimming seventy laps without adequate preparation. When one of the Companions came to the Prophet, and said: 'Oh Prophet of Allah, I love you very much,' the Prophet replied: 'Think very carefully before you say such a thing.' Is the person ready to receive your gift of love and your expression thereof? Is this how you really feel about that person or is it a not very sophisticated means of getting him or her to say that he or she loves you? In other words, does it come from a desire to affirm your partner or your desire to be affirmed? Above all, are you willing to live alongside the consequences of that love and affection?

WHY DOES HE TAKE SO LONG WITH THE MEAT?

Imam Ghazali tells an interesting anecdote from Jewish folklore to illustrate the extent of acceptance:

> Two men had committed themselves to each other in a spiritual relationship to serve Allah and they lived in solitude on the mountainside. One day one of them went to town to purchase some meat. He met a sex worker, went with her and engaged her services. After spending three nights with her, he was too ashamed to return to his brother. Meanwhile, his brother missed him and felt concerned. He came into town and after some inquiries about his whereabouts he found him in what would today be described as a 'compromising situation'. He tried to embrace him but the other denied all knowledge of him, being so ashamed. Then he said: 'Come my brother, for I know your condition and your story. Yes, you were never better loved nor dearer to me than at this moment.'

'Now, when the embarrassed fellow realized that what had happened had not lowered him in his brother's eyes,' concludes Imam Ghazali, 'he got up and went away with him.' Great story.

Imam Ghazali refers to the verse wherein Allah instructs the Prophet (Peace be upon him) to tell those who disobey him that he, the Prophet, is absolved of what they do (Q. 26:216). He says that it is very significant that Allah did not tell the Prophet to say, 'I am absolved of you.' It was to this that Abu al-Darda (May Allah be pleased with him), referred when he was asked: 'Do you not dislike your brother when he has done such and such?' and he replied: 'I only hate what he has done, as for him, he remains my brother.' On some other occasion Abu al-Darda elaborated on this, saying: 'If your brother alters and changes his colour, do not desert him on that account, for your brother will sometimes be crooked and sometimes straight.'

There was much discussion among the early scholars as to whether a person is distinct from his or her actions. Imam Ghazali seems to suggest that this is the case. He also offers an interesting angle on the well-known saying that 'A friend in need is a friend indeed':

> Fulfilment [of the duties of fellowship] includes not neglecting the days of his need and poverty; and poverty in religion is more acute than material poverty. He has been afflicted by calamity and harmed by adversity, in consequence of which he is impoverished in his religion. Therefore, he must be watched and cared for, not neglected. Now he needs constant kindness to be helped to salvation from the disaster that has befallen him. Fellowship is a provision for the vicissitudes and accidents of time. (*The Duties of Brotherhood in Islam*, trans. Holland)

I find the bit about 'the special need of friendship during spiritual poverty' particularly moving. I attribute much of my own spiritual survival to the care of those who refused to abandon me during my spiritual recessions. With hindsight, I could have chosen to impose fewer burdens on that care and could have been less manipulative of it, but what I do know is there is simply no way that I could have survived without it.

This kind of caring acceptance is not quite the same as 'putting up with', which is a condescension that we extend to troublesome neighbours, to colleagues whom we cannot stomach and to our ideological adversaries. The 'I'm chosen, you're frozen but I'll accommodate you until you're defrosted' attitude is not one that we offer our partners or companions, because tolerance is an indifferent and reluctant response to others with whom we have to co-exist. Acceptance, on the other hand, is positive; it is the warm and healing garment of understanding that we clothe our partners, companions or friends in when they shiver in the cold of their inadequacies. I'll tolerate you if I have to co-exist with you but if I'm going to live and grow with you, then I have to accept you . . . warts and all.

Acceptance in a relationship is vital to growth. Often we accept others when and if they change. What we don't understand is that, more often than not, when we accept someone as he or she is, we remove from him or her the burden of having to play games while being terrified of displeasing us. The release of pressures makes people freer to change. In other words, acceptance leads to change, a change that is probably more permanent because the other person determined its nature, extent and pace.

To be accepted for what we are and not for our image, feats, clothes, money, oratory or hairstyle is one of our deepest yearnings and perhaps the most precious gift that we can offer one another. We can then stop turning ourselves upside down and inside out in a desperate attempt to be accepted and get down to the business of living and loving. However, no matter how untiring one's commitment to a relationship, one's cup can, and indeed does, run over. It is always with a sense of deep sadness that one calls it a day and moves on. It is sad when one has to return to the mountain – if one may compare the mountain ascent with a spiritual journey – all alone and possibly even leave one's companion with the sex worker. Yet that has to happen occasionally or else none of us may walk the difficult walk.

Does acceptance mean that we never shun people? No, there are occasions when an individual acts in concert with a broader pattern or scheme to deliberately and consistently undermine all the values that one cherishes. One cannot then argue that such an individual must still benefit from one's friendship. In early Islam we have the example of the Tabuk campaign, when three Companions were spurned by the Prophet and the Muslims, to the extent that even their greetings were met with silence because they made various excuses to delay participating in jihad. Some time ago I read an interview with Omar Henry, 'the first non-White to play test cricket for the Springboks', the national sports team in the era of apartheid. Henry spoke about the 'terrible pain' he experienced when he was rejected as an outcast by the community after he had abandoned the fold of non-racial sport to join a multi-racial team.[1] 'Richly deserved contempt', I told myself. Retaining personal links with these people would have made it infinitely easier for even more to join the ranks of the collaborators with an unjust system and thus set back the course of our people's struggles for justice in South Africa.

While Ghazali's comments with regard to the retention of links are made within the context of personal friendships, the verse from the Qur'an to which he refers speaks of a community sinning. Even when a community or group of people sin, our links with them cannot be severed. What does change is the nature of our engagement with that group of people. Suppose Muslims bear witness to the immorality of economic injustice and a minority racist regime refuses to heed calls for its destruction, then we still say: 'We are absolved of what you do.' We still do not say 'We are absolved of you.' We are not absolved of them because we have a duty to engage them, an engagement of conflict.

As for our friends and partners, we need to remember that we abandon them, not so much because they have fallen into a spiritual or moral void, but because of our inadequacies and because of our inability to pull them out without risking falling into it ourselves. Haste in judging others at a personal level, we need to bear in mind, often reflects unresolved conflicts within ourselves. This, of course, does not imply that one cannot pass judgement on another's action. We must, however, be determined to ensure that it is a principled love for truth and a principled disgust at falsehood that moves us.

TO DUMP OR NOT TO DUMP?

At some point during my sojourn in Birmingham in the United Kingdom, I thought a good bit about my small local circle of Muslim friends and critically questioned what I had in common with them. This questioning led to considerable frustration at what often appeared to be rather empty relationships with friends who were honest religious bigots and unrepentant ethnic and gender chauvinists. So what did I have in common with them? Well, they were funny, they were Muslims and they were Pakistanis, and having lived in Pakistan for eight years and benefited enormously from my stay there, I have always felt an affinity with its people.

So what caused all this critical questioning? Shu'aib Manjra's coming to Birmingham. Here was a South African friend whom I had known for years, who knew and understood a bit about where I came from, who was intelligently religious, critical and witty. In brief, great company. 'Has the time come for me to bid farewell to my Pakistani friends?' I wondered. And, if I am contemplating this, what does it say, not about them, but about me and the way I use people?

Someone once approached Junaid Baghdadi, the famous Sufi, and lamented the scarcity of companions: 'Where am I to find a companion in Allah?' asked the man. Junaid Baghdadi made him repeat this thrice before replying: 'If you want a companion to provide for you and to bear your burden, such, by my life, are few and far between. But if you want a companion in Allah whose burden you will carry and whose pain you will bear, then I have a troop I can introduce you to.' The man was silent.

Now, there is surely a place for just getting together simply for 'some company'. Not every friendship has to be companionship in burden-bearing or heavy sharing. I am also not suggesting a guilt trip whenever you get fed up with someone's company. The point is that meaningful relationships are not based on 'killing time' with a person until someone better or wittier comes along; the heart of a meaningful relationship is the willingness to walk alongside the other and to carry his or her burden and, of course, joy.

In the early days of Islam, the practice of 'twinning' individuals was very common. This practice started with the twinning of the *muhajirun* (exiles) with the *ansar* (literally 'helpers', the Medinese host community) when the former arrived penniless from Mecca. (Which is not surprising given that they had no pennies in those days, but you know what I mean!) This adoption of companions became a feature of Muslim life, in which the two companions, referred to as 'companions in Allah', shared their spiritual, emotional and material resources. Some of the features of this practice could become the basis for pretty exciting and meaningful companionships. Take, for example, the question of a commitment to one's friend. Imam Ja'far al-Sadiq is quoted in this regard as saying: 'The affection of a day is a link; that of a month is kinship and that of a year is a blood tie. If anyone cuts it, Allah will cut him off.' The rewards of such a relationship are often enormous, even though these may be buried in the many inevitable ups and downs. Such a relationship is a commitment that may not be abandoned lightly when the rewards are not immediately visible.

The path of giving without that giving being a subtle manoeuvre to receive is rather difficult. To be there for the other when time and time again the other seems to be incapable of being there for us when we need him or her, is the path of love. Our being 'present' for the other is actually tied up to our humanness. As Ashiek reminded me many years ago, the tree needs to spread its branches for its own survival. In that process of spreading out it supplies shade to the weary traveller. It may appreciate and enjoy that useful function but it is, from its own perspective, not doing a favour to the traveller; it is a question of survival and growth.

A word about choosing friends . . .

We really choose our friends or companions for what we can get from them, even if it's just the thrill of pleasant and intelligent company or being with someone who is good-looking. We somehow regard others as tools of self-enhancement. We see this pretty early in life in the way our teachers select 'the nicer children with straight hair' or 'the 'clever ones' to take messages to the principal's office. We see it in our choice of pageboys and flower girls at weddings and in the qualities that we look for in potential marriage partners.

In this whole thing, does one smell the notion of one's own market value increasing when one is accompanied by an attractive spouse, in the same way that a beautiful garden increases the value of the house? There is far more to our choices of friends, partners and companions than meets the eye. Our choices are the indicators of who we really are, of our values and unfulfilled aspirations. We need to study the qualities that we search for in others very carefully, because it is one of the most valuable doors to self-discovery.

I have witnessed so much tension between partners in personal relationships, including marriage, because the one chooses the other to compensate for qualities that he or she lacked and wanted to see in the other. It is, of course, important to associate with another who could strengthen one in one's own struggle for fulfilment. The problem, however, arises when we do not struggle with our inadequacies but insist on turning the other person upside down and inside out to compensate for them. Such partners do not challenge each other in a creative way to become better Muslims or more balanced persons. Rather, they smother each other in endless rounds of dishonest games that leave both losers.

And the ones who don't brush their teeth? What about those with seemingly little to offer us, the ones who survive, and sometimes die, on the fringes of society, those who have been pushed to the edges by emotional and material poverty? The little girl with a perpetually running nose and dirty fingernails, probably from a background of deprivation, does not give us kicks by her 'cuteness'. The ones who need a loving hand the most get it last and least. The same person, never a candidate for flower girl because of our subconscious rejection or, at best, indifference, becomes an early dropout. (And how many 'dropouts' are not really 'pushed-outs'?)

There are, mercifully, many deeply caring individuals around. However, our relationship with the emotionally unbalanced, the economically exploited or the spiritually impoverished must never lead to smugness, a holier-than-thou attitude. We must guard against emotional and religious self-righteousness because we are with them for ourselves, for our integrity as people. Indeed, many of us are able to reach out to others because some time ago someone found us stunted and marginalized and offered us a crutch and a candle. I remember how, whenever I talked disparagingly about anyone, Brother Norman Wray, my Pakistani guru, would look at me admonishingly and gently remind me: 'There, but for the grace of God, go I'.

THOUGH POVERTY BECAME THEIR LOT . . .

There is a very moving story of unqualified compassion in early Islam. One of the Companions came to the Prophet (Peace be upon him) and complained of hunger. Not having anything to offer himself, he asked some other Companions if there was anyone among them who would feed the man for that evening. One among the *ansar* (host community) volunteered, took the Companion home and told his wife: 'Look, I have accepted this man as a guest of the Prophet. We shall entertain him as best as we can and won't spare anything in doing so.' His wife replied: 'By Allah! We hardly have any food in the house except what is just enough for the children.' The *ansari* then suggested that she lull the children to sleep without feeding them, while he sat along with the guest at the meagre meal. He also asked her to put out the lamp, pretending to set it aright, when they started eating, 'so that the guest may not know of my not sharing the meal with him'. The plan seemed to work and the family stayed hungry, enabling the guest to have his fill. It was in response to this incident, say several commentators of the Qur'an, that the following verse was revealed: 'They prefer others above themselves, though poverty becomes their lot' (Q. 59:9).

Some years ago while we were out in the Tablighi Jama'ah travelling through Pretoria, a local person brought a large watermelon to the mosque for the group, most of whom were having an afternoon nap. A friend, Nazeem Hunter, and I decided to help ourselves to it and left a rather meagre portion for the rest of the group. We were later gently chided by the amir (leader), Boeta Mahmud. '*Astaghfirullah!* (I seek forgiveness from Allah)' he said.'The Companions preferred others above themselves though poverty became their lot. You brothers prefer others above yourselves after you have had your lot!'

After a day or so, someone brought a jug of faluda, a sweet milk beverage, and either I alone, or Nazeem and I, finished the entire jug without informing the group. Later the man came to ask another member of the group for the jug, whereupon they learnt of the faluda for the first time. An argument ensued between myself and Nazeem as to who the culprit was or the extent of our individual culpability. Boeta Mahmud's only response was: '*Astaghfirullah*, the Companions preferred others above themselves though poverty became their lot; you guys prefer others above yourselves after you have had the whole lot!'

Now, the story of the Companion sharing his family's meal with a stranger is quite a contrast to the adage of charity beginning at home, an adage that is not without its virtues. It is important to start at whichever particular point is most useful when one begins to unravel a messy bundle – and this point may well be inside one's own home. However, there is still something to be said for the inseparability of humankind; if someone is starving 'out there' while I have something 'in here', then my own humanity is being compromised if I do not act.

Sharing is a rather tricky matter and something that I know a good bit about, even if only by way of saying what should be avoided.

First, sharing is an act of love, not of sacrifice. Sacrifice is usually an act of duty; giving or doing with a heavy heart and a sense of loss and often imposing a yoke of gratitude on the neck of the receiver. When we perceive the need of the other person, feel that need in our hearts and give because our lives as people with integrity depend on that giving, then our giving becomes an act of love. Giving is a way of living with sanity in an insane world. We give for ourselves; that we may not be diminished by selfishness and greed and that we may grow as persons. This is perhaps one of the meanings of a number of texts from the Qur'an that speak about the way giving is actually a form of multiplying: 'The likeness of those who spend their wealth in Allah's way is as the likeness of a grain of corn which grows seven ears, in every ear a hundred grains' (Q. 2:261).

Second, sharing goes beyond justice. When my brother Ismail and I were small we had this earth-shattering problem of how to divide whatever was given to us. We hit on a great scheme that always worked: the one who cut the apple chose his piece last. This ensured that the cutter achieved a near hundred per cent accuracy, because the other would certainly choose the bigger piece in the event of error. This is rather sad because we pass our whole lives fearing that we'll get the least and manoeuvring to get the most. The reason we insist on an equal share is not that we care about justice and equality, but because we want the bigger share and it's only our acknowledgement that we won't be able to get it that forces us to settle for a compromise – an equal piece.

Justice asks and gives to the extent that it is the right of the recipient. Sharing based on compassion doesn't ask 'What are you entitled to?' It asks 'What do you need from me?' It doesn't say 'I give all the time and what am I getting in return?'; it says 'I give because you need to receive and I need to grow through my receiving.' So many of us confuse the pan-scale, weighing out 'one of mine for one of yours', relationship with love. In a bartering or pan-scale relationship we give and then watch our partner's or companions' responses rather anxiously. I gave you a gift on your birthday and now I await your gift on my birthday. If, for some reason or the other, you are unable to give one, you can forget about getting one on your next birthday; in fact, I may even regret having given you a gift the last time!

The other reason that we are often unable to reciprocate is simply that somewhere, something may have gone wrong with us on that day. When our partners or companions interpret this as a rejection or our indifference to their overtures of affection, or worse still, a rejection of their persons, then this often causes them to withdraw all their overtures of affection . . . at a time when we need it most. Now, I am not suggesting that we become doormats for other people in one-sided relationships. Recognizing the signs of undesired gestures of affection or sharing is often not easy, in part because the other person often doesn't let on. I think that it helps to search for patterns of non-reciprocity rather than isolated cases. Because I have often had great difficulty in picking up those signals, I have now learnt to talk straight and to ask directly whether it is because you are incapacitated in reciprocating or because you want me to move along.

Third, genuine sharing is really an extension of sharing oneself and has little to do with subtle manoeuvres to receive. We will get our returns – well, hopefully – as our brothers and sisters respond to our affection, but they must remain our object, and it is so easy for those returns to become the goal.

Fourth, sharing should never be a conscience rag. When the Qur'an encourages us to spend or to share, it addresses us as people with a sense of morality. This spending or sharing, though, cannot be the sole responsibility of the individual however 'moral' he or she may be. The community is under obligation to extract that wealth if individuals refuse to spend. The development of moral consciousness may be a prior condition for the total success of legal restraints. This, however, does not mean that a state or community governed by the ethos of the Qur'an is going to wait patiently until a particular individual or class feels moral enough to share – certainly not in a society where a few people are dying because of overeating while thousands are dying because of not eating enough.

Selfishness and selflessness are not only personal traits that can be eliminated or strengthened in individuals by appeals to conscience: they are also the causes and results of particular systems. Our inability to see, for example, how capitalism is born from and entrenches selfishness, can cause our discussions on and commitment to sharing and compassion to amount to no more than adding some mint leaves to garnish food which has gone off. It may give the food a nice appearance, but it will still mess up your health. Islam is as much a matter of personal morality as it is of socio-economic spirit and our struggle to establish it is as much a struggle against uncaring and unjust socio-economic systems as it is a struggle against the *nafs* (lower self).

MY BROTHER'S FLESH ON THE MENU?

Much of the preceding pages dealt with our relationships with those close to us or for whose needs we feel some sympathy. What about those whom we just do not like, have difficulty 'stomaching' or with whom we bitterly disagree?

Yes, it is OK to dislike certain attitudes in people and to avoid, and even oppose, those who display annoying, abominable or bullying behaviour. The Prophet (Peace be upon him) told Sa'ad ibn Abi Waqqas (May Allah be pleased with him), one of his Companions: 'I am hoping that you will be a source of benefit for some people and of trouble for others.' South Africa has taught many of us to be wary of the 'love your enemy' language that blunts the anger of the oppressed and is usually little more than a tool in the hands of the powerful, intended to perpetuate their domination. I am, however, equally wary of those who spit venom at others at the drop of a pin and then seek refuge in a hadith referring to 'love for Allah and anger for Allah'. I have heard this hadith invoked far too often as a weapon of personal or organizational warfare.

For the moment though, I would like to focus on the way we relate to those whom we just personally dislike.

To maintain the sanctity of those whom we dislike is a rather difficult. It is a task that often escapes those who, in general terms, are otherwise observant of the requirements of Islamic behaviour. I remember an incident that occurred at a friend's place when I was still at school. Ashiek and I were merrily and mercilessly dissecting the characters of two other friends until the time for prayers approached. We asked his younger brother, Fasiegh, then just entering his teens and going through his own questioning of religion and the presence of Allah in a pain-filled world, to join us. (Ashiek and I were supposedly the guys who were going to ensure that the younger brother stayed on the 'straight path'.) After completing our prayers, Fasiegh casually remarked: 'Right, now that we are finished speaking to Allah, we can continue eating the flesh of our brothers.' We were silent. (If only the silence could have lasted!)

Imam Ghazali narrates a story of Jesus (Peace be upon him) who counselled his disciples by asking them how they would act if they were to see a companion sleeping and the wind blowing his clothes off. They replied that they would screen him and cover him up. Jesus then asked if they would rather 'lay bare his private parts?' When they replied that it was unthinkable that they would do thus, he told them that that was similar to the behaviour of one 'who listens to gossip about his fellow person, then adds to it and passes it on having added some spice to it'.

Some years ago, during the month of Ramadan, I was in Pretoria, where I offered my late evening prayers (*tarawih*). Sitting in one of the centre rows, I noticed a man in front talking to the imam, moving back to discuss something with someone else, and talking again with the imam before he eventually sat down. I did not think anything unusual about this. After twenty prayer units (*raka'at*) had been completed, I left for the ablution area and returned. Having forfeited my place in the centre rows, I slid into the back row. Upon the completion of prayers, I was stopped by three people outside the mosque. They politely inquired about the permissibility, according to Imam Idris ibn al-Shafi'i (May Allah's mercy be upon him), a key Muslim jurist, of reading a brief English summary of the qur'anic text before the commencement of prayer. I pointed out that Imam al-Shafi'i did not have an opinion about this sort of thing and that, on the face of it, there was nothing wrong with it. One of the three objected vehemently to my opinion and, realizing that a pointless argument generating lots of heat and little clarity was about to start, I made some excuse and left with Iqbal, my host.

When I returned to the area after a week the story had taken several new twists. The new version was that I had been involved in a dispute with the imam, staged a walk out and become embroiled in a bitter argument outside the mosque which led to me being hit with a brick and leaving the place covered in blood!

While the story with its growing tail is a rather innocent one, at its core is a very serious issue: the rubbishing of people and of groups whom we do not like or who differ with us in regard to our understanding of Islam. The challenge to the Muslim who desires honesty is to differ with others in their perception of Islam and to hold their persons sacred, not resorting to seeing their different perspectives as an extension of 'their hang-ups' or 'hunger for fame' *ad nauseam*; to look again first of all at our programmes when things go wrong, not blaming them on the real or imaginary manoeuvres of others, or to their being paid Jewish agents. Crediting our opponents with intellectual clarity will force us to grow; labelling whoever disagrees with us as 'confused' or 'vindictive' will entrench a smugness which at best contributes to our own stagnation and could even contribute to our destruction and that of our programmes.

Our unkindness in passing judgement on others is often a reflection of our harshness towards ourselves; our willingness to find the short-comings of others often a reflection of our fears that those shortcomings may be in us. An Arabic proverb says: *'Al-mar'u yaqisu ala nafisihi'* (As a person is himself, so does he perceive others to be). The point here is not whether that particular fault is really in the other person or not, but the reason for our awareness of it, the motivation for our exposing it and the manner in which it is done. An honest examination of these three factors will uncover a wealth of information about us. The despised other is, more often than not, a reflection of the feared and unrecognized self.

Yes, even when we boast of our own achievements or possessions while seemingly denigrating those of others we actually only succeed in revealing our own insecurities. We feel safe in the knowledge of the wrongs, 'sins' or inadequacies of others because it allows us to be blind to our own for a while. And so, desperate as we are to relish the shortcomings of others, we must turn towards ourselves. It is only a car-ing and gentle self-esteem that is going to enable us truly to grow, and thereby change our perception of the disliked other even when we can-not change his or her behaviour.

We need to try to understand what is at the heart of our resentment and anger towards particular people, and to be aware that often the resentment we drag along with us in our lives is actually pretty damag-ing to us. There was a neat little wall display in a Catholic Minor Seminary in Karachi which said: 'Bitterness is like acid; it does more harm to the vessel in which it is stored than to the object on which it is poured.' (OK, OK, I know that they make sophisticated vessels these days; people still come in the old shape though!)

Idris Shah tells an interesting story about misdirected venom in *The Magic Monastery*:

A dervish was sitting by the roadside when a rather pompous courtier passed by with his retinue riding past in the opposite direction. For no apparent reason, the courtier struck the dervish with a cane shouting: 'Out of the way, you miserable wretch!' When they swept past, the dervish rose and called after them 'May you attain all you desire in the world, even to its highest ranks!'

A bystander, much impressed by this scene, approached the devout man and said to him: 'Please tell me whether your words were motivated by generosity of spirit, or because the desires of the world will undoubtedly corrupt that man even more?'

'O Man of bright countenance,' said the dervish, 'has it not occurred to you that I said what I did because people who attain their real desires would not need to ride about striking dervishes?'

Often in our own weakness we are tempted to build our security on the insecurity of others. We then forget that we don't go up by pushing others down and that it is not possible to tear at someone's face without oneself being diminished in the process. Mu'adh ibn Jabal (May Allah be pleased with him) once came to the Prophet and asked him how he, Mu'adh, could cultivate purity of intention and achieve salvation. The Prophet said:

> Follow me, even if you fall somewhat short in what you do. O Mu'adh, guard your tongue from slandering your fellows . . . Attribute your errors to yourself and not to them; do not justify yourself and blame them; do not exalt yourself above them. Do not tear to pieces people's characters so that on the Day of Judgement the dogs of hell do not tear you to pieces. (Muslim)

The discovery of faults in others is easy; understanding the 'whys' extremely difficult. We are so ignorant of the experiences that have gone into the shaping, and sometimes breaking, of the other person that we must withhold judgement of that person, although not necessarily of the action. Indeed, we have no guarantee that, had we been subjected to similar experiences, we would not have had the same hang-ups or have been more unpleasant than those whom we seek to condemn. An old

Native American prayer asks: 'Great Spirit, grant that I do not condemn my fellow person until I have walked a mile in his or her hunting shoes.'

There is this story about a gossipmonger that I heard from Shaikh Fa'ik Gamieldien:

> The gossipmonger relished speaking ill of others. Being of noble conscience, it nevertheless troubled him and so he went to speak to a wise shaikh [not Fa'ik!] about it. After listening patiently, the shaikh instructed him to get a bag of feathers and take it to the highest tower in the town. On a very windy day the man was to empty the bag and then return to the shaikh. After some time the gossipmonger returned to the shaikh to report that he had completed the task as instructed. The shaikh then asked him to go and recover every single feather from wherever the wind had carried it, in every corner of the town: the gutters, the treetops, the chimneys, the drains, and so on. The astonished gossipmonger stared at the shaikh in disbelief and the latter cautioned him saying: 'This, my brother, is the gravity of your problem here and in the hereafter.'

In one of his many brilliant strokes of logic, Imam Ghazali advises the potential slanderer:

> If you examine yourself to see whether there is any open or hidden vice in you and whether you are committing a sin, secretly or publicly and find some, then be sure that the other person's inability to free himself from what you attribute to him is similar to your inability, and his excuse similar to yours. Just as you'd dislike being openly condemned, so he dislikes it. If you veil him, Allah will veil your faults and if you expose him, then know that Allah will expose your faults on the Day of Judgement. If, however, on examining your outer and inner life, you do not come across any vice, any imperfection, you may be sure that your ignorance of your inadequacies is the worst kind of folly, and no inadequacy is greater than folly. If, on the other hand, you are correct in your opinion, thank Allah for it and do not corrupt your perfection by slandering people, for that is the worst of vices.

If this one doesn't work, I can only say: 'Wow! What a tough skin, more akin to hide!'

FOUR

on being a social being

'When I first arrived in the slum,' he told his father, 'one of the first thoughts Kovalski shared with me came from a Brazilian arch-bishop struggling shoulder to shoulder with the poor out in the country and the favellas. According to him, our help serves only to make people more dependent unless it is supported with actions designed to wipe out the actual roots of poverty.'

'Does that mean that it's no use taking them out of their hovels full of crap and setting them up in new housing?'

Max nodded his head sadly.

'I've even come to learn the validity of a strange reality here,' he said. 'In a slum an exploiter is better than Santa Claus . . .' Confronted by his father's stupefied expression, he went on to explain: 'An exploiter forces you to react, whereas Santa Claus immobilizes you.'

Dominique Lapierre, *City of Joy*

If there is one major world religion that is unambiguously identified as having a political agenda, then it is Islam. For most people who are not Muslim this is seen as very disturbing, not least because of the mass media. The truth is that all religions are also the product of socio-political dynamics, both in their origins and in the way they continue to find an expression in everyday life. Furthermore, if politics is really about the access to and exercise of power, then there is precious little in human relationships void of politics. Some of the problems involved in these power dynamics at a personal, organizational and socio-political level are explored in this chapter.

The first section deals with the inalienable relationship between Islam and politics and the importance of de-linking this from the more sensational, but exclusivist and intolerant, political expressions of this relationship. At the other end of the more visible Muslim spectrum is the very strong tendency towards the notion of personal salvation as the way to transform the world. 'Do your personal religious duty to Allah and then He'll sort out the world.' These folks hardly realize that the socio-political roles they play in their daily lives are also contributing to either entrenching the problems of the world or transforming it into a more humane one. This problem, the limitations and even danger of an apolitical personal religiosity, is dealt with in the second section.

The next two sections posit alternatives to these two positions: Islamically grounded personal responses within the context and as a part of a broader challenge to unjust socio-economic systems. While many Muslims warmly welcome the idea of Islam as a faith with very explicit socio-political dimensions, few understand the implications of this at a very personal level. Power is not only something that exists out there in the boardrooms of huge multinational corporations, media centres or parliaments: it also resides deep within me and you and we are never really without any choices.

The idea that one can take control of one's life, and that freedom is not entirely contingent on broader socio-political forces, is looked at in the third section. The fourth focuses on responses to one of the basic causes of social injustice, the drive to well-having at the expense of well-being. The will to have less is posited as one of the fundamental requirements of a life in obedience to Allah, who provides adequately for the needs of all but not the greed of a few.

The last two sections deal more specifically with the question of power and authority and related issues such as manipulation, democracy and accountability. These questions are essential for those of us who find ourselves involved in organizations or social activism. The disadvantaged are not only the financially poor. They are also those used by organizational and political leaders as pawns in their own personal ambitions, as voting fodder by traditional leaders or chiefs in a village and those subjected to the demagoguery of religious leaders who insist that there is no democracy in Islam and that all authority is with God, thereby disempowering all but themselves as the agents of God.

REVELATION OR REVOLUTION?

This was actually the title of a series of talks delivered by a prominent conservative Muslim scholar who seemed to tail me in the northern parts of South Africa during the height of the struggle against apartheid during the eighties, trying to undo my 'damage'. He, of course, argued that religious people ought to support revelation as opposed to revolution.

Religious people often view themselves as a cut above politicians. I want to reflect a bit on the nature of politics and this religious 'aboveness' in an attempt to understand something about the relationship between politics and faith. I do not want to deal at any length with the more obvious and cynical manipulation of religion for short-term political objectives: I want to go beyond this obvious abuse of religion to where it touches us, our beliefs, our theologies, our complicity and our responsibility.

For most of us, politics is about politicians, power games, manipulation, the distortion of truth and carries a host of other sinister connotations. The pejorative associations surrounding it are demonstrated in the commonly heard expression that 'politics is a dirty game'. Politics is about power and, in its most visible form, for many of us, this implies governmental power. If, however, one were to speak to villagers in Pakistan one would find that the world of the feudal lords is the world of power – irrespective of whether their local feudal lord supports the ruling government or not. Similarly, for most women, the world of power is that of men. Power is in the office, in the mosque, in our organizations and all of us – in varying degrees – are involved in power relationships and thus in politics. The only choice that we really have is about what kind of politics we are going to be involved in.

Those of us concerned about human suffering and exploitation need to see how the marginalized can appropriate the same theological categories for liberating action. From the underside of history, the side of the marginalized, politics is not just a power game for the powerful, but a far more inclusive category, open to all human activities.

During the darkest hours of the struggle for liberation in South Africa, the state often argued that there was no need for Muslims to participate in anti-apartheid politics because there was complete freedom of religion. Some Muslims also argued that even under apartheid we had freedom of religion in South Africa. Here they often referred to the way in which our mosques were left untouched by the bulldozers when we were forcibly removed from our ancestral homes under the Group Areas Act. 'We are allowed to pray freely, to build mosques and *madrassahs* [religious schools], to give the *adhan* [call to prayer] and to convert others to Islam,' they argued. 'What more could we ask for, if they do not stop us from practising our religion?'

The accusation that those being moved by their religious convictions to engagement in the liberation struggle were 'using religion for political ends' came from several quarters. For the conservative clergy, going along with the system of apartheid wasn't viewed as politics; opposing it was. Many of them, in fact, had histories of collaboration with the apartheid regime – a regime that epitomized the abuse of religion for political objectives. Even without active collaboration with the regime one could still argue that a conscious silence in the face of the injustice was itself a political act. The example of reactionary clerics in South Africa arguing for withdrawal from politics as a means of legitimating subtle collaboration with power is a story that will resonate in every religious community throughout the world.

I remember the anger and sadness that many of us felt when the apartheid regime's destabilization of Mozambique forced the late President Samora Machel to come to South Africa and sign the Nkomati Accord in 1984. This agreement came about because of superior South African firepower, which killed thousands of Mozambicans and wounded many more through apartheid South African surrogates, and because of the deliberate sabotage of the Mozambican economy. On the afternoon of the signing I had a chat with the most senior figure of the Tablighi Jama'ah in South Africa. He spoke to me about the Accord being the result of 'the blessings of our group's activities' and how 'we were now able to get compensation for our lands confiscated when the communists came to power there'. 'If the suffering of the Mozambican people is the outcome of the blessings of this work,' I thought to myself, 'then how could I possibly be supportive of it?' What lands was he speaking about? Did this man not know that I come from an impoverished and struggling family in the township of Bonteheuwel and that my heart was with the poor who ended up with the confiscated land?

Many a domestic worker from South Africa to Kuwait will bear painful testimony to the moral and spiritual bankruptcy of many of the 'religiously devout'. Years ago, a friend, Abdullah Esau, mockingly remarked that 'at least on the Day of Judgement our domestic workers will not be able to say that we did not introduce them to the Prophet's way of doing things, the *sunnah*. We forced them to sleep on the floor and we forced them to eat left-over food!'

The security police first detained me when I was still in school. Spyker van Wyk, one of the more notorious of the apartheid regime's Security Branch brutes, asked me something that was to stick in my mind for a long time. Being unaware of my involvement with the Tablighi Jama'ah, but very much aware of my political involvement in National Youth Action, a high school group campaigning for equality in education, he wondered why I could not be like *'die mense met die lang jurkies'* (the people with the long gowns). 'What was it about the people with the long gowns that made them so attractive to the security police?', I wondered.

Yet I refuse to believe that it is an 'either–or' story; I have seen too many deeply spiritual people consistently indicating that it is possible to have a warm and intense relationship with Allah as Lord and Sustainer of the universe and, simultaneously, to be concerned about all of Allah's people. I have also seen too many activists, once deeply committed to human values of justice and compassion, losing their souls at the altar of political expedience. I am, therefore, convinced that there must be a path between these two, each which, on their own, often promise little more than political hypocrisy and delusions of spirituality, respectively.

There is, however, something far more fundamental here: the myth of the neat distinction between religion and politics or revelation and revolution. Politics, in its broadest sense, means the determination of human history and the power relations that shape it. While ideas are not always born with an awareness of their political implications, they are never shaped in a political vacuum. This is even more distinctly a fea-ture of Islam. Given that, from its origins, Islam had been inseparably a religion and a polity, it is not surprising that the political struggles among the early Muslims should also have led to the elaboration of theological problems. In another work, *Qur'an, Liberation and Pluralism* (Oxford: Oneworld, 1997), I dealt with how the marginalized can use theological categories for liberation, where politics is not just a power game for the powerful but a far more inclusive category, open to all human activities. In this sense, politics refers to the reality of power in which all persons participate – or work towards participation – in the creation of history, where the distinction between religion and life, spirituality and politics, collapses and all human endeavour is used to achieve dignity and freedom.

Islam as a religion is also a way of life and the ritual forms of worship are a part of religion; they are an important part, but still only a part. If our worship is not linked to our lives and to people's suffering, then it becomes a safe part of religion, a part that all the decision makers in unjust socio-economic structures would want to encourage. The separation between this-worldly and other-worldly matters has never really struck a responsive chord in the world of Islam.

Although many of us abhor the abuse of this connection by Muslim militants, it is certainly one well-founded in the Qur'an. Surah al-Ma'un (Q. 107), for example, supplies an interesting perception of religion (*din*) by defining the rejecter of religion as 'the one who is rough to the orphan' and who 'does not encourage the feeding of the poor'. From this qur'anic chapter it is evident that while religion has much to do with the worshipping of the One God, it is also very much about making the connection between that worship and the suffering of others.

This connection is made on numerous other occasions in the Qur'an, for example when Musa (Peace be upon him) was in exile in Madyan he was offered employment by an elderly man who, after they discussed conditions of employment, told him: 'I shall not make you overwork. You will, *insha Allah*, find me amongst the righteous' (Q. 28:27). Similarly, in Qur'an 90:13–18, after Allah speaks about 'two paths' and the very few who ascend the difficult path, He says that 'as for the steep and difficult path, it is the path of "the freeing of the slave, or giving food upon a day of hunger to an orphan in your family or a needy person in misery"'.

Many 'religious people' would argue that it is not with this connection and with serving others that they have difficulty but with 'politics'. In response to this I would suggest that any religiosity which fails to see the connections between poverty and the socio-political structures which breed and sustain poverty and injustice but then hastens to serve the victims is little more than an extension of those structures, and therefore complicit in the original crime.

To be poor today means more than not to have money. It means being deprived of decision-making power; it means not having access to information and facts about the reality of society, to be marginalized and to exist on the fringes of society. Thus we must go beyond what Max in *The City of Joy* describes as 'playing Santa Claus', giving pieces of bread to the little ones who knock on our doors, peer at us through our TV screens or who offer to wash our car windows at intersections on the roads. The martyred Latin American bishop, Dom Helder Camara, said that when he cared for the poor then people said that he was a saint, but as soon as he asked why people were poor and started addressing the root causes of poverty he was accused of being a communist. We need to appreciate that if we choose solidarity with the poor and the marginalized then our option has a political character in so far as it means attacking the structures that give rise to and sustain injustice.

The choice is not between revelation and revolution, nor is the question whether we should get involved in politics or not, for all of us are already involved. The question is not whether religion can be used for political purposes, either. The question is which religion – that of the feudal lord or of the villager – and for whose objectives: for a narrow class or capital's interest or for God's family – 'the people' and their only home – the earth.

THE *READER'S DIGEST* ISLAM

The *Reader's Digest* is one of those safe magazines, the kind that doctors can put in their waiting rooms without running the risk of upsetting anyone. Besides humour, it focuses on personal initiatives and individual heroism and is welcomed in all societies, including the most repressive. In many ways, the *Reader's Digest* represents a kind of Islam that sits comfortably with everyone who does not want to disturb the peace – even if the peace hides the demons of racism, sexism and economic exploitation.

We are often taught that personal commitment to goodness is the thing; that if I am pious and lead a life of freedom from all 'immoral' practices, then everything around me will be OK. If everyone concerned themselves with being good then society would change: therefore, our task is to work on our faith first and change our own hearts. The analogy that I have often heard from the advocates of this opinion is that of an electrician working on the electrification of a village. While the technicians wire the village, they do not have the privilege of switching the electricity on. When the big day arrives, that honour belongs to some minister. We, they argue, must concentrate on strengthening our faith, until one day when Allah decides to switch on the lights of guidance.

The truth is that there is no point in Islamic history at which there was darkness everywhere until one fine day everyone woke up to be blinded by the light of *hidayah* (guidance). Furthermore, however valuable personal virtue may be, evil is often an extension of entire systems of exploitation and evil. Personal morality or faith within the framework of those systems, or without challenging them and their advocates, is really of little consequence. Allah will not only ask us about the extent to which we did good but also about the extent to which we challenged evil. The following hadith in Bukhari and Tirmidhi alludes to this:

> It has been reported by Nu'man ibn Bashir that the Prophet (Peace be upon him) said: 'There are people who do not transgress the limits of Allah, and there are others who do so. They are like two groups who boarded a ship; one of them settled on the upper deck, and the other, on the lower deck. So, when the people of the lower deck needed water, they said: 'Why should we cause trouble to the people of the upper deck when we can easily have plenty of water by making a hole in our deck?' Now, if the people of the upper deck do not prevent this group from such foolishness, all of them will perish.'

The hadith wherein the Prophet said: 'I swear by Allah that you people cannot attain salvation, unless you prevent the oppressors from oppression', further underlines the futility of personal piety in an exploitative society.

I come from a deeply religious family, one that cherishes all the good old values of respect, decency and stability. We, my mother and her flock, though, lived on the 'wrong side' of South Road in Wynberg; the side that was declared 'White' in 1961. We thus found ourselves carted off to the wastelands of the Cape Flats while the rest of our extended family continued their supposedly respectable, stable and decent lives. It fell to our nuclear family to produce the extended family's first 'gangster'; our family was taunted by the rest for knowing nothing about *'God se gabod'* (God's commandments).

This experience was one of the earliest to make me wonder if sin was purely personal. Did the ruling class share the guilt for the crimes of my brother by uprooting us from Wynberg and dumping us in Bonteheuwel? Did the rest of the *ummah* sin by silence then? Is there not such a thing as social sin when the Qur'an speaks about 'the People of Ad' and 'the People of Thamud' being destroyed? Most Muslims are acquainted with the term *fard kifayah*, an obligation that, if fulfilled by some, absolves the rest, and if unfulfilled, makes everyone culpable. Has the time not passed for us to see beyond the examples of replying to someone's greeting or attending a funeral service? The truth is that there is precious little – if anything at all – which is entirely spiritual, entirely personal, entirely social or entirely whatever.

Very often we only notice the effects and symptoms of problems, without seeing the causes. It's like pimples; one does not see the cause because it is below the skin. Bus fares increase; many people complain but few notice that a year later the bus companies acknowledge huge profits. When the profits are published, they are usually buried in the back sections of the newspaper in complicated language that most of us do not bother to read. Many people are not aware that their tastes and styles are influenced by the marketing and advertising practices of huge companies. Another example is that of the imam in the mosque, who condemns the youth who have taken to drugs but does not see the emptiness that modernity causes in the souls of people. The imam thinks that the 'obvious good' is a scathing sermon whereby drug takers and dealers are going to be dispatched to the lowest pit of hell. How much do his sermons really, and not seemingly, help?

There is another option: to examine how much we and our values contribute to the structures that cause alienation, emptiness and spiritual desolation. Now this path is not easy, because it deprives one of self-righteousness and challenges you to get involved in activism. Any serious attempt to deal with the problem must also mean trying to understand the cause and dealing with it. 'Ah, but that's too complicated,' we say. Let the doctors handle it! This community is ours and we are its doctors, all of us, and we are responsible for looking beyond the skin, to the cause of the pimples. While the path of 'the obvious good' is OK to lullaby a lazy conscience to sleep, it does not do much for our integrity as Muslims and can even damage those whom we think we are trying to help.

Let me use the case of a well-meaning Muslim businessman to illustrate the point: He may decide to give his workers hot soup in winter and be quick to dispense his *zakah* (wealth tax) when the month of Ramadan arrives. However, he underpays his workers and feels that 'at least they have a job': if it were not for him 'where would they have been?' Besides, he feels that he does dispense his *zakah*, so his duty is really complete. He may even argue that it is necessary for poverty to exist, 'or else what will happen to one of the pillars of Islam?' He may never have considered how his exploitative business practices prop up a system that will forever need free soup for the workers. (God forbid the communist thought of making the workers partners in the business!)

Perhaps he has never thought that since he is so keen on upholding one of the pillars of Islam and that (at least according to him), as it might actually collapse if there were none of these poor and miserable people around, he could actually decide to become one of them in order to support that pillar! The truth is that when hunger is the most logical outcome of an entire economic system, the problem needs to be addressed at the level of both the symptoms and the actual causes.

The problem of addressing one or the other or both is reflected in an interesting analogy drawn by a Little Sister of Jesus. The Little Sisters are a group of nuns who believe in just living among the poor, not doing any missionary or social work, just sharing the lives of the poor with all the ups and downs of ordinary life. (Well, OK, the few ups and the countless downs!) They refer to this as the 'gift of presence'. Years ago I met the head of this order when she came to visit her flock in the slums of Korangi on the outskirts of Karachi. I told Sister Iris-Mary, who happened to be from Mannenberg in the Cape, that I saw little point in their 'gift of presence' whereby they do not do anything to organize the community to struggle for a better society. She had a really interesting answer: 'If a child comes running to her mother because she had been battered by a drunken father then the mother has to do two things: she has to wipe the tears and heal the wounds of the child and she has to do something about the alcoholism of the father.' The task of the Little Sisters, she argued, was the first, while the second task was for community workers and political activists.

In my understanding of Islam I have little sympathy for this separation of tasks story, because it goes against the idea of the comprehensiveness of life which, I believe, is rooted in the Unity of Allah. However, one thing is clear from the story: all the handkerchiefs to wipe away the girl's tears and all the mother's ointment is going to do little to solve the problem if nobody is going to work on the father's drinking problem. This is what I mean by trying to discover the hidden forces in our society which really pull the strings and cause the wounds. Oh no, I am not saying that we are victims of eternal conspiracies. Nor do I support the destructive and racist search for a Jew behind every Muslim blunder. I am saying that to live with our eyes open today does not only mean to ask if the burger that one is buying is halal but also to ask where the money is going to end up.

While Islam teaches us that all human beings are free, we must, however, be aware that each of us is also moulded by social institutions and structures. Our personal and social existences are intimately related. It is not only individuals who are cold and uncaring: institutions and structures can also be like that. People make the structures and the structures make people. When we seek to convert people from selfishness to selflessness and from separateness to togetherness, we must also convert the structures.

Many years ago, when I was still at school, I went to hear Professor Fatima Meer, a stalwart in the struggle against apartheid, speak at a symposium on a programme for the social upliftment of the people of the Cape Flats, the really impoverished part of the Cape. 'Any such programme', she said, 'was doomed to failure if it did not recognize that the problems of the Cape Flats is only symptomatic of the problem of Bishopscourt or Houghton, some really wealthy suburbs.' She argued that any programme aimed at uplifting the people of the Cape Flats that did not recognize the link between abundant wealth and devastating poverty was 'tantamount to sprinkling a few drops of perfume over a

heap of cow dung in the hope that the smell will disappear'. This profound indictment of capitalist society and misplaced 'charity' has
remained with me ever since and the 'cow dung' bit has become an
often invoked classic.

Earlier, I argued that our inability to see, for example, how capitalism is born from and entrenches selfishness, can cause charity to
amount to little more than a few drops of perfume. In fact, it could even
be worse: it can lull people into falsely believing that the cow dung is
a heap of scented dried flowers! Unlike many secular lefties though,
I do not believe that sharing has to wait until the revolution: it starts
now, attacking and destroying a system that denies sharing, by person-
alizing it in our lives today.

WHO'S IN CHARGE AROUND HERE?

We sometimes see or feel something that we believe to be unjust but
because it looks so eternal or natural we do not bother to even think of
doing something to change it. Sometimes we are so busy trying to
succeed within the system that it is convenient to ignore the injustice in
it or the values underlying it.

One of the more unpleasant terms common in post-apartheid South
Africa is 'the gravy train'. It refers to being in a senior official post that
carries a very lucrative salary package. Constitutional bodies such as
the Commission on Gender Equality, on which I serve, are among the
wagons of the gravy train. While the Commission comprises people
with a passionate commitment to the poor, it is remarkable that our own
lucrative salaries have never been seriously discussed except in the context of the complaint that we are receiving less than other such bodies.
While this complaint is well founded and reflects the shoddy treatment
that gender equality receives, none of us – including myself – has had
the courage to challenge the entire system that sees a new privileged
class emerging in the name of democracy. Gradually we are being
absorbed . . . While a number of us have found genuinely useful things
to do with our new found wealth, we do so quietly, so as not to upset
the apple cart, rather the gravy train. I am, after all, eligible for another
five years when the current appointment expires.

'The moral high ground' was a crucial element in the liberation
movement's success in mobilizing both our own people and armies of

solidarity activists across the world. While those currently in government are daily compelled to sacrifice much of that moral high ground
at the altar of realpolitik, and many others have long since succumbed
to cynicism a few of us, mercifully, continue to dream on. Come the
next election, I have no doubt that the immorality of the past will continue to be the biggest weapon in the arsenal of the ANC.

The task of the dreamers is to remind those in power that the realities of the socio-economic or geo-political givens within which they are
forced to operate are not the only elements that ought to inform political or economic policy; that, despite all evidence to the contrary, moral
imperatives are not only useful as political weapons. There is also the
vision to which, I would like to believe, all of us were – and a large
number in the government still are – sincerely committed. This is the
vision of a humane society, a world wherein it is safe to be human.

The challenge to reflect on our lives and the forces that shape our
values is very much a part of being Muslim. 'Say: Is the blind person
equal to the sighted? Do you not reflect?' (Q. 6:50). It is only when we
really understand what goes into the making of society and the shaping
of our values that we become capable of taking charge of our own lives.
Critical questioning leads to a greater awareness that our social
environment is unlike our natural environment. While this may sound
obvious, we seldom behave as if it is. We don't question the existence
of our mountains or rivers; their mere presence is sufficient reason for
them continuing to be there and for us to enjoy them. Unlike mountains,
the fact that social norms exist is not sufficient reason for them to be.
Styles of clothing, ways of celebrating weddings, religious festivals, the
arrival of the New Year, and so on, need to be continuously examined.
To argue that one is a helpless victim of social demands and that 'you
cannot help but keep up with the Joneses' is akin to equating our social
environment with our natural environments. We cannot blame our social
environment for what we are because we are, in fact, a part of that environment and, therefore, share in the responsibility for shaping it.

The influence that anything exercises over us does not belong to that
thing in the same way that, for example, light, heat and energy are an
intrinsic part of the sun and cannot be divorced from it. Our relationship with the environment can more appropriately be compared to the
light of the moon. No matter that the moon may appear to be so powerful that the tides of the sea, influenced by it, can cause boats to capsize,

the energy and light do not belong to the moon. The moon's influence is the result of the gravitational link between the earth and the moon. In other words, there is a mutual, yet proportional link.

The power of our environment is only what we have given to it. And because we have given it, we are free to impact upon that power.

In some parts of India, even in this day and age, the height of piety for a widow is to throw her body on the burning pyre where her late husband is being cremated. This act of self-immolation is intended to underlie the meaninglessness of her existence as a separate entity. In South Africa, even today, people refer to their workers, often old enough to be their parents and grandparents, as 'the boy' or 'the girl'. One day, *insha Allah*, these norms may be relegated to the dustbin of history. Today, however, they are very much a part of the lives of these people; they are their social environment. The sane person is, then, not the person who adjusts to these crazy norms, but the one who resists, who refuses to be moulded, because the mould is rotten. The extent of our being Muslim in the world today is, in large measure, gauged by the extent to which we question our social norms and resist them if they do not conform to our values. This is the one freedom that all of us still have; the freedom to respond in our own way to any given situation. We may be stripped of everything, but not of this freedom.

The acceptance of personal responsibility means the emergence of an interventionist Muslim, a Muslim who sees her birth in the twentieth century, in an industrial society, in a racist or sexist environment as part of a plan by Allah in the writing of history. She then questions and reflects on the specific task of her life to change the conditions around her in terms of her Islam. Such a Muslim doesn't settle for keeping pace with the world around but goes around, sometimes quietly and at other times vociferously, determinedly and consistently contributing to the creation of a new world.

Allah's story is being written and He wants us to be the cast. As Allah's scheme for the world is unfolding, He invites us to participate in it when He calls upon us to become His representatives on the earth. 'Lo, We offered the trust unto the heavens and the earth and the hills, but they shirked from bearing it and were afraid of it. And then humankind assumed it' (Q. 33:72). In the garden of humanity there are really no spectators; even the neutral ones are players. Each value that we uphold and by which we live our lives, the positions we take on issues as well as our refusal or unwillingness to do so, all our actions and non-actions, are always in an historical context.

'What can we do other than pray?' is a common sigh among many Muslims, and, indeed, others, when the problems around us seem immense and our courage or will to deal with them lacking. We some-times even claim neutrality. 'Let these Blacks fight it out among themselves' or 'Why should we get involved in *kafir* matters?' are not uncommon expressions. It is really impossible to be neutral with regard to any social issue or problem and simply pray for the eradication of these. Washing one's hands of a social problem or ignoring it simply means being passive inside that problem and, therefore, being a part of it. How do your investment or spending patterns contribute to the eco-nomic injustice that leads to hunger? How do your taxes aid a repressive state machinery? The question is thus not one of involve-ment in social affairs but of whether your involvement is passive and thereby supportive of the dominant and probably unjust status quo or whether your involvement is conscious and part of the work for change that will bring us closer to a new, more humane and just society.

As for praying, Allah, we often forget, does not intervene unilaterally in the affairs of people. Though perfectly capable of changing our con-ditions with 'Be! And it is' (Q. 2:117), Allah links His intervention to the intervention of people. 'Indeed, Allah does not change what is in a people until they change what is in themselves' (Q.13:11).

To be actively engaged with history requires a conscious and an alert way of living. When we become aware that we are free to shape our own responses to events around us then we are able to place our values, attitudes and actions within a broader reality. We will learn to search for the root causes of problems and seek to discover both the personal and the structural consequences of our actions and those of others.

I heard this wonderful story of resistance in the time of the Prophet Yusuf (May Allah be pleased with him). The Qur'an tells the story of the Prophet Yusuf being abandoned in a well by his brothers, who resented the way his exemplary behaviour had endeared him to their father. Found by a passing caravan, he was taken to a slave market to be auctioned. Folklore tells of an elderly woman who was seen making her way to the market with a small bale of wool. When questioned about her plans, she insisted that she had every intention of purchasing the Prophet in order to set him free. They mocked her for her simple-mindedness in presuming that a person could be bought for a measly bale of wool. She replied: 'Let it not be said on the Day of Judgement that Allah's Prophet was being sold on the market as an ordinary slave and that I did not attempt to purchase his freedom!'

The question is not always whether we are going to overcome our social environment, whether we are going to put an end to the abuse of children or be the ones to bring about the liberation of women. Rather, the question is whether we are going to resist wrong and attempt to do what is correct. This is the meaning of being a subject in history rather than an object.

ON BUILDING BURDENS

The Prophet Muhammad (Peace be upon him) is reported to have passed through a street of Medina and seen a new building with a dome. He asked his Companions what it was and they informed him that it was a new house built by an *ansari* (a member of the host community). The Prophet kept quiet and after some time the owner of the new house came to him and greeted him. The Prophet, however, turned his face from him. When the greeting was repeated he again ignored the *ansari*. Upon inquiring about the Prophet's obvious displeasure with him, he was told about the Prophet's inquiry about his new building. He imme-diately went and razed the new building to the ground without bothering to inform the Prophet. When the Prophet passed that way again he inquired about 'that building' and was told of the *ansari*'s raz-ing it to the ground. The Prophet then said that 'every new building is a burden for its owner except that which is absolutely essential'.

In another hadith, the Prophet is reported to have said: 'People say "my property, my property"; while out of his property only that is his which he eats and consumes, and wears out and spends in charity and sends ahead.'

All of us have values and these are usually determined by our social environment. Values, however, as I pointed out earlier in this chapter, are unlike natural phenomena whose existence does not require any kind of critical scrutiny. We speak through our choice of clothes, food, recreation, interior decoration, bank balance and architecture . . . And the messages conveyed by our choices are far more profound and honest than our verbal statements.

These things are not ideologically or religiously neutral; they are extensions of the predominant culture and its underlying values. The phenomenon of fast foods, for example, would never have emerged in a genuinely Islamic society or in other traditional societies. In such societies, the pace of nature is considered, food as seen as gift from nature and/or the Transcendent, people spare a moment in gratitude for the meal that is before them and food is treated with a deep sense of respect. How much and what we eat (three different kinds of food at one meal, junk food or nutritional food), and how we eat (the setting of the table, the cutlery, or whether we sit on the floor and use our fingers) are all reflections of our message. Imposing offices and desks for example, on the surface culturally neutral, afford an aura of importance to the person behind them and a sense of worthlessness and dependence to the person in front of them. Lounge suites with separate chairs and eating from separate plates encourages individuality and distance, whereas two or three eating from one plate, all sitting on the floor, encourages warmth. Distance, however, has to be encouraged in an industrial and capitalist society because such a society can only survive if you view your brother or sister as a potential threat.

The order of Allah is yet to be established, but we can reflect our vision today and we do so in our choices. The threat to our faith as Muslims, then, does not come from the Christian zealot preaching on the train or the naive but well-meaning Jehovah's Witness on the street. The threat is in the attractive ads on TV, the doctor who exploits people's faith in her as an expert on their health to promote a particular company's product, the saleswoman whose uniform resembles that of a nurse and who promotes her company's milk powder at the expense of breastfeeding.

Accumulation, the sister of consumerism, has impoverished us spiritually and humanly. It is essential in a capitalist industrial state that we be stripped of our worth as human beings and that we see our value in terms of what we possess. The capitalist industrial state does not only create enormous holes in our souls but also invents a lot of junk, with essential built-in obsolescence, to fill those holes before we discover them and sit back to wonder why our lives are so empty. They have invented a host of illusionary riches, conveniences and time-saving gadgets, because we need to save time so that we may rest because we have to work hard to pay for the time-saving gadgets and conveniences because we need to save time to rest because we have to work so hard . . .

Well-having – owning material things as a measure of success – appears to have been a dominant value in many societies from the earliest times. Today, however, as never before, it is being actively promoted as the only yardstick of progress and prosperity. The race to acquire more material goods is often exasperating, but we know of no other way to exist with 'dignity'.

I have often wondered why the Israelites in the time of Nabi Musa (Peace be upon him) were so dumb as to worship a golden calf created with their own hands. Looking at our own lives today and at the amount of time, love and energy that we devote to our stone idol (the house), to our metal idol (the car), or to our paper gods (the share certificates), it is no longer so strange that the Israelites, whom Musa led out of the darkness of oppression to the light of liberation, should fall for gimmicks. The difference is, of course, that Samiri, the initiator of the calf-idol idea, acted naively and in isolation. The idols of capitalism and consumerism today are created by a whole class of people whose lives rotate around little other than exploitation for profit.

'But my income is halal', we hasten to proclaim. Yes, that may be so. However, as I said earlier, there is more to the burger than its halal status. The laws of the Shari'ah are only the fibre of a comprehensive order. The skeleton of a fatwa (legal opinion) can only acquire meaning in the blood and flesh of *taqwa* (God consciousness). A fatwa may permit the building of palatial mansions with carpets adorning the walls while two-thirds of the world's population go to bed daily on a half empty stomach, but *taqwa* would never condone it. A fatwa did not ask that the *ansari* demolish the additional structure, but *taqwa* required it. Shari'ah is not sacrosanct by itself, but because it is to lead to the emergence of a social system based on Allah's will. This means that the laws of Islam must never be distorted to destroy the morality of Islam. Referring to the ritual of animal sacrifice, the Qur'an makes it clear that our ritual deeds are valued by their spirit rather than their material or physical dimensions: 'Their flesh reaches not Allah, nor their blood, but it is your righteousness that reaches Him' (Q. 22.37).

But how practical is it to ask people to have less, to lead lives of simplicity, to sacrifice well-having for well-being? This is perhaps not the question. The question is whether there is any other way of living with dignity in an insane world. Allah has given enough for the needs of everyone but certainly not enough for the greed of even a few – unless others die of starvation and the ecological system is destroyed.

We must release ourselves from our burdens. We know that this is not an easy task and that we are not entirely moved by rational or moral considerations. Nor do I want to suggest that this is all that there is to the problem; this is just a challenge to examine our personal roles in the structural causes of poverty and exploitation. For the moment I offer three reasons why we must be challenged.

First, the earth that Allah entrusted to us as an *amanah* (trust) cannot sustain the kind of progress that drives capitalism and consumerism. The USA, for example, uses one-half of the earth's natural resources. Suppose one more country becomes as 'developed' as the USA?

Second, we need to choose well-being over well-having and to combine an intense spiritual restlessness with a deep contentment in material possession if we want to move from the plane of mere existence to leading lives that are fully human and fully Muslim. While Allah insists that we go in search of our sustenance, we cannot equate this with becoming sacrificial lambs at the altar of consumerism and accumulation. Ka'ab ibn Malik (May Allah be pleased with him) narrates that he heard the Prophet saying 'Two hungry wolves let loose among a flock of sheep do not commit more damage than is caused by a person's greed for wealth and prestige to his [her] faith.'

Materialistic ideas of progress and development are the antithesis of the Islamic view because, in Islam, humankind is viewed as essentially a returnee to Allah. It's not as if we are going to return someday; we are always in a state of returning. While this journey must be enjoyed as we struggle to achieve fulfilment, any seasoned traveller will tell us how an overload of luggage hampers many of the joys of travelling.

Third, an existence of accumulation was never characteristic of the life of the Prophet Muhammad. He pleaded with Allah to let him live, die and be raised on the Day of Judgement among the poor. 'Umar (May Allah be pleased with him) tells of a time when he went to visit the Prophet and noticed that there were only pieces of leather and some barley lying in the corner of the room. He looked around and, failing to observe anything else, he started crying. When the Prophet asked him why he was crying, he replied:

> O Prophet of Allah! Why should I not weep? I can see the mat's pattern imprinted on your body and I am also seeing all that you have in this room. O Prophet of Allah! Pray that Allah may grant ample provisions for us. The Persians and the Romans have no faith but their kings live in gardens with streams running in their midst while you live in such dire poverty.

The Prophet, who was resting, sat up and said: 'O 'Umar! Are you still in doubt about this matter? Ease and comfort in the hereafter are much better than in this world.' (Cited in Mohammad Kandhlawi, *Stories of the Sahabah*.)

The Islamic value system, with its bias against things and for beings, can only be given expression when we have a willingness to have less. An interesting question that the Companions were asked by the Prophet on fundraising occasions was not 'How much did you contribute?' but 'How much did you leave behind?' A fascinating little matter for the 'major contributor' to ponder over!

As activists committed to Islam, we cannot wait until the structural causes of poverty are eliminated before the wealthier ones among us decide to have less or the poorer ones among us decide to abandon our dreams of having more. We must do so now, because when the accumulation of material goods means a diminishing of empathy with those injured by an iniquitous system, the destruction of our only home, the earth, and the impoverishment of our inner selves, then we have no alternative but to have less.

WANNA HAVE SOME POWER?

I have often been described as 'a leader' of sorts. There are undoubtedly some who would want to take issue with this description. Perhaps they would even agree with the security cop who, when I was still at school, looked at me and said: *'Jy, 'n leier? Jy lyk meer na 'n luier wat 'n mens an die baby se gat sit!'* (Literally, You a leader (*leier*)? You look more like a nappy (*luier*) round the bottom of a baby!) Be that as it may, the subject of leadership is certainly one on which I have some insights to offer, even if from a negative perspective. (The Tablighis have an interesting one when someone says that he cannot join them because he's still a drunkard, gambler, doesn't pray, still beats his wife or whatever. They tell him: 'You must still come with us; You can tell people "Look at me! Don't become like me!"')

Our personal attitudes towards power, if honestly uncovered, could lead to a wealth of information about our own hang-ups, insecurities and yearnings. The extent to which we deny our self-worth or the way in which we delight in being the conductor of the orchestra must be truthfully looked at if we are to become genuine workers for Allah. The question of leadership underlines the truth of the statement that it is indeed possible to work for Islam and yet move further and further away from Allah as do few other questions.

One can work on Islamic causes driven by the desire for recognition by one's peers and manipulate others in ways calculated to maximize that recognition rather than the pleasure of Allah. On the other side of the coin, we can find ourselves shirking responsibility, also due to a lack of self-esteem, because we hate to be chosen. This can even be disguised as humility or religious modesty. There are number of hadith that indicate that it is not permissible for Muslims, as individuals, to seek leadership or even to desire it. This is not because we negate our Allah-instilled self-worth, but because of the awe with which we view that responsibility. If, however, our brothers and sisters entrust us with leadership, then we assume it and struggle to do a good job, while trying to remain humble in the face of the responsibility that we have assumed.

Often our being in a 'position' causes us to demand respect. We little realize that this demand is demeaning and a negation of our self-worth. We all deserve respect because we are who we are and if respect doesn't come our way then there is something wrong with our state of being. If that state of being is meaningful to those around us then we will command respect. If, on the other hand, that state of being is meaningless or a source of irritation to others, then it is pointless to demand respect.

Imam Ghazali tells a fascinating story of two friends, Abu 'Ali Ribati and 'Abdullah al-Razi, on a journey. During this trip into the desert, 'Abdullah suggested that one of them should be the leader on that trip. Abu 'Ali felt that 'Abdullah should be the leader and the latter agreed. 'Abdullah, the leader, then took a bag filled with provisions for the journey and carried it on his back. When Abu 'Ali asked that the bag be given to him to carry, 'Abdullah said: 'I'm going to carry it, and did you not agree with my being the leader?' When Abu 'Ali replied in the affirmative, 'Abdullah said: 'Well, then you must obey.' That night they were caught by the rain and 'Abdullah stood at Abu 'Ali's head till the morning, shielding him with his cloak. Abu 'Ali sat there, all the time saying to himself: 'If only I had died, rather than said, "You be the leader."'

While it seems that it would have been far more sensible if the two had together decided to share the responsibilities, the idea of leadership as being service for other is unmistakable and praiseworthy. 'Abdullah stands there throughout the night, drenched, but with unqualified dignity.

The amir – with the long 'i' – in Islam is seen as a servant rather than a fellow dishing out instructions, the amir – with the long 'a'. (Muslim history is, of course, by and large, a rather different story.) The authority vested in our leaders or leadership groups comes from the extent of that service rather than the position being occupied. One of the other implications of the amir being the servant is that she emerges from a situation of service. She gets thrown up from that group or community, rather than being imposed by others uninvolved in their struggles. This does not mean that leadership is a reward for service. Our reward is the joy that comes from the involvement and from knowing that we are struggling to please Allah.

One of the lessons that I learnt in the Call of Islam (alas, rather belatedly!), is that leading others doesn't always mean doing work that others could be doing. It often means assisting others in seeing what they are capable of. Indeed, it is dehumanizing to remove a task from another and presume that one is the collective of the group's potential. The essential task of leadership is the awakening of each one in the group to what is best in all of us and to assist each other in actualizing that. The trust of leadership is the trust of enabling, enabling others to become worthy vicegerents of Allah, while struggling to become one oneself, rather than a trust of effective control and authority. This means a willingness to be open and participate in a manner that secures the accomplishment of the goals of the group. To do this we must operate in a manner that helps a group to bring the potential of all its members into full play.

Commitment to the task and creative effort on the part of a group is proportionate to its members feeling free to express ideas and participating in decision-making and goal-setting. Alienation most readily sets in when the leadership appears more concerned with getting a job done than with relating well to the team as co-workers. Since responsibility for getting the job done is as much the group's as it is the leader's, freedom in work and a team spirit is absolutely essential. This also presupposes a good amount of flexibility on the part of the leadership with regard to change, when they are persuaded that changes will be useful for the group and its task.

The way in which we operate is often more important than the end result of our task. Our leadership style and ways of operating must, in fact, become a microcosm of our vision of the order of Allah for the entire universe. If justice, 'people first', openness, and so on are an intrinsic part of that vision, then it must be seen where we work now. The medium is the message. Leadership is responding to the current needs of the group in such a manner that the group is helped to go on with goals that it has collectively determined. To lead is to be of service in such a way that the group is willing to receive that service.

Our work may at times require good business procedures, but any leadership based essentially on that is dehumanizing. When leaders become obsessed with agendas, appointments, checking in and checking out, then they are no longer for people. Leaders obsessed with systems expect people to become for them. In the same way that you can work for Islam and systematically move away from Allah, the leader can work for people and systematically move away from people. Only a deliberate and conscious moving towards an 'us-ness' is going to prevent that.

Leadership is not so much about our titles but about who we really are, what we do, how well we do it and, above all, how good we are at enabling others in the process. I remember a rather unpleasant Call of Islam meeting, towards the end of my involvement with the group, at which I was challenged about my refusal to subject my public-speaking itinerary to the scrutiny and approval of the group. 'Aren't we all equal?' Adli asked. 'No!' I shot back from the hips, firing a volley of qur'anic verses at him to kill his argument – and possibly him if I could have had my way. Alas, he didn't die. I did.

While in the organizational context cited above, Adli was clearly in the right, all people are not unqualifiedly equal. The Qur'an mentions piety, knowledge, participation in struggle as well as precedence in entering islam as qualities that elevate some individuals above others. These are, however, qualities for Allah to consider when dispensing grace or for the community when appointing leaders: they are not meant as crutches to prop up mutilated egos. It is somewhat pathetic (and tragic) when the 'repositories' of these qualities have to remind people of their 'credentials'. Others, even we ourselves, may recognize and respect the qualities of learning, wisdom and leadership in us, but they may never be used to bully those we assume do not have these qualities.

FIVE

on being with the gendered other

> You should really visit our area the next time you come; it's a pity
> that your visit is such a short one. You'd be delighted to know how
> alive Islam is there; you won't find a single woman on our streets!
>
> My guide in Uzbekistan, then part of the Soviet Union, in 1988

Most of the major world religions today are really about males; male
founders, male prophets, male managers of the sacred and male interpreters of the theological and spiritual legacy. Notwithstanding all this,
the vast majority of active and committed adherents to these religions
are women. Men seem to be the producers and women the consumers.
An additional factor that Islam has to deal with is that its historical
heartland, the Orient, is a place where the socio-economic and cultural
marginalization of women remains very stark.

The pressures of modernity and a greater awareness of gender justice have for long compelled Muslims to address the question of
'women in Islam'. The fact that this is a subject of discussion in many
and varied forums without any discussion of 'men in Islam' is itself
rather revealing. As indicated above, the assumption is that the role of
men is an understood and accepted given.

Responses to this awareness of the need for gender justice in Islam
and in Muslim society have been varied. The first insists unequivocal-
ly that 'Allah wills inequality for women'. Examples of this include the
Taliban in Afghanistan and an irregular South African tabloid, the
Majlis, which seem to view women as both a necessary evil for the
release of sexual tension and as invaluable baby-making machines. The
fact that, in their creation myth, woman is made from a broken rib of a
male means that her existence is essentially derivative, that she is

fragile and needs to be hidden, both for her own protection and for that of men, who may fall victim to her inherent predisposition to lead them astray.

The second response is more humane but is nevertheless apologetic and reflects what may be described as a theology of the dole. By this I mean a view of Islam that encourages gentleness towards women; sort of giving them warm soup and blankets while they form a permanent queue outside the citadels of male power with no hope of ever sharing in that power. The interminable refrain here is: 'Islam preaches kindness and gentleness; the problem is with Muslim males and the contemporary interpretation of Islamic law.'

In the last fifty years or so there has been an ever-growing amount of literature dealing with a somewhat more enlightened approach. Among the more contemporary scholars of this third response Fatima Mernissi, Leila Ahmed and Nawaal El Saadawi have engaged in a radical critique of the role of women in Muslim societies. Others such as Riffat Hassan, Amina Wadud, Asghar Ali Engineer and the late Fazlur Rahman have sought to deal with Hadith literature and the Qur'an in order to give them a more gender-friendly gloss.

There is another approach: to view the question through the eyes of justice, not kindness. When unkindness is merely the outcome of an entire system of racial or gender oppression, kindness to the victims is a form of further disempowerment. This approach is thus not interested in tinkering with the details of Muslim Personal Law in order to make it more woman-friendly, except perhaps as a strategic measure of redress in social contexts where women have nothing. Basic questions here would be about the very patriarchal constructions of Muslim Personal Law and, more significantly, about the fact that, however one looks at it, the Qur'an seems to have males as its primary audience.

I am among those who use 'contextualization' and feminist hermeneutics (ways of reading a text) as a means of addressing this problem in the following essays. I often feel though that my approach is rather simplistic and perhaps even somewhat dishonest, in the sense that it is silent on all the theological implications of this path. It's still all that I have at the moment.

After a general overview of the stock Muslim apologetic approaches to the question of gender justice I use the controversial Friday address of Professor Amina Wadud in Cape Town's Claremont Main Road

Mosque in 1994 as a line on which to peg a number of pertinent issues such as male insecurity about the invasion of their bastions of power and the problem of listening when you are engaged in a war, in this case one for gender equality.

In this chapter, unlike the rest of this book, I write consciously as a Muslim male, often using 'we' for Muslim men. I utilize my own insights and the suffering of my late mother to reflect on the relationship between racial oppression and gender oppression, more specifically between apartheid and sexism. This relationship is also evident in the question of violence towards women when we see how it corresponds to the violence that many White farmers inflict upon their Black workers, who are really viewed as part and parcel of their property.

ON MANDELA AND WOMEN

No, this is not about Mandela and Evelynne, Winnie or Graca; it is about the difficulty of reading our religious texts, which seemingly discriminate against 'others': in the case of men, the gendered other – women.

Very few questions get Muslim males, and even some women, to put up barricades of defence and apologia as much as that of the discrimination of women in Muslim society. Our response to the question of gender injustice reveals an enormous amount about ourselves. It reveals our own humanness (or lack thereof), our security or insecurity as males. It also shows the extent to which we are sincerely committed to the call of Allah: 'O you who have attained unto faith, become witness-bearers for Allah in the matter of justice, though this may be against yourselves.' In this case, we – Muslim males – must rise as Allah's witness-bearers for justice.

The dehumanization of women cannot continue unaddressed and the quiet suffering in roles assigned by men must be confronted. For how long can we, Muslim males, pretend that they have no voices of their own? For how long can we continue to seek refuge in spurious sayings of the Prophet (Peace be upon him) that they are of 'faulty intelligence' or 'push them back as Allah has pushed them back'? The emotional, psychological and sexual abuse of women in our societies is real and we need to confront it. We cannot afford to continue lulling ourselves into a false sense of a 'superior Islamic form of gender equality' by our stock responses that Islam was the first to grant women their full rights or that Islamic Shari'ah was, in fact, ahead of other legal systems by according women the right to property ownership and inheritance. While much of this may be true, it does not deal with three fundamental issues: first, what are the rights denied to Muslim women by Muslim men today? Second, how should we view the rights outlined in Shari'ah? Third, how do women seeking gender justice really derive support and inspiration from a tradition whose icons are all either men or isolated women who inevitably draw their 'legitimacy' from their relationship to males: wife, daughter, narrator of traditions, mother of a prophet. Lastly, and perhaps most crucial, is there really any place for gender justice within a theology rooted in a seemingly ahistorical and stable text such as the Qur'an, which is inescapably patriarchal, coming from a Deity that, however that Deity may defy ultimate description, nevertheless employs the male form of the personal pronoun in reference to 'Himself'?

As for the first, we are all familiar with the wide gulf between our rhetoric and practice. We can no longer escape the truth of gender oppression by referring to the West, on the one hand, and Islam, on the other. We need to compare practice with practice and ideal with ideal. What is the point of comparing Western practice with the prophetic society except to delude us into a false sense of moral superiority? We know that the Prophet Muhammad (Peace be upon him) washed and stitched his own clothes and that he shared cooking chores with his wife. We also know that freedom for large numbers of women in most parts of the industrialized world has been reduced to exploitation for commercial gain.

However, all this begs the question: how much of prophetic practice do our males adopt – how many of us can even fry an egg? From where does the practice of dressing little girls in pink and little boys in blue, or of buying cars for the boys and dolls for the girls come? How many of these values of *kufr* (literally, ingratitude, rejection, used to denote heresy) have we not adopted from the very 'West' upon which we heap such richly deserved abuse?

Arguments for the oppression of women are steeped in the logic of 'we have found our ancestors doing it' which was so regularly invoked by the Meccan opponents of the Prophet. Muslim males use the 'Islam has already given it to women, fourteen hundred years ago' argument to deny the fact that, in practice, we withhold even those rights from women in our societies. Indeed, we need to question the very idea of 'giving it' to 'them'. Are human rights a gift awarded to well-behaved little children and as if women ('they') exist outside the world of Islam ('we') in the same way that children are seemingly external to the world of adults? The right to self-respect, dignity and equality comes with our very humanness for, Allah says: 'I have distinguished the children of Adam' (Q. 17.70). If Allah blew of His own spirit into us at the time of creation, then to deny the equality and dignity of women is to deny the presence of that spirit in women.

What of the Qur'an and prophetic practice (*sunnah*) with regards to the rights of women? The Qur'an contains texts which, at a casual perusal, can be strongly egalitarian and others which, also at a casual perusal, can appear to be strongly discriminatory. Let's compare this with the question of discrimination against another form of 'otherness', religious otherness, the idea that people are somewhat less than us because they do not share our religious beliefs. Nelson Mandela, whatever the depth of his humanity and however unbounded his compassion, is regarded as less than a 'Muslim' who beats his wife, abuses his children or even commits murder, because Mandela does not have the appropriate label!

In South Africa there are a number of Muslims who have spent various periods in prison with Nelson Mandela, who comes from a Methodist background. Can these Muslims simply ignore the Qur'anic text that says: 'Do not take the Jews and the Christians as your friends; they are friends unto each other' (Q. 5:51)? If they want to remain Muslims and at the same time remain true to the experience of a shared comradeship in the jails of apartheid then they have seriously to rethink many things connected to this text. What is the context of this verse within the rest of the text? What is the context of its revelation? Who were the specific Jews and Christians referred to in this verse? Under what historical circumstances was this revealed? What are the different meanings of *awliya* (allies)? What is the sense of this verse in the light of other such verses and how do they qualify or amplify each other? What does this verse mean in the light of the basic spirit of the Qur'an which is one of justice and compassion?[1]

Each of us in our lives has known the love, care and dignity of
women and we can never with integrity return to the notion that they are
'inadequate'. Thus we need to ask: 'What does Allah mean when He
says "Men are *qawwamun* over women"' – and *qawwamun* is normally
translated as 'superior' or 'guardians'. In addition to looking at individual texts that seemingly discriminate against women we also need to
look at the assumptions about women and their creation that we often
read into the text. An example of these would be the idea that a woman,
Hawwa (Peace be upon her), was created from the bent rib of a man,
Adam (Peace be upon him), and that women were created for men.

The basic truth in approaching the Qur'an with a view to understanding the role of women and issues of gender justice is that, like any
text, it yields different meanings depending both on the questions being
asked and on the bias of the reader. Let's use a huge wine estate as an
example. Somewhere in the centre of the estate is a palatial mansion of
much historical worth, inhabited by the squire and his family.
Somewhere on the edges, out of view from the passers-by, are the wood
and iron shacks of the workers who rise at four or five in the morning
and return to their hovels late at night; all for a pittance and a few
bottles of cheap wine. While there is only one estate and while the
workers could have a shared existence on it with the squire and his
family, the way they experience the farm will be fundamentally different
from each other. For the one, the farm represents bounty and for the
other misery, even if, in the case of the latter, they may have grown
deeply attached to it in the absence of any awareness that things could
possibly be different.

The point is that reading a text through the eyes of the marginalized
who yearn for justice would yield a meaning in harmony with what
Allah, the Just, desires for all of humankind. This is why the work of
women scholars of Islam such as Fatima Mernissi, Leila Ahmed, Riffat
Hassan and Amina Wadud is so important in the shaping of a new reading of the Qur'an and the Hadith.

As for the prophetic practice, the *sunnah*, the Prophet Muhammad
revolutionized the status of women. We know that until his coming
it was common practice for unwanted females to be buried alive
after birth, the evidence of women was unacceptable and they were
not allowed to inherit. All of this was completely transformed by the

coming of Islam. However, as a prophet and as a revolutionary he had to take cognizance of the social context wherein he was operating. As 'Ali ibn Abi Talib (May Allah be pleased with him) said: 'Address people at the level of their understanding.' The Prophet, therefore, did not abolish slavery but exhorted slave owners to feed and accommodate their slaves exactly as they did themselves. Furthermore, he encouraged the freeing of slaves; the Qur'an suggests that it is an act of great merit, enabling us to be pardoned for our sins (Q. 5:89; 90:13). In the case of slavery, it would be correct to argue that a movement that had to culminate in the freeing of the slaves was set into motion and that the ultimate freedom of all slaves was an inevitable consequence of this movement.

While exhortations to feed and clothe your slaves and to be gentle with your women were courageous and path-breaking at that time we cannot get stuck there, because the objectives towards which the Prophet moved are far more important than the premise from which he started. While kindness, gentleness and compassion are always qualities to be welcomed they can never be substitutes for justice, freedom and equality. Similarly, reforms in women's issues meant that the prophetic intention was the freedom and equality of women. When the Prophet fought against the killing of female babies and insisted on the sacrifice of a ram or a goat to celebrate such a birth, he did not intend to institutionalize one ram or goat for a girl and two for a boy. These were what Joe Slovo, South Africa's celebrated freedom fighter, would have termed 'sunset clauses' in the country's interim constitution, ways for the powerful of yesterday to come to terms with the rising of a new dawn.

My response to the question of male tradition and a stable text is thus to revisit the question of both tradition and text as stable. Both functioned within and were also the products of a given society that Allah wanted to see transformed. It is this transformation and vision of freedom and justice rooted in Allah's will for all people that we grope towards, rather than struggling to hold on to a tradition that is today being presented as unchanging.

Let us not fool ourselves by proclaiming it is not Islamic law that discriminates against women, rather it is only the practice of Muslims. There have, of course, been varied interpretations of the Shari'ah over the ages and in different societies, and some of these have led to a kinder dispensation for women. The truth, however, is that while in a few areas of life Islamic legal thinking has kept up with human progress and produced new insights, in many others, including gender justice, it hasn't. Shari'ah is also a path and a process which, whatever else it may be, involves people with different perspectives, like the farmworker and the landlords. The religious landlords among us – all male – have aborted the process set in motion by the Prophet: we have betrayed the prophetic intention of justice and equality for all Allah's people.

We do not have to be prisoners of our histories. We can also be the heirs of a revolutionary process. There is much in prophetic history that we must claim and build upon for the creation of a world wherein it is safe to be human and woman. The human condition is such that I cannot spit in your face except that I also become diminished in the process. I cannot oppress a woman except that my maleness is also impaired, for my security cannot be built on your insecurity, my promised land cannot be had on land from which you have been dispossessed.

THE GENDER JIHAD

'The first woman ever to do so [addressing males in a mosque] in South Africa' proclaimed the *Cape Times*, a local daily. 'One of the first in South Africa', said another daily. This was in response to a major event on a Friday during August 1994, when Professor Amina Wadud, an eminent Muslim scholar, took to the rostrum in the Claremont Main Road Mosque. While several women had, in fact, previously addressed males in mosques in South Africa, this was the first time that it had been on the occasion of the congregational prayers on a Friday. Although it preceded the more formal ritual of a rehearsed Arabic sermon, in the religious imagination of Muslims it was every bit as significant as the sermon itself.

More committed to transforming gender roles in the community than seeking publicity, and conscious of the major rupture with tradition, the organizers perhaps deliberately downplayed the significance of the event. The extent of this rupture was, however, clearly recognized by the Muslim Judicial Council, the leading body of Muslim clerics in Cape Town, and its supporters. The ensuing furore with its exchange of fisticuffs and anonymous death threats to the organizers and ideologues behind this historic event is thus understandable, even if inexcusable.

The South African Muslim community is one of the most dynamic and exciting in the world of Islam. Some of the most profound thinking on Islam takes place here and every international scholar who visits our shores, of whatever theological or ideological persuasion, leaves deeply impressed by the dynamism of religio-intellectual life among the Muslims here. Our South Africanness has, I believe, been a significant factor in this dynamism, and in many ways the tensions in the South African Muslim community are reflective of those that characterize society at large. Alas, not every believer sees these tensions as 'exciting', for the known is being challenged and the unknown is invariably feared.

The mosque was packed on that Friday and the mood, rather than curious, was euphoric and celebratory. The fact that all the women, who sat downstairs in the space normally reserved for men, were clad in black with only their faces and hands exposed, indicated their own commitment to tradition and to the community even as they were celebrating a rupture in it. These scholars, activists, theologians and academics, far from being 'orientalists', as they are often disparagingly termed, may more appropriately be described as 'South Africanists'. Our initial ideological hinterland was the 'Islamic Movement', the internal description of what is commonly regarded as Muslim fundamentalism.[2] The South African endeavour to rethink Islam for us is, in fact, the result of a marriage between the Islamic Movement idea of a comprehensive Islam and 'the Struggle', the battle against apartheid.

The historic event in the Claremont Main Road Mosque highlights a number of issues that we as contemporary Muslims who desire to remain committed both to our religious heritage and to gender justice need to address.

First, while the debate in the southern parts of the country[3] was about women being allowed to address males in a mosque, many among us have a number of implicit and unstated objectives: women assuming personal responsibility for all aspects of their lives, including officiating in all worship ceremonies in mosques and on the pilgrimage and taking control over their reproductive health, as an intrinsic part of human rights and gender equality. 'Where will it all lead to?', the conservatives ask and point to 'the West' where 'moral chaos reigns' in other religions. We have hitherto avoided this question and just point to the inherently immoral nature of gender discrimination. For how long are we going to ignore the logical theological implications of a comprehensive embrace of human rights and gender justice?

The second issue that the struggle against apartheid also taught us is that people's humanity is in large measure given meaning by the extent to which they, especially the marginalized, are empowered on the one hand and, on the other, the powerful, even the religious ones, are disempowered. When Allah promised to bestow His grace upon and to empower the oppressed among the Israelites he accompanied that promise with another: the disempowerment of the oppressive Pharaoh, Haman and their supporters. An interesting and not entirely unrelated question is whether the disintegration of male religious authority will lead to the disintegration of all religious authority. This may well be, but whatever replaces it can hardly outperform the injustice so regularly perpetrated in the name of religious authority.

Third, does not the emphasis on justice in general, and more specifically gender justice, set this up as the criterion whereby truth is determined? In other words, are we using this to determine the truth of the Qur'an and our traditions rather than truth being determined by the Qur'an and our traditions? While there is nothing intrinsically wrong with holding to one's singular understanding of Islam, we need to walk carefully with ourselves and with others who do not fit into our interpretation of what this single understanding is all about. Did Allah not say 'And We have created the world in truth so that every soul shall earn what it has earned and that it may not be wronged' (Q. 45:22)?

Fourth, most Muslims have not begun to think through the issues connected to gender justice, although the conversations of ordinary Muslim women often contain horrendous tales of wife battering, sexual abuse and wife abandonment. They are convinced that the redressing of all their pain is located within traditional notions of the male being the sultan in the home and that they merely require a gentle sultan who observes Islamic morality. More recently, in one of South Africa's northern provinces, thousands of Muslim women signed a petition in support of a radio station which demands the right to keep women off the air. How connected to ordinary women and their concerns are these progressive Muslims? Will this be another case of the masses cheering while their 'liberators' are being fed to the lions?

I recently had a rather chastening experience at our mosque. The women congregants at our mosque prayed upstairs until the day of the Amina Wadud sermon, when they came downstairs. Since then they have prayed alongside the males, from the third row to the last, with a rope separating them from the men. The front two rows were, however, reserved for the men in a manner that was never articulated or discussed. Upon the death in Ramadan 1998 of a dear friend and gender activist, Shamima Shaikh, an event that I deal with later in this chapter, I delivered an obituary in our mosque. I concluded by asking if we could do two things to honour her memory and her work. I asked that the men go home and seriously reflect on the nature of their relationships with the women in their lives and that we remove another symbol of gender discrimination in our mosque, by enabling the women to move to the front two rows.

The following evening I went early with a friend, Firdawsa, to set up a bench between the pulpit and a pillar to separate the genders from the first row. The world did not cave in and the women tentatively sent the young girls to occupy the first row. On the second evening we repeated our action and this time some of the women occupied the front row. On the third day I went to Pretoria where I worked. When I returned to Cape Town after a few days everyone had reverted to the position of four years earlier. I felt a bit like a presumptuous White trade unionist wanting to organize Black farmworkers in a couple of days and then fleeing back to the comfort of his trendy suburb after a nice speech to the workers, leaving them to deal with the farmers. Just what and who gives you the right to act as this big-time gender equality activist?

These are just some of the questions that I have been thinking about for quite some time and have even begun to address. In many ways, the reluctance to answer them publicly in an unambiguous manner comes from the fact I am not a disengaged thinker who enjoys being radical. I am interested in transforming my community and to do so I must combine courage with prudence – not that I have had any notable success in this regard. Furthermore, I believe in the value of raising questions and just leaving them there. What I am certain about is that the marginalization and oppression of women must end, and that one of our weapons to end it is Islam.

While the struggle for gender equality is about justice and human rights for women, it cannot be regarded as a women's struggle any more than the battle against anti-Semitism is a Jewish struggle, or that of non-racialism a struggle belonging to Blacks. While violence against women may physically and legally be a woman's problem, morally and Islamically it is very much that of men. In the words of Maryam Rajavi:

> In a society where women are second-class citizens, deprived of their genuine rights how can any man claim to be free and not suspect his own humanity? . . . Are men not in bondage too? I believe that they are. Of course, their situation is different. They are enchained by their quest to dominate women and impose their will on them and inevitably on society and history. (*Islam and Women's Equality*)

All of us, whether in our offices, bedrooms, kitchens, mosques or boardrooms participate in the shaping of the images and assumptions which oppress or liberate the other – and thus ourselves.

IT'S JUST A DARK BLOB OUT THERE

Yes, I was also there. I sat in the front row. I was there from beginning to end. The next evening I visited my cousin and met her fiancé for the first time. 'Did you hear about this woman [Amina Wadud], Mawlana?' he wanted to know. More interested in how 'this woman' was being viewed by ordinary Muslims, I asked him to tell me more, without saying anything about my presence at the controversial event. 'She delivered the sermon; from the pulpit, to crown it all! What's more, she announced that she's available to perform anyone's marriage; they must just phone to make an appointment.' I just said 'Wow!' and went on to ask him how his imam and congregation were planning to respond to all of this. He informed me that they were going to rise up, organize buses, protest outside the mosque on the following Friday and mobilize the community in an attempt to unseat the imam and the current mosque committee.

The truth is, of course, that Professor Wadud spoke before the formal sermon and answered questions after the prayers. (And, no, she did not offer to perform marriages.) Yet, here was this guy in an absolute fit about what he had heard. Did he listen when he heard? Did his imam listen when he heard? They say that in any war truth is always the first casualty. How sad, our inability to listen to others, the haste with which we pigeonhole others and then casually proceeded to rubbish them . . . and then do untold damage to our own souls in the process.

Have you ever felt misunderstood? Have your motives ever been questioned? Have you ever yearned for someone to understand you as you really are? Have you ever felt angry because you felt that someone had deliberately been misrepresenting you? Have you ever wondered 'Why on earth couldn't they come to me to ask me?'

Let us look at ourselves and know that the yearnings of other people are no less than ours. Let us speak the truth about people, especially if we disagree with them. Know that falsehood destroys; above all, it destroys the person engaged in it. Know that the refusal to confront someone calmly and frankly with our arguments is a reflection of our own lack of courage and perhaps the feebleness of our faith. Know that the haste with which we resort to tackling the person and avoiding the ball does not say much for our ability as sportspersons. I know that it is difficult to be nice to the other side when it appears as if they are about to destroy all that we hold dear, when it seems as if they want to abandon long-held interpretations of Islam that we have come to think of as Islam itself. It is difficult to listen to the other when we feel threatened. It is however, always preferable to pay less attention to horror stories and approach the people involved directly.

At a conference entitled 'Islam and Civil Society' in Pretoria, Mawlana Goga, the principal of a girls' *madrassah*, came up to me and raised some questions about the sermon that I had just delivered during the congregational prayers. Soon afterwards we were joined by several other senior students from the Newcastle Darul Ulum, a major traditional seminary. Initially, I did not know what to say; it was as if we were speaking different languages. I simply could not deal with their questions because they came from a mindset from which I feel completely alienated. Postmodernist Islam was talking, not conversing, with traditional Islam. In a very non-judgemental way I told them of my difficulty. We then went on to speak about the need for us to talk and listen to each other. Listening to them, I became aware of my own intellectual arrogance, of the convenience with which I stereotype traditional scholars. I also understand how much of my own thinking is intrinsically linked to a worldview that is genuinely threatening to all forms of traditional discourse. I should, therefore, not be surprised when people react; anyone who feels threatened reacts. And they jolly well have a right to react. Yet I was moved by their courage to come from Newcastle to listen, not to be taught, but to listen. I, too, realized afresh the need to listen to those who disagree with me.

I know that the other side is not any less human than mine. They also bleed when pricked; they also raise their voices when their arguments run out of logic; they, too, go home after the fight outside the mosque and wonder whether it was worth it. Sometimes, of course, they cover their uncertainties by even more strident pamphlets or slogans. Their 'other side', my side, is equally uncertain. Often we think of the other side as just a big dark blob out there: 'modernists', 'academics', 'mullahs', 'clerics', 'feminists' . . . Listen to any insider and a completely different picture, a myriad of diverse internal voices, emerges. Listen carefully to yourself and while a single voice is usually clearly audible most of the time, you'll often hear several radios broadcasting on the same frequency. Sometimes, of course, when the war is on, the different sides pretend that they are solid blocs; the truth, however, moves somewhere in between.

There is far more greyness in our positions than our adversaries or we are wont to admit. We only pretend that our position or that of the other side is rock solid. (And any student of basic geology will tell you that not even rocks are solid.) We talk about the 'ulama [*clergy*] say' as if there is a solid 'ulama opinion. (There may well be, if we think that only our side has 'ulama and the others only have charlatans.) Only if we care to listen can we discern the diversity of opinions in our own hearts and in the voices around us. I have no illusions about the difficulty of listening. How can we listen when we are engaged in a war, especially if that is a war for our faith?

Let us also not forget that for both sides in the gender jihad it is a question of faith. There are many sensitive women who simply cannot, with any self-respect, live alongside the idea of a God who reduces them to half of men. For them, and for the men who identify with them, it thus very much a question of faith, and a very personal and deeply held one too. At times, it may even appear to be immoral to call for a culture of listening. Could we listen to the cops brutalizing us and murdering our kids during the seventies and eighties in South Africa? Should we have? Where would our struggle have been if we decided to pause and listen to them? Can we ask women to listen to men who have abused them, dehumanized them for so long? The amazing thing is that most women committed to gender equality are still prepared to listen. None of them are saying that they want a complete transfer of power.

As for we males, what is it about us that makes us feel so privileged? I recently heard a Christian minister from Atlanta, Georgia, say something really telling, even if somewhat crude: 'I refuse to preach in a church which does not allow women to preach there,' he said. 'In effect, they are telling me that I am OK because of something between my legs which women do not have and, frankly, I do not think that that is enough reason for me to qualify to preach!'

We need to ask what exactly it is that we are afraid of; is it really women speaking in mosques? Is it the loss of our own faith at the hands of 'modernists', the uncertainty as to where all of these 'new ideas' will lead? Is it the loss of power that we as males exercise over women? Is it the loss of authority that we as religious leaders exercise over people? Is it our own sense of masculinity that is being threatened? If it is, then is it not more rewarding to look deep into ourselves and personal histories and study this hunger for power, this desire for authority and our own deep-seated sexual insecurity?

There is much truth in the idea that those who shout loudest against something usually feel most personally threatened by it – and often this 'it' that they feel threatened by is actually or feared to be located deep within themselves. In the same way that fanatics resort to screaming certainties as a way of camouflaging their own doubts, our fear of the gendered or sexual other and the resulting chauvinism is often a shield against our own deep-seated real or feared internal other.

If I may revert to the tale of my cousin's fiancé who ranted against 'the woman who preached in the mosque'. In a curious twist to this tale, this engagement with my cousin collapsed soon after, when a neighbour produced a photograph of her fiancé in another role – as a very stylishly dressed woman! Rather than reacting so angrily against women preaching in mosques or leading the prayers we need to ask ourselves: what are we really defending and what are we really afraid of?

THE FALL OF MAN

During the 1980s, a Muslim tabloid which originates in the Eastern Cape gave my views on the role of Muslims in the struggle against apartheid rather extravagant, uncharitable coverage, for about eight consecutive issues devoting most of the front page and virtually the entire centre spread to them! Now that's called 'publicity'. The tabloid used rather strong language to dissect what it regarded as my 'baseless and false' views on Islam and the struggle for freedom.

Throughout this period they never failed to be respectful of my person and to refer to me by my theological title 'Mawlana' (literally 'our protector' or 'our friend', usually meaning 'priest'). Subsequently though, they really flipped and referred to me as 'an ignoramus masquerading as a Mawlana'. That's extraordinary. They suffered me an enormous amount until then and the question is, what really caused them to banish me so unceremoniously from the fraternity of those who manage the sacred? Women, as always held responsible for the fall of man, were responsible for my descent from a 'Mawlana with baseless opinions' to 'an ignoramus masquerading as a Mawlana'. (Well, at least, the issue of women. I had publicly argued that the qur'anic permissibility to marry four wives was no longer applicable.)

For me though, it is not just an issue such as the permissibility of beef or cheese consumption, nor of whether you need to see the moon with the naked eye or not before you can commence with the fast of Ramadan, all issues which rear their heads from time to time in the community and then disappear. The suffering of women, like that of any injustice, is a part of our existence, of what we live for and, for far too many, die for.

My mother was one of those too many. She started working as child at a 'steam laundry' in Wynberg and literally ended her life working as an ironer in Parow. She complained bitterly about the ever-present watchful eyes of 'the supervisor', 'the shop steward' and the boss. There was the crazy run for the train in the mornings, long before the sun was up, while the bosses were still having cups of coffee and browsing through their morning newspapers. Long and tiring hours on the factory floor were eased by non-stop piped music. Production, production, and more production were all that the bosses cared about. What did she get in return? A measly weekly wage and a silly box of chocolates near

Christmas, at 'breaking up'. (It's not just the factory that 'breaks up' at that time of the year, it's also the workers reaching breaking point.)

Returning home from the factory was another ordeal. In earlier years, coming home from the steam laundry in Wynberg meant a short, calm walk down Batts Road; afterwards it meant standing third class in two overcrowded trains and a long walk through sandy bush in Bonteheuwel. How did she land up in Bonteheuwel where there is no variety in the sandy hills? Our previous home was on the wrong side of the road. They came in 1961 and declared our side of South Road 'White'; Milford Road, with its Coloured and Black population, was flattened. Thus we ended up in a matchbox house among the sand dunes and the Port Jackson trees.

Alas, apartheid and capitalism were not the only forces that ravaged her existence and ensured that she lived only into her early fifties. She had six sons. My father abandoned our family when I was a few weeks old and my mother had to rear all six of us. As is usually the case with desperate struggles for the life of a family, the pivotal person was a woman. My brothers were 'helpful' but the essential task of cooking, cleaning, washing, ironing and the countless odds and ends were still hers. We were, after all, 'men' and although our helping out was useful, that was not to be our major calling in life. 'The man is the sultan of the house' is a creed even my mother adhered to. The trauma of six sultans in one palace is another story. My mother's place was in the kitchen, in the house, in the township of Bonteheuwel, in the factory and in apartheid South Africa. It was a place that she accepted, but it still stank.

How often have we not used the acceptance of oppression and the fear of freedom as justification for the perpetuation of injustice? Women often don't want men in their kitchens, so it is convenient for us to stay out of them. This is similar to the reasoning applied to 'boys' or 'girls', sometimes old enough to be our grandparents, who work as domestic servants and accept eating in the backyard. The argument that 'they prefer it this way' is commonly heard in White and upper-class Muslim homes. Benevolent madams may even add: 'In fact, we have invited him/her to sit at the table with us on numerous occasions but he/she always refuses; that's just the way they are.'

Every single argument, religious or cultural, that is employed to keep women in the kitchen or in the house has a parallel in racist discourse. 'Our traditional way of life', 'Allah made them inferior', 'No, they are not inferior, merely different', 'What would happen if women were to control the world?', 'The ideal for women is to be at home, necessity brings them to the factories.' (Remember apartheid's 'The ideal for Blacks is to remain in the homelands, necessity brings them to the cities'?) Sexism also parallels liberal racist discourse: 'Of course, women can govern, if they are capable.' On the other hand, we assume, often rather mistakenly, that men are capable of governing and never add 'if they are capable'.

The similarity between resistance to gender and racial justice was also brought to the fore in the recent battles of conservative communities to resist integration at a school level. 'Our greatest fear is losing our culture, it is what we are, our being, our salvation,' said a spokesman for one such community. 'Rather poignant,' I thought when I first read the heading to a story in a local paper, until it struck me that it was the distraught father of a pupil at the formerly all-White Potgietersrus Primary School, desperate to protect his daughter from the onslaught of the natives . . . They refused to 'cave in' to the government's demand that the school be integrated. Rather than accepting the twelve Black pupils who had applied for admission they withdrew their children and sought refuge in the local Apostolic Faith Mission church building, in a frantic but futile last stand for 'the Afrikaans culture and religion which we have struggled to uphold'.

The rest of us marvelled at the naiveté of those who hope to hold back the waves of equality by putting their little racist fingers in the hole of the dike. It was a father protecting his daughter, the old theme of the patriarch who is duty-bound to protect his vulnerable female ward in the name of religion and culture. Yet the vast majority of South Africans instinctively recognized that this man and his ilk should not be allowed to get away with it in our country, not in this day and age. It is not that most South Africans have a problem with Afrikaner culture or religion, only with a particular manifestation of them. And if they insist that their appreciation of their culture and religion is the only authentic one and that those who do not share their bigotry do not count, then they have only themselves to be held responsible if outsiders reject the whole lot.

Sadly, Potties, as Potgietersrus is fondly called by its inhabitants, is not only in the Northern Province; it is all around and within us. There are men, and even some women, who are desperate to hold back the waves of gender equality and justice for all. And, like the Potties man, they make moving appeals to religion, culture and biology. Like the Potties man, who blames the conspiring external devilish communist forces who have undermined tradition, the chauvinists blame the pornography-peddling West with its unsolicited and undesired White cultural interventions. ('We are Africans; this feminist stuff is White poison', 'We are Muslims; women's equality is Western rubbish'.) Like the Potties man, they are so blinded by the prospects of losing power and the spectre of their own liberation from their prisons of fear of the 'other', Black or woman, that they fail to see that underneath all this is a rather simple quest: justice. Like the Potties man who insists on the separation of the races, natural chauvinists complain about the dangers of overlooking physiological differences. Referring to the obsession with these differences, Maryam Rajavi says: 'The real danger throughout history lies in overemphasizing these differences to justify and legitimize discrimination against women' *(Islam and Women's Equality)*.

There is a marked difference though: unlike the response of disdainful bemusement, outrage and extensive press coverage which greeted the Battle of Potties, the rearguard reaction of chauvinists to the entrenchment of gender equality and the subjection of religious and traditional personal law to the Bill of Rights is given careful and even sympathetic consideration. Gender inequality is so deeply ingrained in our society that many of those deeply offended by racial discrimination continue to accept sex discrimination. The Constitutional Assembly acted with enormous courage and integrity in this regard. It did not succumb to the need to keep African traditional leaders as a supporting electoral prop in rural areas, or to 'keep minority religious groups happy'. Instead, it strengthened the gender equality clauses in the Bill of Rights so that they would not be subjected to discriminatory traditional or religious laws in any way.

Does the Constitutional Assembly's position signify a lack of respect for religion and does it constitute interference in the religious beliefs of our country's citizens? The new South Africa is in some ways the product of, simultaneously, a contempt and a deep reverence for religion, and this is also reflected in the country's Bill of Rights. It was a contempt for all expressions of religion that fostered and justified racial discrimination, exclusivism, exploitation and oppression. (And there were expressions of all our country's religions that did exactly this. The fact that the man from Potties could find refuge for his daughter in a house of God testifies to this.)[4] Conversely, the new South Africa came about through the active labour of numerous men and women who, moved by their indomitable faith in a just God, sought to give active expression to the dream of a country wherein all God's people would be fully human and fully alive. It is this reverence for all God's people, what the Quakers call 'that of God in all of us', that is the highest religious value, which the Bill of Rights seeks to uphold when it insists that gender equality cannot be subjected to exclusivist and discriminatory interpretations of religious or traditional law.

As for the question of interference in religious beliefs, undoubtedly, yes, the country's Bill of Rights does constitute interference, in the same way that the state interfered in the religious beliefs of the man from Potties. If he decides that racism and a denial of the humanity of others are intrinsic to his religious beliefs then it's really regrettable. We can rejoice in the fact that there are numerous Christians and not so numerous Afrikaners who prefer to focus on the inclusive and the just strands in their religious heritage and culture. If some Blacks, Muslims, Jews, Catholics and others insist that a denial of the full humanity to women is an intrinsic part of their tradition, then tough. Mercifully, there are numerous Blacks and religious believers who insist that justice, being intrinsic to the God that they worship, is an inseparable part of their faiths.

CALLING ALL MARRIED COUPLES!

Bendorff is a small picturesque village somewhere in the north-western part of Germany. To my knowledge, the population is largely German and the Muslim population is rather small. Yet this was the place where I performed my most extraordinary 'Id al-Adha prayers. I was invited by the German Muslim League to come and celebrate the festival commemorating the willingness of the Prophet Abraham (Peace be upon him) to sacrifice his son and to speak about Abraham as a symbol of religious pluralism.

Early that morning I set off for the chapel where the prayers were being conducted.[5] With the benches pushed aside, carpets neatly laid out, the crucifixes covered by sheets, there were the Muslims –

Bosnians, Germans, Iranians, Palestinians and Egyptians – sitting in a circle praising Allah by chanting the *takbir* (the customary praising of Allah). They were now joined by a brother from a distant corner of the world, South Africa.

Women! There were women making up about one half the circle! And they were chanting along with the men! What an extraordinary sight! And there was more to come. I joined the group in the *takbir* and wondered about the world of Islam, the diversity of this community of Muhammad, the many manifestations of the desire to submit to the will of Allah. The chanting of the *takbir* was different from 'ours'. (Wherever I have travelled I have found a chant different from 'ours'.) Yet there we were proclaiming the greatness of Allah. And I wondered: 'What is "ours"? South African? Malay/Indonesian? Cape Townian?'

My mind kept on wandering to something that Mawlana Abdul Kader Osman said during our student days in Pakistan: 'The Qur'an speaks about light (*nur*) and darknesses (*zulumat*) because while truth is only one, there are many forms of falsehood and innovation.' Taken to its logical conclusion, even shaking hands on 'Id day was a manifestation of falsehood and innovation because there is no proof that the Prophet (Peace be upon him) shook hands or embraced after the 'Id prayers (I must say that AK, as we called him, was a rather consistent fellow; after the 'Id prayers he marched off straight to his room and refused any offer of a handshake or an embrace!) And these women? And the kids merrily running around from mummy to daddy and then back to mummy . . . the leader of the group, Bashir Dultz, who is a prominent Sufi shaikh, gently smiling at them?

The time for prayers came and everyone stood up. 'Can all the married couples come to the centre please,' the imam requested. 'What on earth is this about?' some wondered. Quite simple, really; the married couples were going to form the connection between the rows. At the end of each male row the female row began and everything was 'OK' where the two sides met, with the imam standing somewhere in the centre in front of the husband. (No, not the imam's husband! Relax, the imam was a male; I'm referring to the husband of the connecting woman in the front row.)

'Does anybody have any problems with this arrangement?' the imam asked. Silence. With the prayers concluded there were handshakes and even embraces all round. (Yes, yes, I mean all round!) I spoke to some

of them afterwards. I was particularly intrigued by the informality of
some of the women. Body parts were covered, as was the hair, but a
woman wearing jeans, admittedly not tight fitting, during prayer?
Surely, that's a bit heavy? I very politely asked Huda Salah, an
Egyptian Muslim, about her jeans and whether she really thought them
appropriate for prayers. 'I will be glad to answer your question', she
said, 'on condition that you assure me that you asked the brothers who
are wearing jeans the same question.'

The point is that often we say that men are also expected to dress
modestly, that men must also 'lower their gazes', that men must also
cover their private parts, and so on, but we're not really serious about
it. (When did I ever hear men being criticized for wearing tight-fitting
clothes during prayers or at other times?) It's a bit like the rhetoric of
many Muslim businessmen when confronted with questions of
exploitation: 'Islam is against both capitalism and socialism,' they say.
Scratching below the surface one quickly discovers that they really
believe that capitalism isn't such a big problem. In their daily business
practices? It's just great!

Fatima Mernissi, in her inimitable style, tells an interesting story
about her childhood at the time of the Second World War: 'The
Allemane [Germans] forced the Jews to wear something yellow whenever they stepped out into the streets, just as the Muslim men asked the
women to wear a veil, so that they could be spotted immediately.'
Mernissi and her cousin, Samir, speculated furiously about why the
Allemane were after the Jews and eventually her mother came up with
a master stroke:

> It could be the same thing as with women here, no one really
> knows why men force us to wear veils. Something to do with dif-
> ference maybe. Fear of difference makes people behave in very
> strange ways. The Allemane must feel safer when they are with
> themselves, just like the men in the medina [city] who get nervous
> whenever the women appear . . . Crazy world. (*The Harem Within*)

We are terrified of our own weakness. Most of us feel so terribly in-
adequate as persons that we require another species to feel superior to.
It is, of course, unfashionable, at least in public, to feel superior to the
Blacks, the Berbers, the Bushies, the Pathans, the Miabhais or the

Kashmiris. Thank heavens, women will always be around! (If not, we'll always have the Jews to fall back on, of course.) Unable to assume responsibility for our vulnerabilities, we blame women and they end up carrying the burden of both their own fall – after being pushed by us – and our fall.

And then we say that women are the weaker sex?

THE COURAGE TO BE MAD

A very dear and very mad friend of ours, Shamima Shaikh, one of South Africa's leading Muslim gender equality activists passed away in early 1998, when her physical body succumbed to cancer. Shamima was thirty-seven and left behind her husband, Na'eem Jeenah, and two sons, Minhaj and Shir'ah, aged nine and seven.

Shamima was a member of the National Executive of the Muslim Youth Movement and former editor of the progressive Muslim monthly *Al Qalam*. More recently, at a time when other co-religionists were denying women the right to be on air, she served as chairperson of Muslim Community Broadcasting Trust, which runs The Voice, a Johannesburg Muslim community radio station. It was, however, as a gender activist within the Muslim community that she made her mark. She spearheaded the formation of the Gender Desk of the Muslim Youth Movement. In this capacity she rapidly became a thorn in the flesh of conservative Muslim clerics on the now defunct Muslim Personal Law Board, who were keen to develop and implement a set of Shari'ah laws that would entrench gender inequality.

In an event that drew widespread controversy in the Muslim community, she led a rebellion of Muslim women worshippers at the 23rd Street Mosque in Johannesburg in 1994. Throughout the month of Ramadan she and a number of other women prayed upstairs in the mosque. When she arrived on the twenty-seventh night, the most spiritually significant one for Muslims, the upstairs was occupied by men and a tent was set up outside for the use of women. Braving numerous angry offended men with fragile egos, she led a group of comrades to reoccupy their space. On another occasion, she and a friend just decided to pray outside the mosque in pouring rain after being denied entry. By then she had acquired the well-deserved description as 'that mad Shaikh woman'. Yet, to friend and foe Shamima was the epitome of

gentleness and politeness. If ever there was a passionate fighter for justice who fought every battle with a smile and much laughter, she was one.

In the same way that for anyone committed to gender justice a
woman's place cannot be confined to bedrooms and kitchens, she ultimately became frustrated with being an 'upstairs' woman. In a
little-known move, unprecedented in the world of Islam, she and a
number of comrades – male and female – started an 'alternative' congregation where gender equality and all its implications for Islamic
thought and practice were the norm.

Shamima first learnt that she had cancer about three years ago.
Nothing changed for her. Her life was full of laughter, courage and the
will to change the world and she merrily continued. 'If the last hour
strikes and finds you carrying a sapling to the grove for planting,' said
the Prophet Muhammed, 'go ahead and plant it.' Her hour had struck
but her planting continued unabated. Knowing that her life was rapidly
ebbing away she delivered a lecture on 'The Qur'an and Woman', with
great difficulty, in Durban three weeks before her demise.

She inspired us and taught us that there is nothing inevitable in life.
She insisted that while death may be inevitable we are free to shape our
responses to it. She chose not to undergo various forms of chemo-
therapy and other than resorting to some traditional and homeopathic
options, was determined not to return to her Lord kicking and screaming.
A poem, presented by a cousin and posted at the entrance to her bed-
room said it all:

What Cancer Cannot Do

Cancer is so limited
It cannot cripple love,
It cannot shatter hope,
It cannot corrode faith,
It cannot destroy peace,
It cannot kill friendship,
It cannot suppress memories,
It cannot silence courage,
It cannot invade the soul,
It cannot steal eternal life,
It cannot conquer the spirit.

The day of her death and burial was a day of relentless pushing of the religio-cultural limits. Shamima's death was testimony to the qur'anic verse that says 'Do not say about those who are slain in the path of God that they are dead; nay they are alive . . .' She had requested that a close female friend lead her funeral prayers. (As part of her obsession with retrieving subversive theological and juristic memories which accorded women a more just place in the Islamic scheme of things, she had come across a report that the funeral prayers for Imam Idris ibn al-Shafi'i (May Allah have mercy on him), a revered Islamic jurist, were led by a woman.) Thus it came to pass that for the first time in the last few centuries a Muslim's funeral service, albeit at her home, was led by a woman and followed by women and men.

At another service in the nearby mosque later, her husband led the *salah* (prayer) despite the presence of a number of theologians and clerics. A large number of women attended the funeral prayers at the mosque. (And no, they did not go upstairs, nor to an outside tent.) It was heartrending to see so many women in the twilight of their earthly lives entering the house of Allah for the very first time. And when her physical remains arrived at her final earthly resting-place, in the town where she was reared, Pietersburg, the women were again there to offer the funeral prayers and be present at the burial. While a narrow pathway separated the women mourners (mostly clad in black) from the men (mostly clad in white) who surrounded the grave, it was nevertheless a historic occasion.

Seeing the black-robed women observers separated by a narrow pathway from the male participants at the graveyard, I was reminded of a curious phenomenon at Boulders Bay, a beach near Cape Town. Here one can see scores of penguins on the shore. They quietly stare at the numerous visitors separated from them by a rope lying in the sand, and they rarely cross the rope. The difference, of course, was that the human beings face them while here, at the funeral, we had our backs turned to the 'other' and we all faced the centre of our attention, Shamima.

Do we always have to make a fuss about the presence of women? Do we always have to panic when they enter 'our' sacred space?

After arriving in Pietersburg, I took a walk to the local mosque to offer the *asr* (late afternoon) prayers – and who did I observe in the mosque in the male section? A woman! Her legs and arms were exposed and she wore a T-shirt with a rather low neckline which left little to the imagination. Oh, it's OK. Relax. She was not there to pray. She was only the Black cleaner. (Remember that apartheid years poster of a startled White priest walking into his church and finding a Black man? 'What on earth are you doing here?' asks the priest. 'Father, I'm the new cleaner,' replies the man. 'Sorry, for a moment, I thought that you came to pray,' responds the visibly relieved priest.)

So we can deal with women, but we need to reduce them to half human beings in order to feel less threatened before doing so. (In some ways, I am reminded of the way most Muslim communities deal with gay people. They are welcome as flamboyant camp singers at weddings on the Indo-Pak subcontinent, hairdressers for the bride, handy to come and do the washing and ironing. All of these are acceptable at a social level and passed over in silence at a theological level, as long as they are very clearly effeminate, obviously 'funny' and 'know their place'. Heaven forbid that they try to be just 'ordinary' and 'normal' and visit our homes or befriend us like any other human being. It's then that the roof caves in.)

Shamima, we do not have to pledge that we will pick up the battles where you left off. About that you have no doubt. We can pledge to try to do so with the gentleness and love with which you fought them.

What a life! What a way of passing on! What a death!

'If this be madness, God,' her husband Na'eem, prayed at her funeral service, 'Give us all the courage to be mad.'

Amin.

SIX

on the self in a world of otherness

The story is told of a rabbi whose disciples were debating the question of when precisely 'daylight' commenced. The one ventured the proposal: 'It is when one can see the difference between a sheep and a goat at a distance.' Another suggested: 'It is when you can see the difference between a fig tree and an olive tree at a distance.' And so it went on. When they eventually asked the rabbi for his view, he said: 'When one human being looks into the face of another and says: "This is my sister" or "this is my brother" then the night is over and the day has begun.'

Klippies Kritzinger, *Believers in the Future*

A student recently asked me if I was 'a staunch Muslim'. I felt a bit like Alice in Wonderland when she was asked by the caterpillar 'And who are you?' She replied: 'I . . . I hardly know, Sir, just at present, at least I know who I was when I got up this morning, but I think that I must have changed several times since then.' I replied: 'Well, it depends on what you mean by "staunch", what you mean by "Muslim" and on the particular moment that you are asking the question or want the answer to apply to.'

We all comprise multiple identities, depending on where we come from, what we believe in, where we are and whom we are interacting with at a particular moment. Often we insist on identity as a fixed and unchanging category. A closer look, though, shows that we and the way in which we view ourselves are really ever-changing. The insistence on viewing identity as stable usually reflects our insecurity, our fear of the unknown parts of our selves emerging when the label is peeled off, and so we hold on desperately to the label although the contents of our selves are in a regular state of flux. In the words of Salman Rushdie:

> We have come to understand our own selves as composites, often
> contradictory, even internally incompatible. We have understood
> that each of us is many different people . . . The nineteenth-
> century concept of integrated self has been replaced by this
> jostling crowd of 'I's. And yet, unless we are damaged, or
> deranged, we usually have a relatively clear sense of who we are.
> I agree with my many selves to call all of them 'me'. (*Time
> Magazine,* 11 August 1997)

The idea that there is no stable self is considered in the first section of
this chapter, where various forms of otherness within the house of
Islam are looked at through the prism of the many displays of 'official'
Islam as well as 'popular' Muslim spirituality in a Cairo mosque. Still
on the subject of the 'internal other', the second section deals with our
relationship with those inside the house of Islam who do not share our
perspective of what Islam 'really' is or how best to work on really
getting it into our lives. We all have our inside-outsiders; the ones who
share our labels but whom we cannot stomach. The way we deal with
others is really a reflection of the way we deal with ourselves. The last
section of this chapter thus deals with the etiquette of differing with
others and the importance of holding one's adversary sacred despite
the differences.

While we are rather generous in both the speed and frequency with
which we hurl the epithet *munafiq* (hypocrite) at our inside-others,
much of our difficulty in the contemporary world is with the religious
other; those who do not share the Muslim label with us. For Muslims,
this label is obviously very important. 'He named you muslims before
this and here', says the Qur'an (Q. 22:78). Thus 'muslim' is also a
label, a form of identity. However, the Qur'an also refers to 'muslims'
before the Prophet (Peace be upon him). In other words, there is an entity
called muslim outside the group of people who followed the Prophet,
for the word refers to anyone, or indeed, anything that submits to the
will of Allah. Regrettably though, rather than describing a person with
certain characteristics, the term now only refers to a certain social
group, a group that views itself as the chosen of Allah.

The second part of this chapter deals with the problem of religious
labels and of a compassionate God who looks at the deeds of people
rather than their labels.

KNOCK, KNOCK – IT'S THE *MALBOET* (AND HE'S KNOCKING FOR ME!)

When I was a child ('was'? Am I not a still a child? Do I not carry my child 'other' within my adult 'self'?) the community had a man who was the announcer, known as the *malboet.* He would knock on doors and, in a mixture of Afrikaans, Cape Dutch and Malayu, invite the household to a religious gathering, a mosque meeting or a funeral. We always had mixed feelings about the coming of the *malboet;* besides the mixed bag of languages that he used, he was also a mixed bag of grief and joy.

Notions of mixed bags defy religious categories of Black and White, yet our religious lives abound with mixed bags.

The city was Cairo; the sermon (*khutbah*) rather bland, not surprising for an official mosque run by the Egyptian Department of Religious Affairs and Endowments. The preacher (*khatib*) was certainly knowledgeable and somewhat liberal. He spoke about the 'ease and convenience' of Islam; quoting the Prophet (Peace be upon him), he said: 'Make things convenient for people and do not impose difficulties upon them; give them glad tidings and don't frighten them away.' In what I thought was a veiled reference to the Egyptian Muslim militants, he added another hadith: 'Whoever seeks to complicate this affair of ours [i.e., Islam] will find himself overwhelmed by it.'

And the mosque? The Mosque of Husain, directly opposite the famous Azhar Mosque. The Azhar University, the oldest extant university in the world, is a bastion of Muslim orthodoxy, whatever orthodoxy may be on a particular day. When the monarchy ruled Egypt, the Azhar duly pronounced such a system in conformity with Islam; when King Faruq was overthrown in 1952 it denounced the monarchy and supported the new republicanism; when Gamal Abdul Nasser introduced socialism, the Azhar followed suit with its supportive fatwas saying that socialism was an intrinsic part of Islam. And so it was with the wars and peace treaty with Israel . . . How fluid, crooked and wide the path of the firm, straight and narrow!

Well, some things are predictable in the world of Islam. It is actually quite nice to walk into a mosque thousands of miles away from one's own (what is one's own?) and know exactly what's up and what to do next. Occasionally, in our encounters with our own 'other' we get a bit disturbed. Sometimes we see the 'other' praying differently and mutter something soothing about all four of the Sunni schools of jurisprudence being 'on the truth'. Sometimes I hear of other Muslims slaughtering a black chicken to ward off some evil spirit and I just shake my head at this 'heresy' – merrily forgetting how my very orthodox late mother liberally sprinkled salt in the corners of the house to ward off the same evil spirits. They just don't make orthodoxy like they used to, do they?

Anyway, back to the Mosque of Husain in Cairo. All notions of normality were ruthlessly interrupted when the formal congregational prayers came to an end. With the official managers of the sacred safely departed into their air-conditioned offices, the masses took over and the mosque was rapidly transformed into a veritable feast (or fleamarket) of Sufi (or quasi-Sufi) groups doing their own thing; the ever-changing Azharite 'orthodoxy' made way for the 'heretical'. One group formed two long lines straddling the length the mosque and facing each other, chanting while swaying backwards and forwards. Another, all wearing red sashes, sat in a square, conducted by a leader in a gentle almost hypnotic, chant. Then there were several circles, some wearing green turbans, others white caps with a green crescent, and so on. *'Ya Hay! Ya Qayyum! Ya Haqq!'* (Oh Living! Oh Eternal! Oh Truth!) As if there were some kind of limit to the extent to which the mosque itself can handle 'otherness', the dances were reserved for its outer precincts. Here they were, the swirling dervishes, dancing and chanting, spinning like the tops of our childhood, in long dresses which resembled the 'stiffening' which women wore underneath their dresses in our childhood.

What had I walked into? I like *gadats*, our local Cape Town liturgical gatherings, but what was this? Hovering between my eternally dual, rather multiple, identities as a fascinated outsider, confused insider and a host of in-betweens, I wandered from group to group. When someone from within one of the groups beckoned me to join them, I quickly walked away – somewhat frightened – a bit like a child when confronted with the unknown 'other'.

I had had no prior knowledge of the place and had ended up there simply because that was the area where I had been told I could buy some commentaries of the Qur'an. I had noticed large sections of the crowd moving in a particular direction and followed suit. This was a shrine; a place where the Master of the Martyrs, the Prophet's grandson

Husain (May Allah be pleased with him), was buried.[1] The crowds thronged around, touched and kissed the brass handles of the shrine's outer perimeter and then wiped their faces. *'Ya Husain! Ya Husain!'* was the lament. Much louder was the chant *'Allahumma salli ala Muhammad'* (O God, bestow your blessings upon Muhammad!) which had a desperate ring to it. It was as if they wanted to exorcize any notion that their reverence for Husain could upstage that of the Prophet.

I always get lost in these situations – not that I am found in others. I was in the presence of our master, Husain. What should I say? What should I pray? What should I think? And all these people around me? (Including the man and his two children saying 'cheese' while posing in front of the shrine and another uncle taking photos of them.) Am I of one of them or the perpetual other? The blood of Karbala, the betrayal of the heritage of Islam, the courage of Husain and the mess of this *ummah* (community) were some of the images that scraped through my guts.

And then I noticed the women, the eternal spectators. Heads covered and uncovered, long dresses and short dresses, make-up and no make-up; there they were, the other other. Some gave the impression of being serious devotees while others appeared to have popped in quickly on their way to a wedding or the beach. Some part of the mosque, in addition to a section upstairs, seemed to have been set aside for women so that they could view the shrine from a half door.

Always more comfortable with the text, I hurriedly sought refuge in a nearby bookshop, where I bought my commentaries.

The haunting question is 'What is Islam?' The Qur'an and *sunnah*? Yes, yes, but through whose eyes? Is any set of beliefs or ideas really located only in a text and the historical memory of how that text was lived out? Is memory not always shaped by the ever-changing personal reality and history of every individual? What do the experiences of all of these people count for? Do they and their practices not also contribute to the shaping and reshaping of Islam, of the interpretations of the text? Here I was sitting in a taxi with volumes of Rashid Rida, Ibn al-Arabi and al-Tabari; each with his unique expositions on the meaning of the text. Weren't all those 'funny things' that I just witnessed another, albeit non-written, elaboration of the text?

I raised some of these questions that evening at a gathering that the celebrated Islamic philosopher, Hassan Hanafi, hosted for me. 'Islam is one', offered Salim al-Awwa, the jurist. 'Everyone takes from it what

he or she finds relevant and useful. The more one takes from it the better a Muslim one actually becomes . . . The bits that each one takes from
it, though,' he concluded, 'should not be confused with the whole.'
Sounds OK.

My problem is not so much how and what we take from it as what
we bring to 'it', how our bringing actually transforms 'it', whether we
and 'it' are utterly distinct and if, in fact, there is an 'it'. Are the self
and other really two entirely different things? Does the substance of
faith not carry something of our own lives in it? Are elaborations of the
text utterly distinct from the text itself?

Back to the *malboet* and his announcements.

Now I know that with the passing on of every person something of
me also passes on, and that the birth of a person is also in a sense my
birth, that I am because you are, that otherness is a condition of selfhood. I also know that celebrating and esteeming otherness is, in fact,
a celebration of the self.

GO SLOWLY WITH THE MUD!

When we return from haj or the lesser pilgrimage (*umrah*), or hear others
upon their return, we nearly always detect relief to be back with our
'own', and we seldom reflect on this 'otherness' within ourselves, the
diversity in the worlds of Islam and the many islams that we have seen
on our journey. We see only our own version, insisting that it be
written with a capital letter. We are terrified of having the childlike
memories of a singular Islam shattered by the reality of multiplicity.

Some years ago I was asked to mediate in a community conflict that
had been raging for some years in the area of Bonteheuwel, the township near Cape Town that I come from. A public meeting in the mosque
turned quite rowdy. In an attempt to give both sides an equal hearing,
I proposed that they sat on different sides. To a person they were hor-
rified at the way their disunity would become visible and I, of course,
bore the brunt of their anger. It's a bit like when you are four years old
and are beginning to realize that Father Christmas is not real, yet you
cannot confront the realization, so your smart alec brother, who has
taken it upon himself to shatter your dreams, becomes the object of
your anger.

In my travels throughout the world where Muslims live, whenever I have been asked to address a congregation, as a matter of courtesy I ask the imam or the committee inviting me to suggest a topic. Nine times out of ten, the response will be 'the unity of the Muslims'. Few aspirations seem to be as sacred to Muslims as the quest for unity. There will always be differences among – and equally significant, within – us, simply because we are people. Yes, we are Muslims and we do have a lot in common, but Muslims are also people. If in a single family there is so much diversity, how can it be any different among people all over the world with diverse regional and personal histories? Our desperation for a single understanding of Islam is, in fact, a reflection of our desperation for wholeness. While there is nothing intrinsically wrong with this, we need to walk carefully with ourselves and with others who do not fit into our understandings of what this single understanding is all about.

I often wonder if the dismissal of otherness and the call for unity by leaders does not hide their own yearning for power and control over even greater numbers than their present limited followings. For several years while the official Iranian delegation was allowed its annual demonstrations during haj, the major slogan they chanted was: *'Ya ayyuha'l-muslimun, ittahidu, ittahidu'* (O Muslims, Unite! Unite!). They and their supporters chanted their slogans carrying photographs of the late Ayatollah Khomeini. Wasn't the implied message 'unite under our leader, on our terms'? It is difficult to come to any other con-clusion if one bears in mind that the revolutionary discourse in Iran is essentially exclusivist and makes little or no space for anyone who dis-agrees with it. (The line is, of course, that all Muslims will agree and those who don't aren't really Muslims but CIA–Zionist–Saudi agents.)

The insistence on confining 'us-ness' to our little groups and con-signing all else to the damned 'other' category is sometimes intrinsic to the very foundations of many of our movements or organizations. Some years ago Mawlana Shah Ahmad Noorani of the Jama'at i Ulama i Pakistan, a Barelvi group,[2] claimed that the Prophet himself (Peace be upon him) was the founder of his group. It is also commonly believed in Tablighi Jama'ah circles that the late Mawlana Muhammad Ilyas, the founder of this Deobandi movement, was instructed by the Prophet to establish it. I am not commenting on the truth or otherwise of these claims. There is, after all, no known way of judging the truth of a dream. What I am saying is that if one believes that one is acting on the direct instructions of the Prophet, then it's impossible, even wrong, to accommodate those who disagree with you.

What is wrong with uniting under them or anyone else if their programme or opinions are entirely based on the Qur'an and the *sunnah*? Nothing really, except that the Qur'an and the *sunnah* require interpreters and interpreters are people. During the Battle of Siffin, 'Ali ibn Abi Talib (May Allah be pleased with him) was confronted with precisely this problem. Mu'awiyah, who opposed him, insisted that the dispute be brought to the Qur'an for arbitration. 'When Mu'awiyah proposed that the Qur'an decides between us,' 'Ali ibn Abi Talib said:

> I could not turn my face away from the Book of Allah, for the Almighty, the Powerful has declared 'and if you are at variance over any matter, refer it to unto God and the Prophet'. This is the Qur'an written in lines and within two covers. It does not speak with its own tongue; it needs interpreters and interpreters are people.

To thus argue that all I, my group or leader say is simply what the Qur'an says, and that our understanding of it squares one hundred per cent with what Allah had intended it to mean is to have a somewhat exaggerated opinion of ourselves, our group or its leader. The question is not whether there will always be differences among us, but how we deal with them.

Whenever one of my Pakistani lecturers, Mawlana Anwarullah, was approached by someone abusing another group, he would politely ask: *'Aap kia bechte hain?'* (What are you selling?) It's all very well ranting and raving about the foul smell in the shop next door, its expensive prices, its rotten goods, or about the shopkeeper's lack of consultation before he launched a certain product. Any customer is bound to get tired of a promotion based entirely on denouncing the guy next door. Pray, tell us, what are you selling?

In fact, obsession with the bad in the other in all likelihood hides a problem with the self. The point is made in the following joke submitted by Charles Tomberg to the humour service to which I subscribe. (OK, the point is not very well made but you don't need a watertight excuse to tell a joke, do you?)

A man walked into Joe's Barber Shop for his haircut. As he snips away, Joe asks 'What's up?' The man proceeds to explain he's taking a holiday in Rome.

'Rome?!' Joe says, 'Why would you want to go there? It's a crowded dirty city full of Italians! You'd be crazy to go to Rome! So how ya getting there?'

'We're taking TWA,' the man replies.

'TWA?!' yells Joe. 'They're a terrible airline. Their planes are old, their flight attendants are ugly and they're always late! So where you staying in Rome?'

The man says: 'We'll be at the downtown International Marriot.'

'That dump?!' says Joe. 'That's the worst hotel in the city! The rooms are small, the service is surly and slow and they're over-priced! So whatcha doing when you get there?'

The man says 'We're going to go see the Vatican and hope to see the Pope.'

'Ha! That's rich!' laughs Joe. 'You and a million other people trying to see him. He'll look the size of an ant. Boy, good luck on this trip. You're going to need it!'

A month later, the man bumps into Joe, who says, 'Well, how did that trip to Rome turn out? Betcha TWA gave you the worst flight of your life!'

'No, quite the opposite,' explained the man. 'Not only were we on time in one of their brand new planes, but it was full and they bumped us up to first class. The food and wine were wonderful, and I had a beautiful twenty-eight-year-old flight attendant who waited on me hand and foot!'

'Hmmm,' Joe says. 'Well, I bet the hotel was just like I described.'

'No, quite the opposite! They'd just finished a twenty-five-million-dollar remodelling. It's the finest hotel in Rome, now. They were overbooked, so they apologized and gave us the presidential suite for no extra charge!'

'Well,' Joe mumbles, 'I know you didn't get to see the Pope!'

'Actually, we were quite lucky. As we toured the Vatican, a Swiss guard tapped me on the shoulder and explained the Pope likes to meet some of the visitors personally, and if I'd be so kind as to step into this private room and wait, the Pope would personally greet me. Sure enough, after five minutes the Pope walked through the door and shook my hand. I knelt down as he spoke a few words to me.'

Impressed, Joe asks, 'Tell me, please! What'd he say?'

'Oh, not much really. Just "Where'd you get that awful haircut?"'

Perhaps Joe has also had a sneaking suspicion that he was not good at his job. We need to rethink our own programmes and ways of doing things when things go wrong and not blame failures on the real or imaginary manoeuvres of others. We need to focus on our ideas and programmes rather than denouncing everybody else and their ideas. Moreover, the mess ups that we see in our neighbour's shop are more often than not a reflection of what has gone wrong in our own shop.

We need to be balanced in our views about the people with whom we work and about those with whom we refuse to work; the people who disagree with us are not necessarily the brothers or sisters of Satan nor are the people with whom we agree angels. There is no White person or Black person; people are only found in various degrees of combinations; if there is anything essential about the human condition then it is greyness.

I have for many years kept my hair very short. In fact, in Pakistan the barber used to come along to the *madrassah* every Friday morning and, for the equivalent of two and a half cents, would shave anybody's head. I was a regular customer. A lecturer, Mawlana Bakhsh, who was fond of me, praised me in class as a 'self-effacing "Sufi" who doesn't care about looks'. On the other hand, some of the South Africans who distrusted my political views attacked my 'hypocrisy': 'He talks so much about solidarity with the darkies [Blacks], but is embarrassed about his *kroeskop* [curly hair].'

If truth be told, I wasn't the sweet little angel my friendly lecturer made me out to be; nor was I the hypocritical devil my unfriendly compatriots made me out to be: just a very human youngster with what seemed like an incurable dandruff problem!

Some years ago I told this story in Winnipeg in Canada. The next day a dermatologist presented me with a year's supply of anti-dandruff stuff that sorted my dandruff problem out. I still keep my hair short though. Mawlana Bakhsh, my friendly lecturer, was right, after all!

ON ANTS AND ELEPHANTS

During a recent visit to Bonteheuwel I delivered the Friday sermon, and was astounded at how absolutism has ravaged the Muslim community. For several years they have witnessed ongoing battles between a former imam and his ever-changing group of supporters on the one hand and the various committees in charge of the mosque or trying to take charge, on the other. Each side insisted that it was one hundred per cent righteous and claimed that its opponents were one hundred per cent evil.

I spoke about how the ants get trampled underneath when the elephants fight, about the need to value the contribution of those who have preceded us even if we disagree with them and implored them to speak gently to each other. 'Remember,' I said, 'Allah told Moses to speak gently to Pharaoh; none of you is better than Moses, nor any of the people with whom you differ worse than Pharaoh.' Several people cried. I was desperate for those who refuse to see that there is another side to their story to abandon their false gods of self-righteousness. If only they could for a moment enter the broken and devastated soul of the community to witness the consequences of the battle of the elephants. If only the committed Muslim were to spare a thought for those on whose behalf we claim to be waging our organizational wars. If only we could come to terms with what it is in our psyches that really drives our commitments, to see something more in our people than useful fodder for our exclusivist ideas.

Real unity and respect are based upon a refusal to engage in the blanket rubbishing of those with whom we disagree; it is a respect and tolerance of other opinions that most ordinary Muslims desperately long for. The groups, organizations or individuals that we disagree with are seldom the unmitigated disasters that we make them out to be. How can I not value the miraculous personal transformation brought about in the lives of numerous individuals by the Tablighi Jama'ah, individuals who would otherwise have been consigned to existences of unspeakable crimes? And who am I to denounce the *mawluds* (celebrations of the Prophet's birthday) and other spiritual circles that – certainly in the

Cape – have played a crucial role in our very survival as Muslims. (Some theologians may today debate the correctness or otherwise of *bid'ah* (religious innovation) and its different forms. Any historian of Islam in South Africa will, however, tell you that these theologians wouldn't have been around as Muslims if it weren't precisely for those very activities vilified today.)

Wasn't it the Arabic Study Circle, and later the Muslim Youth Movement, that first introduced South Africans to the use of the Qur'an as a book of guidance to be approached in the mess that our country was in? Wasn't it Qiblah that first insisted that Islam offered a revolutionary path for South Africa at a time when many of their detractors were quietly benefiting from collaboration with the apartheid regime? While each of these tendencies or groups have their problem areas, I still think that it is crucial to be truthful about the contribution that they have made to Islam in South Africa. I and my understanding of Islam are not the axis around which the earth rotates, however much I may desire it to be the case.

I loved my ten years in the Tablighi Jama'ah but it was the absolutism, the idea that only we and our programme mattered, that drove me out. 'This is the equivalent of the ark of the Prophet Noah (Peace be upon him), *la raiba fihi* [there is no doubt in it]', Qureshi Saheb, an elderly companion of the late Mawlana Ilyas (May Allah have mercy upon him), the movement's founder, told me in Raiwind, Pakistan. I could not handle the idea of Allah's assuring statement at the beginning of Surah al-Baqarah about the truth of the Qur'an being applied to a contemporary understanding of the Prophet's methodology, however pious and sincere that understanding. I do not wish to suggest that seeing good in everyone does not mean taking sides. On the contrary, as Mawlana Zakariyyah Kandhlawi (May Allah have mercy upon him) writes in the *Tablighi Nisab*, the reader of the Tablighi Jama'ah, 'I do not trust the man who is on good terms with all his neighbours.' I am only saying that we should not blind ourselves to the good that may possibly be in others. I find a statement attributed to Imam Idris ibn al-Shafi'i (May Allah have mercy upon him) very helpful in this regard: 'I am correct with the possibility of being in error; my opponent is in error with the possibility of being correct.' Just a little space is asked for to allow the 'other' to be.

I have little doubt that my views on pluralism, allowing and valuing other perspectives and ideas, will be hard to swallow for many a committed Muslim. There are some of us for whom our movements, organizations and opinions are the sum total of our lives, and we are proud of them. We have invested an enormous amount of time and emotional energy in them. To suggest that the path or opinions of others may also be worth something and may possibly also be rooted in Qur'an and *sunnah* could even mean the loss of our identity and the sense of security that comes with certainty. I understand and value a passionate commitment to a particular path. Despite this, we need to spare a thought for what our absolutism and organizational arrogance do to the ordinary person in whose name we denounce each other.

LONG LIVE MRS BATISTA!

When one says 'Sometimes I ask myself . . .' then one is actually reflecting one's own multiple identities. When I raise issues in this book without answering them, it is not intended to take the mickey out of my readers. They are serious questions and I sincerely ask them of myself. Sometimes we answer people so eloquently during the day and roam the beaches at night in search of answers to the very same questions. We can fool all the people all the time but it's a bit more difficult to fool ourselves. Quite simply, I want to show that it is possible for people to hold certain positions and yet know that there are many holes in their arguments; that one can stand apart from one's views and be critical of them. There is, however, something more serious than this: we are people and therefore participants in a process never-ending, mostly unconscious of constantly being reshaped.

My task is to ask the questions, to try to find answers, to struggle to live alongside the truths that I do discover and to embrace the many questions that continue to live on. Where is all this thinking going to end up, why do we have to ask so many questions? Because I want to live with myself, with my faith and in my environment and to do so means that I cannot run away from the questions.

Once, a Companion of the Prophet (Peace be upon him) came to him and complained of a pain in the stomach. The Prophet advised him to

take some honey because the Qur'an says that therein is a cure for all
illnesses. After a week or two the Prophet asked him how his stomach
was and the Companion replied that it was still aching. The Prophet is
reported to have said 'Allah has spoken the truth and your stomach
has lied.'

Let me relate this story to a real life and personal story. Life was
tough in Bonteheuwel where we lived as victims of the Group Areas
Act. Many a winter month saw my brother and me going to school
barefoot. Often there was nothing to eat at home and we frequently
resorted to scavenging for thrown away apple cores and the like in the
gutters. Mrs Ellen Batista (May Allah have mercy upon her), a devout
Catholic woman, was my mother's constant companion throughout
these difficult years. The wire fence separating our yards were not too
high and with a deft climb both Mrs Batista and my mother could nego-
tiate their quite substantial frames over the fence. When age prevented
them from doing that, they had to make do with walking up to the fence
and sounding their peculiar call: 'Cooweeee!'. The other would come
to the fence to be 'present'. Sometimes it was 'a cup of sugar' required,
at other times it was just a bit of fish oil and two rand 'until Friday' or
a chat. (Well after we had moved out of Bonteheuwel and some years
after my mother had died, just before the festival of 'Id one of us would
sneak into what had been our backyard and sound the familiar call from
the darkness. When we visited Mrs Batista on the occasion of 'Id a few
days later, she would recount how she had distinctly heard my mother's
call 'a few night's ago'. She knew that this was the 'omen' that we
would be visiting her.)

This was our context, our reality, our pain and joy. Let's say this was
our stomach.

On the other hand, there was the Qur'an, which says that Muslims
must not befriend the *kuffar*, the Christians and the Jews and that in the
end they will all end up in hell.[3] What do I do now? As a Muslim I cannot say that the Qur'an does not speak the truth. Do I say that our
suffering and poverty, on the one hand, and Mrs Batista's help and companionship, on the other, are not real? (Is my stomach lying?) Now many
illnesses are imaginary, but poverty and hunger, to those who know it, are
real. People die of it. Do we continue to benefit from Mrs Batista and yet
in our hearts believe that the best deal that she can get in the hereafter is

to be a servant of the Muslims in Paradise? Many people can actually live with the idea of a God who is as unjust as this; I cannot.

There are two other ways out. The more popular and the easier one is to ignore the Qur'an and carry on as if it has nothing to say about the situation. Ignore the honey and run to the doctor. The other way out is much more difficult, requires a lot of work and, above all, means having to take Allah and the Qur'an seriously. It means rethinking the meaning of the Qur'an and trying to find out what a particular text means in your situation. What did it mean in the Prophet's time? When was it revealed? About whom was it revealed? To whom is it addressed? What do the words (in Mrs Batista's case) 'islam' (submission to Allah's will), *iman* (faith), *kufr* (rejection; heresy) and friendship mean in the Qur'an? What did they mean before Islam? Did they relate to a specific situation or to a general situation? Is Allah interested in labels or in deeds? If your answer is 'labels', then what does it say about you that your perception of God is so small-minded?

Suppose I present two tins to my audience, one containing rubbish and the other a delicacy. The tin containing rubbish is marked 'delicacy' while the one marked 'rubbish' contains the delicacy. Which tin is more valuable to those in the audience who have the ability to see beyond the labels? (Now I know that there are some nutters who go around collecting labels, either as a hobby or to return in exchange for a free product. Here, however, I am not talking about a God that is into marketing gimmicks!)

All this may be rather complicated. However, one does not have the right to condemn others who are determined to be true to both the pain in their stomachs and the Qur'an just because one does not have the time or the inclination to think it all through, to do the research, to study the Qur'an, Arabic, the Prophet's life and the sickness. Walk away from the questions if you want to, but do so silently and with respect towards those who have the courage to grapple with them.

Questions and questioning can be fun and we have many in our community who have pained the religious establishment no end with their persistent and nagging questions – often for the sheer heck of it. I do not share the enthusiasm of those who insist on letting a million thoughts bloom just for the fun of diversity and pluralism, a kind of scholarship which often claims to not take sides because this is the perfect ideology for the modern bourgeois mind. Such a pluralism makes a genial confusion in which one tries to enjoy the pleasures of difference without ever committing oneself to any particular vision of resistance, liberation and hope. (David Tracy, *Plurality and Ambiguity*)

As I argued in *Qur'an, Liberation and Pluralism*, for those who struggle to survive on the margins of society, living under the yoke of oppression and struggling with those from other religions who are equally oppressed in the hope of liberation, a pluralism of splendid intellectual neutrality is not an option. We need to ask what causes are being advanced by our commitment to pluralism. In order for thinking and rethinking to be meaningful and connected to the ethos of Islam these must flow from, and lead to involvement.

The theological search for a place for Mrs Batista under Allah's shade, therefore, does not come from a perverse sense of taunting traditional Muslim exclusivist understandings of faith and entry into the ranks of the flock. Rather, it is part of the struggle to create a world where people are judged by their deeds and not by their ethnic, religious or sexual labels: in brief, a world of justice.

ACCESS TO OUR WATERHOLES?

The oppression of the Harijans in India is something widely known to most of us. The curse of untouchability has for centuries been a blot on the conscience of India. 'It is rooted in Hinduism,' most Muslims hasten to add. 'We have none of this racism and exploitation in Islam', and in our arrogance we fail to distinguish between our faith and our practice.

In the Punjab region of undivided India a fairly common phenomenon among the Harijans was conversion to Christianity; a hopeful escape from the indignities of the caste system and the hope of possible favours from their new co-religionists, the British ruling class. Many of these Punjabis were sweepers: 'They belong to the sweeper community', as one would say on the subcontinent. Now, of course, upward social mobility in this area is extremely slow and, for generations, it may even be non-existent. Sweepers would thus remain sweepers, the personification of dirt on the subcontinent, and so would their children, Christian or not.

When undivided India became the Republic of India and the Islamic Republic of Pakistan in 1948, what happened to these Punjabi Christians in Pakistan? Muslims treated them in exactly the same manner as they had been treated for centuries by the upper-caste Hindus. Muslims, especially in the more remote rural areas, routinely deny them drinking water, permission to eat in roadside cafes, and so on. When Muslims are asked why they force the (Punjabi) Christians to walk miles for water, they respond by saying 'These people are Christian.'

Now the Punjabi Christians, the sweeper community, are dark skinned and speak Punjabi and some Urdu. There is, however, another Christian community in Pakistan, the Goans. They are of Portuguese–Indian descent, speak English and are usually fair skinned. These Christians are esteemed guests at Muslim functions and are highly sought after as secretaries, air stewards and business partners. When the guilty Muslims are asked about this rather obvious contradiction, they stare at you as if you have two heads but no brains.

In the village of Padre Jo Goth in the province of Sindh this endless anxiety and humiliation over drinking water was the lot of the local Punjabi Christians until a German church agency decided to fund the boring and construction of wells for their fellow Christians. What wonderful Christian charity! That is, until the wells were completed and the Christians denied the 'unclean and unsaved' Hindus access to their wells!

I have little doubt that those Muslims did not act the way they did because they were Muslims, nor did those Christians act the way they did because they were Christians. The point is that their prejudices, correctly or not, were, for them at least, sustained by their respective religions.

Many of us will hasten to say that this has nothing to do with our religions. Perhaps such disclaimers should be a bit less swift. Listen to Shaikh Kishk in Egypt, Ahmad Deedat in South Africa, Jimmy Swaggart in the USA and the followers of Rabbi Kahane in Jerusalem; see how many of their co-religionists are swayed by them. These people are as much an intrinsic part of one's heritage, they draw as much from our wells as you and I. We may denounce them, attempt to compensate for their ignorance, even pray that they die of piles and become infested with the fleas of ten thousand camels. They will, however, forever remain a part of our baggage.

Often our prejudices about the other are a way of holding on to what we perceive as the known. Many Muslims feel that Deedat's multitude of anti-Christian, Jewish and Hindu videotapes have told us all that there is to be told about the other and we are comfortable with that. There are times when questions about the importance of correct dogma surface, about the importance of labels to a God whom we believe sees beyond labels and looks at the hearts of people. Instead of pursuing these questions we hasten back and seek refuge in the known: order another of those Deedat tapes.

In our ignorance and fear of the other we elevate group solidarity to the level of absolutes which take the place of Allah as an object of worship. Thus the commitment to the clan and, the invariable corollary, the demonizing of the other acquire a greater value than truth and our beliefs. I have often wondered about the way we may be actually be committing *shirk* (heresy) by elevating the community above our commitment to be a 'witness-bearer to justice for Allah – though this may be against yourselves' (Q. 5:135). The injunctions of Allah not to 'conceal evidence, for whosoever does this has a sinful heart' (Q. 2:142) and not to 'cover the truth with falsehood while you know' (Q. 2:283) are often of little consequence.

Some years ago I attended the annual summer school of the Centre for Islam and Muslim–Christian Relations in Birmingham, where speakers from the two traditions usually make presentations on a similar topic. A Muslim speaker dealt with the plight of Muslims in the United Kingdom and a Christian with that of Christians in Pakistan. While the Christians accepted the criticism of the Muslims, this openness was regrettably not reciprocated. As someone who had lived in Pakistan for about eight years and who had had considerable experience with the Christians there, I defended the position of the Christians. I also pointed out that, if anything, the Christian speaker had considerably downplayed the extent of their own social oppression.

Until then, I had been leading the formal *salah* (prayer) for the Muslims present. When that session ended and we went to the prayer room I found two of the other participants encouraging each other to proceed with leading the prayers, despite my presence. Immediately after the prayers they all made haste somewhere, leaving me rather isolated. Much later, I approached a fellow Muslim imam who was also a

Pakistani, who had always come across to me as rather balanced, and wanted to know what I had done wrong. 'Surely,' I said, 'you know that I spoke the truth? What did I do to deserve this ostracism?' 'You are right,' said he, 'but you should not have said what you did about us in front of them!'

The underlying assumption in this defensive posturing is that the other is the enemy and that we are here first to defend ourselves and second, hopefully, to win some over to our side. It is, of course, not difficult to perceive of the other as the enemy. We are not mere individuals but carry our histories with us and Muslims are still living through centuries of misrepresentation of Islam, the collusion between colonialism and so-called objective scholarship to reduce Islam and the Qur'an to figments of a sensuous pretender's imagination. There is also our own experience as part of the colonized world exploited by the West, which regards its culture as normative and all else as aberrations.

For Muslims this experience of colonialism with all its underlying assumptions of the superiority of Western cultural and religious norms is not the mere baggage of history. So many in the West today object to Muslim women wearing scarves in their schools, while it never occurred to Westerners to wear loincloths when they came to Africa. This battle continues and many of the powers-that-be have identified Islam as the enemy. Given the materially based values, the absence of any political morality and the chauvinistic jingoism of triumphalist capitalism, I would have been disappointed if Islam were not viewed as an enemy by these powers.

It is, however, the fear of Islam by ordinary men and women that troubles me. Their prejudices and fears, too, are usually based on the unknown. When they are based on the known then it is a known processed by the mass media, which is owned and controlled by the powerful. While the dispossessed have their fears and prejudices, the powerful in the West have the economic and military power to transform fear and prejudice into potent weapons for destruction and 'defence'.

For us, people committed to the noblest in our religious heritage, though, the question is not merely one of the survival of our own. Today our survival depends on the survival of the other, much as the survival of the human race depends on the survival of the ecosystem. We have gone beyond 'no man is an island unto himself' to 'no entity

is an island unto itself'. A vague and sentimental sense of attachment
to the clan is not going to see us through the turbulent future of a world
threatened by the gradual re-emergence of Nazism, environmental dev-
astation and a triumphalist New World Order based on the economic
exploitation of the Two-Thirds World, a world where women continue
just to survive on the margins of dignity.

There are many ways of dying. There is, however, only one way to
live: through discovering what the self and other is really about, to
understand how much of the other is really reflected in us and to find
out what it is that we have in common in the struggle to recreate a world
of justice, a world of dignity for all the inhabitants of the earth.

THE JEWS! WATCH OUT FOR THE JEWS!

The propensity for seeing bogeys and the multitude of conspiracy theories based thereon is rather widespread. Nazism would have been a
dead duck without it; so would Stalinism. In the USA, yesterday's
McCarthyism and much of today's religious and political right wing are
reflective of a long tradition of conspiratorial thinking.

Conspiracy theories seem to abound wherever and whenever public
life is under stress. When that stress merges with a deep-rooted religiosity, one ends up with a rather potent concoction of some really
imaginative theories. When Muslims girls in Egypt 'discovered' the
sign of the cross on their veils there was 'a scramble for explanations',
to quote a Cairo newspaper. Some people said that Christians had
sprayed a chemical onto the veiled women's clothes and this material
assumed the form of a small cross no larger than an ant; as soon as the
clothing was moistened, the size of the cross would increase to about
three centimetres. Others offered another interpretation, which held that
the cloth had been imported from Israel and that it was scientifically
treated to form crosses with the purpose of stirring up dissension
between Muslims and Christians.

In Iran, during the early days of the revolution supporters of the
American embassy takeover argued that their intention was to flush out
the nest of espionage controlling all the anti-Islam conspiracies. Others
who opposed it argued that the very takeover was a conspiracy;
Washington was behind the seizure of its diplomats, with the deliberate

intention of isolating Iran diplomatically! Still in Tehran, the *New York Times* reported a taxi driver's reason for the interminable traffic jams: he thought that the city's notorious traffic jams were the handiwork of American agents. 'They get people to do unnecessary things and make the drivers frustrated and lose their tempers,' he explained.

But then, who knows? The report in which these pieces appeared itself could be a part of the Zionist conspiracy against Islam. If it were a factual report then how do we know that the taxi driver wasn't planted there to present a ridiculous picture of Islam to a Western journalist. (Oh gosh! Why do I confuse Iran with Islam all of a sudden? Oh well, it's all the same, isn't it? Whites and Western civilization/Christianity, Blacks and communists, Zionism and Jews, Arabs and Islam. Hold it! Aren't you talking about Iran? Iran's population surely isn't Arab? Well, these people are all the same, aren't they?)

The problem is that very often conspiracy theories do have some germs in reality. The problem is not with conspiracy theories that originate in reality but with 'reality' that originates in such theories – and here the convergence between far left, far right and fatalistic religious traditionalism is rather stark. Such theories are, in fact, an integral part of extremist discourse. Steeped in theory, rigid in principled positions and unable to undertake the shifts in religious or political paradigms necessitated by any courtship with grassroots reality, these believers have to delay engaging that reality. The implication of this mode of thinking is 'Whatever we do is of little consequence, so we confine ourselves to our well-worn mental [for they can hardly be described as 'intellectual'] constructs'.

Conspiracy theories are often reflective of an inability or refusal to acknowledge complex or unacceptable reasons for certain events. However, what we need to address is the fact of the raw material that we supply for conspiracy theorists to manipulate and exploit. Laying it all at the door of the all-purpose bogeyman means not confronting realities, which in turn means not facing critical problems, much less solving them.

The curious thing is the way the conspiratorial mind latches on to snatches of reality – sometimes even mirages – to construct an entire worldview or political philosophy. Racism, religious chauvinism or romantic self-perceptions often underpin much of this worldview. Conspiratorialists are thus able to don the armour of light, of God or of justice, brandishing our swords, candles or 'one bullet'[4] against the forces of darkness.

The business of recognizing the integrity of the other is more complex and daunting and invariably introduces the notion, however vague, that there may possibly be something to his or her programme, ideas and beliefs. Allowing the other space in which to be means conceding some of my space, and when my entire universe is located within my own theoretical or religious constructions or beliefs then to give way is to cave in. When we refuse to do this the other invariably becomes a victim of us and our theories. Such was the case of Salamat Masih, an eleven-year-old Pakistani. In his words, as given in newspaper reports:

> The thing started over pigeons. The feudal lord's mansion is right next to our hut. My two pet pigeons had gone there and were captured. The name of the boy whom I had fought with over the pigeons, the feudal lord's son, is Zahid. He is eight years old.

Next, words reportedly insulting the Prophet (Peace be upon him) were found in the local mosque and the eight-year-old Zahid claims that he saw Salamat Masih writing them:

> The morning after the fight, as I was arranging water for the buffalo, after breakfast, they came. I thought that they came to complain to my mother about the fight. Instead they accused me with the writing of these words. I denied it, but the boy who was with them was told to say that he had actually seen me doing it. They told me that if I wanted to be spared, I should name Rama [Rahmat Masih]. They had gathered the entire village there, I was beaten and forced to name Rama. The next day about three villages got together and took out a demonstration against us. My uncle and I was summonsed and sent to jail. Rama was also caught.

This is how the tragic, heartrending story of a Pakistani Christian, Salamat Masih, begins. Salamat was eleven years old when the fight over the pigeons occurred. Three years on, at the age of fourteen, he was on death row in Pakistan. Salamat's one uncle, Manzoor Masih, was also charged for co-authoring the scrap of paper. Rahmat Masih (Rama), another Christian, was resented because he refused to work for the local feudal lord and exercised independence by cultivating his own small plot of land. Because of the 'Christian conspiracy' against Islam, a number of churches and schools run by Christian religious orders have since been burnt in Pakistan. Manzoor has since been killed by a Muslim priest, Maulvi Fazlul Haq, in broad daylight at a bus stop outside the court. Meanwhile, Rahmat and Salamat have been sentenced to death for insulting the Prophet.

Don't ask me how it is possible. Anyone who has lived in Pakistan with his or her eyes, ears and heart open will understand that it is possible. It does not matter that Salamat Masih was a dropout from kindergarten. (Yes, this is also possible in Pakistan!) It does not matter that he is totally illiterate and only learnt to write his name in prison during his three-year period awaiting trial. An accusation was made, the priests cried that Islam was under threat, worked people up into a frenzy and none cared about the truth. The only thing that mattered to ordinary Muslims was that the Prophet was being insulted and that they are the 'defenders of the faith'. The only thing that mattered to the priests was that they had power over the masses. The only thing that mattered to the feudal lord was that his honour as the only real man on the block needed to be protected.

'I am glad that I never learnt to write. Today, if I have some hope that I may someday be a free person again, it is because I cannot write,' said Salamat, shortly before his trial. A simple truth, my brother Salamat, but it is not truth that they are interested in. Hundreds of priests and their followers surrounded the court during the trial and demanded the death penalty. If the judges declined to find them guilty, then, it was clear, the mob would find the accused as well as the judges guilty – and sentence them all to death. The judges played safe and found both Salamat and Rahmat guilty.

Since then an entire Christian village, including a church, has been bulldozed, Christian children in several villages, until then allowed to attend school, although forced to sit separately and behind the Muslims, were banned from a number of schools. Police have entered and desecrated churches in attempts to flush out protesters against the death sentence of Salamat and Rahmat . . .

Oh, how we imprison others in our ignorance of who they and we really are! 'You've seen the picture of Jesus and the lamb in some Christian homes? Jesus was hanged because he stole a lamb,' some

Hindu kids told me in Pakistan. 'Sir, do you know why the Sunnis fold their hands during the prayers?' 'Because they hide their little idols in them', my Shi'ite students told me. (I always refrained from telling them what I was, not that I actually knew!) 'The Shi'ites do not believe in this Qur'an; they believe that the goat belonging to the Prophet's wife, 'A'isha, ate ten chapters,' the venerable Mawlana Badi'uzzaman taught our third-year class in Karachi. (I did wonder how the goat managed to devour a neat ten chapters and call it quits right there!)

'Women lead the prayers in the Claremont Main Road mosque.' 'A Christian priest preaches every evening in the month of Ramadan.' 'The men and the women stand together during the prayers.' These local lies are, of course, much milder and I dare not equate them with the lies surrounding Salamat and Rahmat Masih as they faced death row, before international pressure forced Pakistan to allow them into exile. Yet, people were prepared to kill in the Claremont Main Road on the basis of lies. Referring to the anniversary of the Battle of Badr on the preceding Saturday, they chanted 'Today [Saturday] is Badr, tomorrow it is Claremont Main Road!' For those lies they proclaimed their willingness to die and to kill.

How strange that people can actually be prepared to die and kill for their commitment to what they see as the truth, and yet for this commitment to be based on lies and denial. When confronted with the oppression of Christian Pakistanis most Muslim Pakistanis vehemently deny it. 'It is just anti-Islamic propaganda.' (And I recall the days when the oppression of Blacks in South Africa was 'just communist propaganda' to many Indians and most Whites.) 'I have lived in Pakistan for twenty years and I know that it is not true,' proclaimed a German Muslim sister in Frankfurt when I spoke about how Pakistani Christians were denied drinking water in the villages and often had to walk long distances for water. Where did you live, my sister? Whom did you live with? What did you choose to see? How many South Africans of White or Indo-Pak origin have even been inside a Black township or a Black home? Yes, I do not deny that you may have been there, but where there? From which perspective did you check things out? What side were you on?

It is not enough to say that you were on the side of Islam and the truth. Whose Islam and whose truth were you defending? The Islam of blind tradition, echoing the Quraysh of pre-Islamic paganism ('We have found our forebears doing this'), or the Islam of dynamism, reason and creativity? The Islam of the Shah or of the oppressed? The truth of the powerful or the powerless? The truth of men with fragile egos or that of battered women? The Islam of the feudal lords and the priests or that of Asma Jehangir, the Muslim lawyer who defended Salamat Masih?

To rise and become Allah's witness for justice, even though this may be against the male chauvinist, the racist, the powerful self . . . the Qur'an's insistence that we rise for justice 'though this may be against your self' is a powerful invitation to examine and to challenge the self and the many selves within us – both as a community and as individuals. To embrace the challenge of unravelling the complex and threatening other in order to assume responsibility for what happens to us and then do something about it . . .

SEVEN

on being a new south african muslim

Our message wants to take us forward into the twenty-first century so that we are able to creatively meet the manifold challenges which await us. Islam is a living faith, a dynamic religion that has firm principles but also sufficient flexibility to adapt to all times and conditions. This message seeks to continuously reinterpret and rethink the tradition of Islam in terms of contemporary challenges.

Imam Abdur Rashied Omar

South Africa is an exciting country and Islam in South Africa offers much that progressive Muslims elsewhere can get excited about. The qur'anic support for struggling for justice alongside people of other faiths, for example, is one such area that I dealt with extensively in *Qur'an, Liberation and Pluralism*. Thus, while this chapter has a peculiarly South African feel it nonetheless offers insights to other Muslims, particularly those living in predominantly non-Muslim societies.

And now we in South Africa have arrived – or at least we have left the darkness of racial oppression. The collapse of the old and the dawn of the new presented manifold challenges for the committed Muslim who took his or her South Africanness as earnestly as his or her commitment to faith. In this chapter some of these challenges are reflected upon in the light of my earlier stated commitment to rethinking Islam in terms of the objectives of the law, rather than the law itself.

The first section deals with the historic elections of 1994 and the response of some Muslims who felt that they could only be adequately represented in Parliament by a Muslim party. This is a position of religious apartheid that is also being advocated in other parts of the world. While I clearly reject this option, I nevertheless acknowledge that there are a number of ingredients in the new South African cake that sit rather uncomfortably with Islamic theology as it is currently understood by the vast majority of Muslims. Some of these dilemmas and questions are reflected upon in a tentative manner in the second section of this chapter.

The next two sections deal with the democratic and secular nature of the new constitution and its entrenched Bill of Rights, both of which evoked considerable debate among Muslims. The theological anguish when we woke up to discover that demanding our own rights also meant acceding to those of others, the romantic notion of an Islamic state for South Africa and the idea that popular sovereignty means a denial of divine sovereignty are looked at here.

Among the more unsavoury products of a society kept in chains for so long is the fact that when the doors of freedom are flung open one has little control over the demons that are let loose. The loosening of the state's authority and the expectation that adults were really meant to take charge of their own personal lives and guiding morality was accompanied a proliferation in the sex industry and, more specifically, a steep rise in the drug trade and crime in general. Muslims were in the forefront of the public struggle against gangsterism and drug abuse. This struggle saw the rise to prominence of the controversial Muslim group, People Against Gangsterism and Drugs (Pagad). Many of these problems were the immediate products of the socio-economic policies of the apartheid regime, which, it is now coming to light, had its own illicit drug-dealing operations running to generate income for their struggle against 'terrorism'. Yet those bereft of political insight found it convenient to blame democracy and posit simplistic solutions – termed 'Islamic' – such as chopping off hands, castrating rapists and hanging murderers.

While numerous committed South African Muslims are making a significant contribution to the reconstruction of our society, several segments of the community display a haunting fear of the light of democracy and freedom. Some of these responses are looked at in three sections, one dealing with the case of Radio Islam, which was compelled to close because it refused to allow women's voices to be broadcast, another dealing with crime in general and the third with the death penalty.

The last part of this chapter deals with the process of coming to terms with our nation's violent past and the mechanism set up to deal with it: the Truth and Reconciliation Commission (TRC). I latch on to the question of Muslim indifference to the TRC to look at what I regard as the major challenges facing progressive Islam in South Africa today.

ON THE BRINK OF FREEDOM?

For years we waited, not a patient waiting, but an anticipation with enormous determination, an anticipation characterized by struggle, by martyrdom, by torture and, yes, also by deep laughter and joy. More than three hundred years of racist minority rule were about to end. The moment in the life of our nation arrived where, for the first time in more than three centuries, our people as a nation and communities were going to take charge of their own lives.

Well, some folks just had to spoil it. Forget about 'housing for all', 'universal adult employment' and 'equality before the law', 'Women's Rights are Human Rights!', and so on. 'What's in it for me as a Coloured, Indian or Muslim?' 'How can I now seize the moment and make sure that all the inhabitants of my cocoon can remain protected?' This, alas, was the key concern of some Muslims who organized themselves into two Muslim parties.

'A vote for the Africa Muslim Party [AMP] is a vote for Islam!' proclaimed the placards stuck up outside the 23rd Street Mosque in Johannesburg during the month of Ramadan in 1994. The party was being unofficially launched on the twenty-seventh night of Ramadan, the Night of Power (*laylah al-qadr*). With the mosque filled, the women were suitably shoved into a tent set up for them. Later that evening, the wife of a prominent supporter of the AMP encouraged other women in the tent to add their signatures to a list, saying 'It's only the usual form that we sign on Big Nights.' There was no such thing as a 'usual form that we sign on Big Nights'; it was a petition indicating support for the AMP, which could be used to secure it financial support from the state's electoral kitty.

Less than a week before that a number of Muslims had gathered in the same mosque to discuss the idea of the formation of a Muslim party. Tough; many who came were sadly deluded. The only talk accommodated was what kind of support one could offer the party. Everyone who questioned the wisdom behind the move was treated as an enemy of Islam. The Party of the Muslims had arrived! Had it? 'Now no one has an excuse to abstain from voting or for voting for one of the *kuffar* parties!' Really?

For a number of reasons, I do not buy into the idea of a Muslim political party to cater for the needs of Muslims only. The idea is based on the false assumption that the socio-political interests of all Muslims are identical. One should vote for them, they argue, merely because we all carry the Muslim label. The struggle against apartheid had taught us only too well that there are Muslims and 'muslims'. (Just the day after 'Big Night', a 'brother' at the University of Witwatersrand had argued with me that the women should not pray *jumu'ah*, the Friday congregational prayers, on the lawns with the men. He argued that 'the Jews, Hindus and Blacks will see our sisters and the next thing is that the same thing that happened to them in Bosnia will happen here'. Upon being asked whether he was saying that the women of Bosnia had invited the mass rapes on to themselves, he calmly replied in the affirmative. How could such a heartless specimen of humankind ever be a Muslim, I wondered.)

The truth is that there are various expressions of islam in the literal sense of submission to the will of Allah (and shades of *kufr* in the garb of Islam, as the above incident illustrates). The founders and backers of the Muslim political parties understand this only too well. In various parts of the world, many of these individuals have been in the forefront of a struggle for expressions of Islam which differ from that of the establishment clergy. Indeed, several of them have been victims of the same fascist logic from some clergy quarters to which they now want to subject others. Their slogan, 'A vote for the Africa Muslim Party is a vote for Islam', is really invoking the same logic. The implication is that those who do not vote at all are boycotting Islam and others who vote against the AMP are voting against Islam.

Muslim parties are really a negative response to social insecurity and fears of the 'unknown'. In some ways these parties represent a Muslim laager. The idea is to retreat into the comfort of well-worn clichés about Islam having all the solutions and the Qur'an being our only constitution. This position shows no understanding of the complexities of the problems facing our country, nor any appreciation of how Islam translates into tangible and practical policies for governing a modern state. In South Africa many Muslims supporting these parties were also afraid of developments after the elections. This fear has its roots in the 'unknown' and propaganda about the 'unknown'. The question is, of course, why were the vast majority of the people of our land, their leaders and their aspirations, were 'unknown' and feared by these Muslims? If they were ever serious about Islam playing a role in this country how come they do not have more knowledge between and contact with the people of this land?

No, some of them argue, we are not retreating into a laager; we want to reach out to 'these people' and give them the message of Islam. Well, where were you in their hour of desperation when 'they' were being murdered, detained and baton charged and their houses bulldozed? If one's Islam did not lead one to active and ongoing solidarity with the victims of apartheid then there are serious questions about the nature of one's Islam. Do the people of this country really need an Islam that sits comfortably with injustice and economic exploitation, an Islam that preaches pie in the sky for Blacks while Indians and others have it on earth?

'Look at how the moral standards have deteriorated,' many a Muslim partyite argues. 'At least the Muslim parties will take a clear stand as far as morality is concerned.'

First, I doubt if the people of South Africa have any need for moral lessons from a people whose morality is confined to sex, abortion and alcohol but is silent on questions of hunger and exploitation. (The very notion of moral standards having 'deteriorated' seems to imply that things were better before. This understanding of 'things being better before' can only emerge from people who cared precious little for the suffering of the oppressed majority in our land.)

Second, while Muslims have every right to articulate the Islamic view of personal morality, it is important to understand that this morality is intrinsically related to a comprehensive Islamic moral–ethical worldview. In the same way that one does not demand amputation of thieves' hands in a poverty-ridden society, one cannot insist on capital punishment as the norm in a society which is not governed by the laws and values of Islam. The Shari'ah injunctions and Islamic morality are parts of an ever-developing whole and while the fundamental principles

of *tawhid* and justice are eternal, the way that these are to be con-
cretized in society has always been subject to human interpretation. To
isolate the rules from their context and argue for their artificial trans-
plantation into a non-Islamic society is to reduce an entire worldview
to a set of punishments.

Third, while the vast majority of Muslims feel strongly about issues of
personal sexual morality, abortion and alcohol (admittedly, not strongly
enough to actually live alongside the injunctions of Islam in this regard),
it is important to remember that these norms are peculiar to Muslims and
other religionists who share their views on these issues. Can we really
expect a government representing all the people of this country to implement laws that are peculiar to us and our worldview? Where does it stop?
Will the brother from Wits expect an ANC government to enforce his
appreciation of Islamic morality that prohibits women from praying
behind men? What does it say about our own self-confidence and the
strength of our institutions when we have to rely on the power of a non-
Islamic state to uphold the moral standards peculiar to Muslims?

Some will, of course, argue that we are not alone in this battle for
morality and that others share our concerns. Indeed, there were several
right-wing Christian parties contesting the elections on similar issues.
The only problem is that this argument destroys the very basis of the
existence of the Muslim parties, which is that they are the only ones
with the answers to problems of our country. There were many of us,
deeply committed Muslims with a passionate concern for our land, its
people and their fears and aspirations, who refuse to be members of a
community which exists on the margins of society, thumping Bibles or
copies of the Qur'an at the rest of the nation in hypocritical displays of
self-righteousness.

Some years ago I was a guest at the home of Muslim family which
owns a large cosmetic company. I really thought it curious that there were
no signs of any of their products – ranging from toothpaste to hair sham-
poos – in their own bathroom and wondered if they truly believed in their
company's advertisements, which adorn many a billboard in the town.

Why should we join a bunch of people who arrogantly offer a religious product to the nation when they and their followers show a
reluctance to use the product in their own lives? Is it not in our dealings
with others, in our commitment to alleviate their suffering and in our

willingness to serve all people that our Islam becomes manifest? The choice facing Muslims is one of an Islam that sits comfortably with the people of this land and that speaks to their hopes and fears, on the one hand and, on the other, an Islam of religious chauvinists who do not care tuppence for people except as customers in their shops or mere objects to receive their religious videotapes or pamphlets. Until we are able to demonstrate to others that the ideas and beliefs peculiar to us are actually working for us, we need to work alongside them on the ideals that we have in common. These are the ideals of jobs and housing for all, security, peace and justice.

TELL US ABOUT YOUR GLASSES

At the time when our country's new constitution was being debated, for many a religious person in South Africa, it appeared as if the time for demands had dawned. Rarely around to demand anything of the apartheid regime, they took to the streets demanding a return to all sorts of norms under the guise of 'morality'.

The most significant question in examining all these demands is the kind of glasses that we wear when discussing the constitution, the Bill of Rights and religion. If we can have clarity as to where we stand regarding the underlying ideological/theological assumptions that shape our religious views, then we will reach the core of the issue: religion has not only been a tool in battles, it is itself a battleground. This appreciation will assist us to locate ourselves and at least understand where those who differ with us come from.

There is a basic truth which underlines my approach to all three of these issues: our present political set-up came about as a result of the struggle of men and women of different religious backgrounds and numerous men and women of no religious commitment whatsoever. The essential drive behind this struggle was one for justice. This means that those with a simple commitment to fairness will not allow any one group to run away with all the fruits of that struggle, least of all those who opposed the struggle for justice or who did not care for it at all.

In the current wave of demands around issues of abortion, the death penalty and gay rights coming from some sectors of the religious community much is made of the 'majority of the people of our land' being

Christian or, in the slightly more accommodating version, 'believers'. This is a remarkable shift in the thinking of people who have never really cared about the demands of the majority of our people under the apartheid regime. Furthermore, given that all of our communities are deeply divided on just about every issue under the sun, we need to question the assumption of a universal Muslim, Hindu or Jewish opinion 'out there'.

I believe that clarity around the nature of the country's constitution, our identity and of our religious commitment will go some way towards ensuring that we live as children of our age and as committed Muslims.

In a democracy, a constitution is essentially a contract between a state and its citizens, and among all the citizens of the state. In such a state, because a constitution demands the loyalty of all its citizens, it must embody what the citizens have in common with each other and be shaped by that commonality. As human beings we have different levels of existences; I, for example, am a Muslim, male, a South African citizen. The constitution's essential task is to focus on our commonality as citizens while allowing maximum space to foster the other aspects of any individual's identity, however he or she may wish to identify him or herself. It goes without saying that this accords with universally accepted provisions for the protection of minors and that this space does not invade that of others. In all these other aspects of identity, the responsibility of a state cannot extend to granting any group an advantage over another. This is more so the case when the post-apartheid South African state has come into being with the collective efforts and struggle of diverse racial, religious and gender groupings. Should the post-apartheid state actually favour one group over the other, including religious over non-religious, it would be violating the very ethos of justice that brought it into being.[1]

One of the problems to emerge from our different and overlapping identities is that we use a single language to articulate emotions, facts, beliefs at these various levels. Acknowledging that the constitution is a contract between citizens and the state, and not between citizens and the Entity that some may chose to recognize as the Supreme Being, it is useful to bear in mind that our language actually relates to this world. While the language of the constitution may be absolute, it does not embrace all that the word 'absolute' implies for a religious believer. A constitution may correctly say that the will of the people is sovereign, without this being a comment on the sovereignty of a Transcendent Being. Christian Zulus are, after all, not faulted for acknowledging both Goodwill Zwelithini and Jesus as king/King, nor does a Muslim resorting to electrical power imply that he or she does not recognize the power of Allah.

The fact that I am contributing towards upholding the country's constitution does not mean that I do not accept the Qur'an as the ultimate guide in the life of Muslim. I just do not wish to confuse oranges with horses. Our people have always been the repositories of scriptures. Among ourselves, as South African Muslims we have never had any quarrel about the Qur'an; nor has the history of religion in our country ever been about the content of scripture. Rather, the debate has been about its diverse uses and the many approaches to it. (Remember how qur'anic verses such as 'Obey Allah, the Prophet and those in authority among you' were used to support the apartheid regime? It's a long time ago, isn't it? And now it's so difficult to find anyone who was not a part of the struggle. But then we live in a period in which memories are short and knives long.)

Speaking as one who has made some contribution to our struggle for justice, I am also aware of the enormous strength that many of us have derived from our religious traditions. Many of us have earned the right to argue for the consideration of our religious values in our country's constitution. For example, as a Muslim, I believe in a comprehensive faith with a comprehensive morality. I refuse to confine my understanding of morality to sex; there is something rather obscene about a theology that has been deafening in its silence on all the injustices that have visited our land and only awakens to questions of sex and sexuality. Given that I believe that there is more to human life than the sexual impulse, I will argue that a comprehensive sense of religious morality must inform the constitution. This morality will embrace the quest for justice and equality; it will view exploitation, poverty and hunger as immoral.

Religion has a lot to say about the intrinsic worth of human beings, the requirement of reciprocity in social relations (to do unto others as one would have done unto oneself). Its exhortations to compassion, reconciliation and justice are values that we have in common with non-religionists, and which we can offer to the country. We do not have to offer them as arrogantly held superior values, but as a part of our deeply religious selves that we manifest in our own lives. Religious people often confuse the truths that they believe in with themselves as the believers in those truths. The supposed superiority of your beliefs does not put you into a superior position, and so we ought to walk a bit more humbly. Let all religious people remember that we are being taken seriously by this government because of the spirit of nation-building and inclusiveness. Let us not abuse this inclusiveness in order to exclude others who are not religious or who do not welcome our restriction of morality to sex, the death penalty and abortion.

Some Muslim groups have argued for incorporation of qur'anic injunctions into our country's constitution and I wonder if this not perhaps part of our butterfly dance of escapism and digression from our inability or refusal to live our faith out in our daily lives. Is our insistence on transferring responsibility for our morality to a secular state not really a sign of a deep lack of self-confidence belying the verbal protestations of religious superiority? While the broad moral guidelines of our faith should inform all our thinking, including that of politicians among the Muslims, the idea that any community's scripture should shape the country's constitution or its Bill of Rights is rather problematic. In a country of diverse religious beliefs or of no such beliefs, whose scripture are we going to use? Given the role that Marxists have played in our liberation struggle, proportionately a more noble one than that of many a Muslim, shouldn't *Das Kapital* also be considered as an authoritative scripture?

The Qur'an asks that the 'believers avoid the friendship of Jews and Christians'. If taken literally, both the Bible and the Qur'an reject notions of gender equality. Some schools of Islamic legal thought denounce masturbation as sinful. Can we, in all reasonableness, expect the state to patrol people's toilets and bedrooms? Can we, in all fairness, ask the state to regulate the relationship between Muslims and their Jewish and Christian neighbours? Can we have scarf police for Muslim women? Must sin in the eyes of God, Jehovah, Jah or Allah translate into a crime in civil society? If so, whose religious scripture are we going to adopt?

Suppose a miracle takes place and we actually agree on one sacred scripture. We will still end up with the problem of people and their very different ways of seeing things. There is the question of text and that of context. What did a particular word mean in the original language? What did it mean to its first hearers or readers? What was the context of this revelation? About whom was it revealed? Is it a general or specific rule? Is the application of the rule significant or the underlying principle? Is the text abrogated or not? These are questions that have vexed exegetes for centuries. It does seem rather unfair to expect political leaders to sort out more than two thousand years of diverse exegetical opinions on diverse religious scriptures.

It is, of course, true that some may claim there is no question of interpretation. These people usually imply that the only true meaning is actually their interpretation. This understanding of scripture, I suggest, has more to do with battles for political control over the minds of ordinary believers than with any serious theological thinking. While the relatively common experiences of people may minimize their divergent outlooks in different historical periods, diversity is never negated.

The absolute and undisputed reference point for Muslims is the Qur'an and, for Sunni Muslims, the Prophet's definitive conduct. The unavoidable point of departure from which these criteria are approached, however, is one's self and the conditions wherein that self is located. Ignoring the ambiguities of language and history and their impact on interpretation results in there being no effective distinction between normative Islamic morality and what the believer 'thinks' it to be. Both traditionalism and fundamentalism deny any personal or historical frame of reference in the first instance. While they will insist that normative Islamic morality is 'to be judged solely by the Qur'an and the Prophet's conduct' throughout their discourse they simultaneously imply 'and we are the only ones who have correctly understood it'.

SWITCH OFF IF YOU GET TURNED ON!

Every religious or ideological community has its 'only us' brigades. Post-apartheid South Africa spawned two particularly controversial versions in the Muslim community. One was Radio Islam, a community radio station run by Taliban-supporting clerics who proclaimed it to be 'the only Islamic radio station in the world', and the other is People

Against Gangsterism and Drugs (Pagad), which claims to be the only solution to our country's crime problems. Here I want to deal with some of the issues brought to the fore by Radio Islam's refusal to allow the voices of women over the air. The second issue, our responses to escalating crime, follows in the next section.

The state was the only entity allowed to broadcast publicly under the apartheid regime. Currently, numerous community organizations have taken to the air and there are a number of Muslim radio stations in the country. Regulated by the Independent Broadcasting Authority (IBA), which also licenses these radios, all of them are bound to uphold and nurture the basic ethos of the constitution and its Bill of Rights. Radio Islam, broadcasting to large parts of the country, subsequently violated its licence agreement by refusing to air the voices of women. A case was brought against them by a group of Muslim youth supported by the country's Commission on Gender Equality (CGE), the constitutional organ to promote, defend and protect gender equality.

Radio Islam, however, insisted on its position that a woman's voice is *awrah* (a part of a person's being which has to be concealed) and a potential source of evil. ('What won't these men get up to once they are tuned in or turned on and unleashed by the allure of the female presenter's voice?') It also implied that this was the only truly Islamic position and that the whole world of Islam was wrong on this score. (Rather like the mother watching the regiment on a march past and commenting on how the entire regiment, other than her son, was out of step!) Some of us suggested that a simple answer was for the radio to adopt a slogan for all the adherents of their interpretation of Islam: 'If you get turned on, you switch off!'

After months of a mini jihad in which the silence of women on the air was decreed to be a fundamental issue in Islamic law, the radio relented and agreed to phasing in women's voices to the extent that they would eventually get four hours a day. (Some mischievous fellow suggested that the radio planned a women's slot on cooking, in which a woman would come and offer a recipe on how to boil water: 'Let the water boil for two hours' – silence for two hours – 'Now let the water cool down for an hour' – silence – 'Now pour the water slowly down the drain' – silence for an hour until a man's voice comes on to resume normal broadcasting.)

The IBA and the CGE were more than a little bewildered about how a fundamental religious position could change in few months. They were also somewhat confused about a religious law which allows women to be on the air for four hours a day but not twelve. The IBA finally found that Radio Islam still did not intend to offer substantive equality to women and it was therefore, denied a licence to continue broadcasting.

Needless to say, I was not an avid listener to this radio station. After several calls from friends to react to the interminable invective and slander that Radio Islam heaped on me as a Commissioner on Gender Equality, and after several death threats, the Commission subpoenaed a number of tapes. I listened to them and other than being amused by the funny parts about my being a paid up member of the Jewish Board of Deputies and so on, I really felt sad at the fear of an open society that the radio and numerous callers displayed. In Chapter 2 I spoke about Victor Frankl – no apologies for citing a Jew – who made some profound observations about his fellow prisoners in the Nazi concentration camp at Auschwitz. Some of those prisoners, despite having yearned desperately for their freedom, had been held captive for so long that when they were eventually released they walked into the sunlight, blinked nervously and then silently walked back into the familiar darkness of the prisons to which they had been accustomed for so long.

In its appeals for survival, Radio Islam employed a curious mix of arguments, ranging from democracy to scripture: the vast majority of its listeners – mostly women – didn't want women on the air, their democratic right to this, the Shari'ah demands that women be silent, the constitution protects freedom of religion, and so on. The contradictions were glossed over, as were the diverse voices within their own ranks. Where does democracy fit in when your interpretation is the last word? Why appeal to a constitution that you regard as inherently evil? What are the implications of insisting on your peculiar and somewhat 'bizarre' rights to discriminate against women for other minority communities who may come with equally 'bizarre' demands? The matter is now headed for the High Court, where Radio Islam will square it off with the Commission on Gender Equality to decide the significant issue of the clash between two fundamental rights, the freedom of religion and the right to gender equality.

Numerous Muslims, some relatively enlightened in matters unrelated to gender, were deeply upset that it was a Muslim group that first initiated the formal complaint of gender discrimination with the IBA and the CGE, and much of the invective directed at me was because I was expected to stand by 'the community'. 'Why do we have to wash our dirty linen in front of the non-Muslim public?' is the regular lament. Who is 'the community'? Is there any recognition of the linen being dirty, let alone a willingness to wash it? Is justice not a greater demand than community cohesion? How does one mediate when one side claims to be speaking for Allah, because to change positions would imply a God who can change His mind?

It is remarkable that a community comprising less than two per cent of the country's population has so much confidence in its own beliefs that it can intervene substantially in the national debate on issues of religion, gender equality and freedom of expression. I have always been astounded at this indomitable belief in the superiority of our own product throughout the world of Islam, including those parts where we are a numerically insignificant part of the population. In few parts of the world, though, is the volley of Muslim demands viewed as just another integral and legitimate part of the socio-political landscape, as is the case in South Africa. This testifies to the spirit of inclusivity of our new democratic society. This inclusivity though, imposes certain obligations upon us.

First, we cannot allow pride to become religious arrogance. We do so when we miscalculate our own importance and confuse the putative superiority of the principles of our faith with our track record as a socio-historical community.

Second, our inability to deal with internal pluralism should not lead us to misinterpret the ability of others to listen to us as a sign of the strength of our truths and the weakness of theirs, rather than the depth of their commitment to listen to all sides.

Third, we need to reflect on the nature of the actual rather than the verbal messages that we transmit to the broader society. Looking at the quality of Muslim religious life around us, one actually sees little trace in personal and community lives of attempts to live alongside the injunctions of the Qur'an, even in the limited sense as interpreted by those who argue for incorporating Islamic ethical norms or the puta- tively Islamic penal code.

Exclusivist groups will always be a threatened species in an open society and their fears of leaving their prisons are thus well founded. However, in a nation that has fought so long and so hard for ideals of justice for all, there can be no safe haven for those who continue to believe that one human being, by accident of race or gender, is superior to another.

CRIME OUT THERE? OR IN HERE?

In a newsagent, the man watches as his four-year-old daughter, thinking she is unobserved, slips a pencil into her pocket. He instinctively slaps her on her hand and, becoming aware of the unwelcome attention from the other shoppers, somewhat embarrassed, mumbles more kindly to the girl: 'Please don't ever do this again; Daddy will bring you a pencil from work tomorrow night.' This concocted story has probably played itself out in numerous ways in all of our lives and, without stretching it too far, reflects a number of issues in the crime crisis currently gnawing away at our nation's soul.

In Pagad, with its slogan 'Kill the [drug] merchant, kill!', we see encapsulated the instinctive and often simplistic response and 'solution' to crime and violence in our society. The rise of the liberal democratic state that upholds the human rights of all, including criminals and gangsters, has been blamed by a large section of the population and they have called for the return of the death penalty. Others, including the gangsters, have laid the blame at poverty's door.

The rise of the liberal democratic state has certainly loosened the reins of the state and many of the police – steeped in a jackboot culture of *skiet, skop en doner* (shoot, kick and beat) – are still paralysed about what goes and what doesn't in the new South Africa. Furthermore, while the state now guarantees all sorts of rights to all its citizens, we have not seen a concomitant commitment to protect the lives and property of citizens, which is the primary function of the state.

The problem, however, is not the liberal democratic state itself, nor is the solution a return to totalitarianism with its slogans of death to all dissidents and social delinquents. Many Muslims whose only experience of life abroad is either their country of origin or a few months in Saudi Arabia on pilgrimage often resort to the rather glib response that 'in Mecca people can leave their shops unattended and unlocked when they close for prayers because thieves have their hands amputated!'

A few years ago I was in Sweden for a conference which lasted a few days. Afterwards a friend, Patrice, and I were invited to spend a weekend at the home of one of the organizers. When we arrived at her house, unattended for nearly a week, she headed straight for the door and opened it without unlocking it. To our astonishment she said, 'Oh, people do not lock their doors here!' And this was in Sweden, with all its liberal laws, its prisons resembling small hotels, where they don't murder murderers or rape rapists.

The problem is not one of poverty, either, for the people of Bolivia, Palestine or Bangladesh are much poorer than our poorest and yet one is still free to walk around in those places at any time of the night. The problem is rooted in the systematic cheapening of human life by the apartheid regime and the accompanying destruction of any sense of morality, the growth of a self-centred utilitarian culture where people just see themselves and their own needs.

However, we are dealing with the South African nation: a miracle nation, a nation that turned all predictions of a drawn-out, bloody and dirty race war on its head. The people of our land refused to adjust to decades of enforced discrimination and doggedly pursued their own agenda of liberation. The point is that while, in the long run, only a vast improvement in our socio-economic position will bring about a fundamental change in the crime situation, we are not entirely powerless and can do an enormous amount to turn things around. For this, all of us – victims and perpetrators – need the willingness to own the problem and a determined bid to be a part of a humane solution, one that will not see the remedy aggravating the disease.

Some of our public responses to drugs and gangsterism really reflect on us as the prisoners of deep-seated anger and bitterness. We have, in fact, become victims who have internalized the cheapening of the human spirit that the apartheid system so desperately sought. Just when we thought that the beast had been slain we find that it had entered our innards. Desperate to exorcize the beast, we find an enemy 'out there' in the shape of gangsters and drug merchants, against whom we direct our venom without fully appreciating the source of the venom.

There may well be an enemy out there, as many a victim of gang-sterism and drugs will testify, but that is only a part of the story; we, the criminals and the victims, are the Siamese twins given birth to by yesterday's regime. Drug merchants require customers; gangsters require willing customers who will buy their stolen merchandise: here lies the rub. Blame the collapse of sexual morality on the freedom of the streets that sex workers seem to be enjoying if you will, but it takes two, at least two, to tango.

A refusal to recognize the way selfhood is tied up to the despised other and that the seat of the venom is the self is dangerous because, if we do not come to terms with its presence, we will be engaged in an eternal search for external entities on which to unleash it. 'Where are we going to clean up next?' becomes a driving quest. Yet venom, as I said earlier, is like acid: it does more harm to the vessel in which it is stored than to the object on which it is poured. This means a refusal to divide the world into 'them' and 'us'. The problem is not 'out there', nor are the solutions. Manenberg, an impoverished township where Rashied Staggie, a prominent gang leader, is a celebrated hero, is only a reflection, even if unwelcome and ugly, of Gatesville, the middle-class area where Pagad meets. Similarly, as far as Pagad is concerned, it is not 'them', Iranian or Libyan influence, at work as much of the media speculated. Pagad is but another organic part of our community venting its own anger at the seeming inability or unwillingness of the state to move against those wreaking havoc with our lives.

The wave of Muslim activism against drug peddling and gangsterism raises a number of interesting questions about Muslims, Islamic law and religio-moral minorities. First, the Qur'an, for Muslims the unadul-terated and direct word of God, is explicit in its sanctioning of an array of physical measures, including the amputation of hands, whipping and the death penalty for a number of crimes ranging from theft to murder. Muslims in general, therefore, have always been unapologetic about this. However, like all texts once disconnected from their contexts, the words of the Qur'an so easily become very pliable tools in the hands of those not fully appreciative of the underlying profoundly human and compassionate ethos of these injunctions.

Second, the authority to judge an accused, to exact retribution and to determine the nature of that retribution in an Islamic society is clearly defined: it lies with the state and its organs. Neither the text of the

Qur'an, nor Muslim jurists over the years have ever sanctioned the application of the Islamic penal system by non-state authorities. Traditional Islamic jurisprudence categorizes the state as one of three types: the 'abode of Islam' where the ruling authority is Muslim and the laws of Islam prevail, the 'abode of war' where the state is actively antagonistic towards Muslims, and the 'abode of peace' where Muslims are living in freedom despite the state not being Muslim. Those arguing that South Africa is anything but the abode of peace in terms of Islamic jurisprudence would be hard pressed to find a Muslim jurist to argue their case.

This brings me to a third phenomenon, the overwhelming support in the Muslim community for the torching of Rashaad Staggie, a notorious gang leader, and the twin of Rashied, in September 1996 during a Pagad march.[2] Despite the general underlying sentiments that this was justified by Islam, with a number expressing the desire for an 'Islamic state', the simple question, 'What does the Shari'ah, Islamic Law, say?' was completely ignored. Confronted with the fact that all Muslim jurists unanimously concur that the killing of Staggie cannot be condoned in terms of the Shari'ah, many attacked the track record of the jurists in fighting crime. The assumption seems to be that because the interpreters of the law did not do anything about enforcing it, then the law may be ignored. The problem though is that, for Muslims, the lawgiver is God, who cannot be ignored.

Furthermore, 'frustration' or 'anger', however legitimate, has never been the basis of any legal decision or crusade in Islam. The Prophet Muhammad (Peace be upon him) was asked: 'Which of the three strives in the path of Allah? One who fights in order that he displays his bravery, or one who fights out of a sense of anger or one who fights in order to show off?' He replied: 'He who fights so that the word of Allah is exalted, is the one who strives in the cause of Allah.' This is why the insititution of the qadi, the judge, is so entrenched in Islam: so that a dispassionate mind can intervene between the accused and the 'anger' of the people.

What is happening is that 'the community', rather than the law and the text, seems to have become the criterion by which truth and error are determined. This poses an interesting dilemma to liberation theologians like myself who have consistently argued that this is commendable. It should also pose a serious dilemma to those who justify Staggie's killing in the name of Islam: how does one reconcile abandoning the Shari'ah in the name of affirming Islam? Isn't one, in effect, identifying with postmodernist Muslims who argue that one can, in fact, lead a life of submission to God (the literal meaning of the Arabic word *islam*) without buying into all the legal stuff that accompanies normative Islam?

Lastly, there is the question of fidelity to the directly revealed word from God. It is understandable that one should desire that everyone live alongside it. The problem is of the method of extending this to others who do not share your appreciation of the word of God, and of whether one has the right to do so. 'The Word of God', say some Zionists, 'has given us Greater Israel': we see the horrendous consequence that this has for the Palestinians and Lebanese who daily have to experience the oppression of other's commitment to their narrow interpretation of their sacred texts. Nearer home, one can well imagine what would happen to many Muslims if deeply committed vegetarians or environmentalists felt compelled to impose their morality and started torching meat peddlers because of the suffering that meat-eating inflicts on animals and the damage it causes to the environment.

To return to the issue of crime, at a more private and quiet level more and more South Africans are resorting to an equally questionable and – sometimes literally self-defeating – response to the problem of the cheapening of human life. Arm yourself to the teeth. Current estimates suggest that there are seven million guns floating around in the hands of civilians, one for every six South Africans. In 1997 eleven thousand people were murdered with guns and 24,700 attempted murders involved guns. Given that 18,000 licensed guns are stolen each year and that people are far more likely to be killed by their own guns than protected by them, one shudders at the foolhardiness of it all. In this spectacle of gun-owner falling victim to his (nearly always his) own gun is reflected the symbiotic relationship between self and other and, once again, the inseparability of our destinies.

Is this what we fought for? Is this what so many of our martyrs laid down their lives for? A society where everyone is armed to the teeth, ready to exact the ultimate penalty at the slightest provocation?

At a deeply personal level we need to be aware that much of our self-respect is measured by the extent to which we own our responses to all life's situations. While the most horrific manifestations of crime may be 'out there', its beginnings are often in here, inside our own behaviour. This means refusing to succumb to a culture of walking away with impunity from your office with pencils for your kids, proudly displaying the stolen video that you bought for peanuts or omitting through sheer laziness to pay your TV licence.

No matter how efficient a state is, morality is not something that it can ever enforce, if this is indeed desirable. Nor is it achieved by slapped wrists or other forms of violence: morality is primarily taught by example, and only becomes effective once it is owned by people. At a social level, owning the problem means a commitment to strengthening the organs of civil society. A quiet, ongoing and determined involvement in community-based anti-crime forums, neighbourhood watches and police forums must become the litmus test of our concern for the proliferation of drugs and the rise of gangsterism. While some of these forums have the potential to become trigger-happy images of the enemy they are intended to tackle, this will only happen with the complicit consent of those ordinary citizens who throw up their hands in despair and pietistic lamentation.

ON MURDERING MURDERERS

In Pakistan, Tara Masih, the legendary state executioner, recently passed away and, following tradition, his son succeeded him. As the surname 'Masih' denotes, the family is Christian, as all executioners, whippers and lashers in Pakistan have traditionally been. What we are witnessing here is a repeat of 'tradition' whereby all sweepers throughout the country are Christians. Here, as elsewhere on the subcontinent, sweeping is a vocation that you are born to if you are a Punjabi Christian or a lower-caste Hindu. Muslims in Pakistan and upper-caste Hindus in India do not clear their own blocked domestic sewage pipes. 'Call the sweeper' is the standard response. In this society, the sweepers are the personification of dirt and only they, common wisdom goes, ought to handle dirt.

Society does not relish the prospect of living alongside the consequences of its own sewage. Let the dehumanized other, the 'non-us' handle it. (The sweeper also never has a name. He or she is simply 'the *jamadaar*'.) The sewage and foul odours that the sweeper removes enable us to feel a bit better about ourselves, to forget about that vulnerable specimen of humanity suspended on a toilet seat.

Is this why we hang people?

The post-apartheid escalation in crime throughout South Africa has led to a rise in the clamour for the return of capital punishment. Inasmuch as this clamouring is about murderers and rapists and the punishment that their deeds warrant, it is also about ourselves and society's ways of coping with its unpleasant by-products. Until the moratorium placed on hangings and the subsequent judgement against capital punishment by the Constitutional Court, South Africa found itself in extraordinary company: along with the USA, China, Iran and Iraq we were at the very top of the league in executing criminals.

Let us consider the arguments in favour of capital punishment in the light of our attempts to forge a society based on justice and reconciliation. First, a number of surveys indicate that the majority of South Africans support the reintroduction of capital punishment; many of its advocates have called for a referendum on the issue. South Africa is a parliamentary democracy, in which we elect our representatives for broadly conforming to most, never all, of our views. Where would the political and religious right wing be today if the present government were to listen to 'the vast majority of our people' who are now being so regularly invoked in support of capital punishment? In jail and the dustbins of history, I suspect. Why does the religious and political right wing expect the state to uphold the best in our humanness when it comes to reconciliation and forgiveness for uniformed murderers in the service of a universally despised apartheid regime, yet want the state to unleash the most primitive instincts within us for murderers without uniforms?

Second, it is argued that the death penalty deters. If this were indeed the case, then how come that apartheid South Africa's hanging figures increased annually? Malaysia's hanging rate has increased at an average of 115 per cent every year since the death penalty was introduced for drug possession. (A while ago I heard the Malaysian Prime Minister arguing that to stop the hangings now would be an injustice to all those already hanged!) In Saudi Arabia, the 'beheading days', previously confined to Fridays, have now been extended to every day of the week to cope with the increase. The justification for capital punishment in the face of overwhelming evidence that it does not deter seems to be rooted in people's most atavistic, primordial instincts for revenge.

Surely such responses have little or no place in a civilized society? Abu Hurairah (May Allah be pleased with him) relates that someone asked the Prophet (Peace be upon him) to advise him. He said: 'Do not yield to anger.' The man repeated his request several times. Every time the Prophet said: 'Do not yield to anger.'

Third, advocates for the death penalty argue that this is the retribution that society must exact for murder. Why do we then not rape rapists? Is it because deep down we realize that something of our humanness will be severely impaired, that there is something abominable about stooping to the level of the lowest among us?

Many Muslims instinctively respond positively to right-wing rhetoric on law and order in general and, more specifically, on calls to apply the death penalty for a number of crimes. Believing this to be 'Islamic', many also think that this will somehow contribute to the Islamization of society. The Islamic penal system was applicable to a certain kind of society where retribution for various crimes often spanned generations. 'An eye for an eye' is not a prescription but a limitation. Thus the Qur'an says 'And in *qisas* [just retribution] there is life for you, O people of understanding' (Q. 2:170). In other words, the kind of endless retribution exacted upon generations had to be terminated. This is one of the reasons that the punishments defined in the Qur'an are called *hudud Allah* (the limits of Allah). If the death penalty were a divine prescription then the question of blood money would not have arisen.

Given the extent of socio-economic disparity which exists today, it is evident that any insistence on the death penalty – even in majority Muslim states – means that only the wealthy will be allowed to get away. (That is if their bribes, expensive lawyers or diplomatic representatives have not already managed to secure them their release, a mistrial or a not guilty verdict.) The truth is that, for whatever reasons, the death rows of the world are occupied by the poor and the exploited.

Why should we not hang people?

First, so that we do not become dehumanized. I believe that the Qur'an set into motion a revolution that was intended to enhance the quality of life for every human being and to facilitate his or her journey to Allah. This is a God who does not place anyone beyond redemption. My doing so limits my own humanity because our fates are interwoven.

Second, error is intrinsic to human beings. We know, for example, about Kirk Bloodsworth who spent nine years on death row in the USA after being sentenced to death for the murder and rape of a nine-year-old girl. Now recently developed DNA tests done by the FBI and an independent laboratory prove that he was innocent. A few years ago, the discovery of large-scale police corruption and tampering with evidence in one police district in England led to the re-opening of a number of cases, and some convictions were set aside. What if those convicted had been hanged?

We may argue that society invariably makes mistakes, but what if those mistakes were with my life? It is true that no system is faultless but capital punishment closes the door eternally on any attempt to repair the fault. Thurgod Marshall, one of the former luminaries of the USA Supreme Court, in the famous case of Firman versus Georgia said:

> If the American people knew that capital punishment is no more a deterrent than life imprisonment, that most prisoners upon release become law-abiding citizens, that the death penalty itself may stimulate criminal activity, that it is imposed discriminatorily, that there is evidence that innocent people have been executed, that this wreaks havoc on the criminal justice system, then most Americans would be offended by the death penalty.

Is it too much to ask that South Africans, who know so much about people's inhumanity to others, be offended by it? Will someone save Tara Masih Jr from all the deaths that his own humanity must surely undergo every time he lets that floorboard drop?

FINDERS KEEPERS, LOSERS WEEPERS?

When a society has gone through as much trauma as South African society and when a people have been as horribly oppressed as the Black people of this country then the need to address the past is indisputable. In the words of Nelson Mandela in *Justice in Transition*, 'to close our eyes and pretend none of this ever happened would be to maintain at the core of our society a source of pain, division and hatred and violence. Only the disclosure of truth and the search for justice can create the moral climate in which reconciliation and peace will flourish.' The South African nightmare is like a childhood trauma and will 're-appear as nightmares and neuroses until he [the child] brings it out in the open and looks at it' (Mariono Grondona, *Time Magazine*, 22 May 1995).

To deal with the challenge of a healing closure of the past, the granting of amnesty for all politically motivated crimes, and the task of uncovering the full truth of last phase of our country's nightmare, the Truth and Reconciliation Commission (TRC) was established by the new constitution. After nearly two years of investigations, hearings, and controversy at the time of writing in 1998 it is ready to hand its report to the President.[3]

We have watched the proceedings and have wept with the families and victims. The simplicity of their demands – 'I just want the hand of my husband back that is being kept in a bottle somewhere,' said one grieving widow – has left us stunned and humbled at the capacity of people to forgive. We have been deeply moved by the unbounded humanity of its Chairperson, Archbishop Desmond Tutu, and thoroughly impressed by the competence with which the whole thing is being conducted.

So how far did South Africans get?

The TRC is the result of party political negotiations, as Tutu has often reminded us when confronted with some of the inherent weaknesses such as its predisposition towards reconciliation rather than justice. While the TRC is genuinely an attempt to deal with the wounds of the past, it is also an ideological tool of realpolitik in which ordinary citizens cannot be allowed to upset an agenda of nation-building and a 'positive investor climate'. (It's quite fascinating that this mechanism is being hailed by all and sundry in the industrial world – the same world that is vigorously supportive of any move to hound and punish Nazi criminals, even if they are well into their eighties. Is the message somehow that Jewish lives are more significant than Black lives, that the savage Blacks cannot be trusted not to give free rein to their barbarism but that Whites can be trusted to pursue their killers and exact nothing more than justice?)

Various spokespersons of the Commission have often said that its essential focus is on the victims. We have seen the remarkable way that they have been dealt with: the homage being paid to victims and their families, the way they are being truly heard and the earnest manner in which the Commission pushes the relevant authorities for compensation and other requests to be handled expeditiously. However, in the absence of a clear focus on justice as the other side of the coin, one cannot help but wonder if this talk on focusing on the victims does not have the effect, even if unintended, of allowing the perpetrators to get away.

Many families of the victims of the apartheid regime's killing machinery have been reluctant to make submissions to the TRC and their unease or rejection reflects those of many other South Africans. One such family is that of the martyred Imam Abdullah Haron, murdered by the security police in 1969. Other families, such as those of Steve Bantu Biko and Griffiths and Victoria Mxenge have lodged full-scale but unsuccessful legal challenges against the TRC's competence and lost their own rights to justice in court. For these families it is not a choice between justice and reconciliation; it's an assumption that reconciliation is premised on justice. If the victims were truly the essential focus of the TRC then why should we not allow the various victims and families to determine their own way of being reconciled? Why should these families be coerced – subtly or otherwise – to become part of what is for many of us a cathartic and very healing process if they insist that this is not the way in which they are going to be healed. If the incredible request for 'a bursary for my daughter' or 'the return of my husband's hand' is all that is asked by some, why should others be expected to relinquish their quest for justice – even if it is as basic as Mrs Rebecca Truter's demand that her son's murderer's state pension be stopped 'so he can feel how I struggle'. Surely the yearning for justice is not any less human than that for reconciliation?

While justice is a moral value with intrinsic worth that requires no external validation, whether religious, ideological, nation-building or whatever, this is not the case with reconciliation. There cannot be any doubt that our country is sorely in need of healing and of the crucial importance of reconciliation in this process. What is called into question is the meaningfulness of reconciliation without justice. Will a process whereby a committee grants amnesty to murderers, often living on huge state pensions, while the families of the victims shed 'rivers of tears' in front of the TRC not give a new twist to the cruel adage 'finders keepers, losers weepers'?

While the TRC has been careful to avoid casting any aspersions on those families or victims reluctant or unwilling to come forward and has never sought to undermine them, we still need to be aware that a peculiarly Christian version of forgiveness and reconciliation is being played out. It is not a version that finds a resonance in all South Africans, or even among all Christians. This is a version that seeks stability rather than justice and that derives its strength from a Christ who asks the Father to forgive his persecutors even as he is being crucified. While many may find the idea of unqualified forgiveness truly moving and believe that their own humanity is enhanced by forgiving those who trespass against them, I am sceptical about translating all of this into social and political terms.

If truth be told, the only truths we were told were those the perpetrators feared were going to come out in any case. The agents of the apartheid regime confessed only to the barest minimum required to get them off the hook. As for reconciliation, those who needed to hear those truths most of all, the Whites of South Africa, were essentially absent throughout the proceedings.

And the Muslims? Where did we fit into all of this? What did we make of it all?

One of the Commissioners is a Muslim, as is the judge who headed the Amnesty Committee, while several Muslims testified in their personal capacities. I gave evidence at the religious hearings on the suffering of Muslims under apartheid, their role in defending it and their contribution to our liberation from it, as did Imam Hassan Solomon of the Muslim Judicial Council. Besides widespread coverage of my presentation and what was rather mistakenly seen as Solomon's rejoinder the following day, the entire event passed Muslims by, as a community. The TRC itself and the issues raised by it and its way of operating were really non-issues in the community.

There were two exceptions to this indifference. The first involved some concerted, albeit largely unsuccessful, efforts by Imam Abdur Rashied Omar of the Claremont Main Road Mosque to interest the congregation in the TRC and its work, and the second was an attempt by *Al Qalam*, the Muslim monthly, to cover the work of the TRC on a regular basis. Many non-Muslims critically committed to the reconciliation process and fully aware of the significance of Muslims as both victims of, perpetrators and liberators from apartheid expressed concern about this indifference. I was persuaded by Fr Michael Lapsley to host a discussion for Muslims on this indifference. Twelve people were invited, ten promised to come and one, Soraya Bosch (May Allah have mercy upon her), pitched up.

In what I regard as the two most significant reasons for this indifference lie the major challenges for progressive Muslims in South Africa today. Many of us defined our theology and our located our organizational programmes in terms of opposition to the state. The haemorrhaging that our support base experienced as a result of the death of apartheid has exposed the shallowness of our commitment to a thoroughly contextual or South African Islam. Furthermore, the disappearance of key activists and thinkers into state structures and the inability to nurture new blood have contributed to the general absence of Muslims as a community from crucial forums such as the TRC. This absence has also had several other negative implications. Muslims can conveneniently slump into their own obsession with narrow community issues such as when to celebrate 'Id, reactionary elements are able to dominate the public image of Islam and there is a lack of organizational discipline on and support for individual progressive Muslim thinkers. Furthermore, in the absence of strong organizations with a solid infrastructure and a long term vision, many attempts by progressive Muslim individuals to keep the flag flying are viewed as 'ego trips' or 'priming the Muslim electorate for the next elections'.

The second challenge relates to the larger South African society. Very few of those involved in the struggle for freedom realized that this was really a struggle against all forms of injustice. It was a struggle for 'the least' (as in the saying of Jesus – Peace be upon him – 'What you do unto the least of my brothers, you have done unto me'). There are, therefore, many Christians who do not understand that Christianity as a privileged religion and discourse must make way for a more humble religion which regards all the other faiths of our country as equals. I believe that this problem was reflected in the Christianization of the TRC process and that it contributed significantly to the Muslim willingness to remain on the sidelines. (On the day of my testimony, I spoke critically of the symbolism of having Jews, Muslim and Hindus coming to testify to an all-Christian panel, headed by an Archbishop sitting under a huge crucifix in a church hall.)

Our challenge is thus to persistently remind others of our presence and of the value of the religious heritage that we bring along with us, but to do so in such a manner that they would want to embrace us as partners in the reconstruction of our nation.

CONCLUSION

what's on your agenda?

The boarding down the Broadway displayed in large red letter-
ing: 'Do you want to be saved?' . . . Had it read 'Do you want to
be safe?' millions of people would have said 'Yes, Yes, Yes, we
want to be safe', and another barricade would have gone up. The
soul is imprisoned, protected, nothing can get in to hurt it, but then
it can't get out either. . . . Come outside if you wanted to make
progress. 'Coming outside' was dangerous, very dangerous, but
it had to be done; there was no other way.

Fynn, *Mister God, This Is Anna*

The letter below raises a number of questions that were also posed in the
concluding chapter of my book *Qur'an, Pluralism and Liberation*, where
they were also left unanswered. This letter first appeared in *Al Qalam* and
responses ranged from 'even Farid Esack is beginning to see through his
own ignorance' to the more perceptive one from Abdul Kader Tayob:
'I'm not going to fall for this trap; this guy just wants us to discuss his
views again.'(AK will forgive the misquote. If however, he insists on a
proper citation, then the reader may subsititute the 't' in 'trap' with a 'c'.)
One of the readers of the original manuscript of this book, Nasiema
Cassiem, wrote the following note alongside the letter: 'Even though I
feel that it is good enough to just ask questions, shouldn't an attempt be
made to provide answers? Or would this drive you insane or to para-
noia?' Well, Nasiema, thanks for the challenge, which I will partially
take up, and also for the reminder to request my readers that if anyone
finds some of my marbles they should kindly return them to me, care
of my publishers.

Dear Farid,

Is this how one spells your name? Your mother, I recall, spelt it with an 'e' before the 'd'. Is this a part of your dumping tradition? I have been a regular reader of your views in various papers since you started writing. Of late, I have also been reading letters to the editor of *Al Qalam* criticizing your views and those of your fellow travellers in enlightenment/confusion/darkness who grace/soil the pages of this paper. None of you ever bother to respond to these criticisms. Is it an intellectual contempt for those whom you regard as lesser mortals? Given your pretence to humility, one would have expected at least some acknowledgement that you read what your critics have to say, perhaps even an attempt to really listen.

First, can you spell out exactly where the Qur'an and Hadith fit into your thinking? While there is an occasional sprinkling of verses from the Qur'an in your written work, you hardly cite Hadith. One gets the impression that for you and your like, the text – or rather, some parts of the text – is invoked to support your own views instead of the text shaping your views. You will, no doubt, argue that there is no such thing as the text shaping views and that the text is inevitably and invariably used as justification for views already held by the reader. This may be so. The point is that in the tradition of Islamic scholarship no one consciously argues from this premise. In truth, you and your like have placed yourselves outside tradition.

There is a blatancy about the challenges that you throw out in your writings and utterances, which most of us sense and yet are unable to articulate, a sense of disdain for this community and its traditions without having the courage to abandon it. Instead, you hang around and subvert it from within. The anger that you saw around the Claremont Main Road Mosque at the time of the Amina Wadud controversy and the hooliganism that you lamented is admittedly a reflection of intolerance in the community. It is, however, also a growing anger at the blatancy of your theological challenges and disdain that you and your like display towards the community and its traditions.

Second, is there for you anything really unique about Islam that makes you hold on to it and desire it as a faith for others to follow? Increasingly you are adopting a broadly humanistic perspective that can really be argued for from any or even no religious perspective. One gets the impression that the only reason your articles are flavoured with some Arabic or Urdu words is because your audience is Muslim, not because you are writing from an Islamic perspective.

Last week, on national radio, it was left to a Christian to caution you against substituting religion for a secular humanism that desperately seeks to curry favour with the politically correct flavour of the month. Some time ago you wrote about the 'humanum', the truly human, as an ethical criterion. Are you not, in fact, elevating the humanum as the criterion of right and wrong, just and unjust, instead of the will of Allah as expounded in the Qur'an and elaborated in the *sunnah*? Your project is rethinking Islam. Where do you 'rethinkers' draw the line? Postmodernity does not believe in such a thing as lines, does it? Tell us about your boundaries. Where do your equality and justice stop if they do stop anywhere? Gay marriages? Women leading the Friday congregational prayers? A Hindu priest conducting a marriage ceremony in a mosque (with a bit of fire to add character)? In fact, why have any kind of marriages? Isn't that too defined a relationship, too confined a union for postmodernity? Why have the formal prayers at all? It's a tradition with little rational basis, isn't it? What's the point of one bow and two prostrations? Why don't you postmodernists just cancel the whole thing? Come on, tell us what's on your agenda.

In the heyday of Stalinism in South Africa you courageously criticized your comrades in the Communist Party for their two-stage theory. According to this theory, the first stage of the revolution is a national democratic one whereby all the socio-economic formations will be mobilized for democracy, etc. Afterwards, in the second stage, the communist society will be built. In the first stage, though, not everyone is told what the ultimate goals of the revolution will be. You spoke about the dishonesty of getting people to board a bus whose destination is known to only the driver and a select few passengers.

You are pretty neat with all your questions, merely outlining frameworks for possible solutions, what Mohammed Arkoun calls 'heuristic lines of thinking'. I smell that underneath all your 'frameworks for possible solutions' lie definite answers, for which you and your like don't have the guts to stand up and be counted.

What's this thing with 'pluralism', the other flag that you wave so regularly? Aren't you really asking for space in which to promote ideas alien to Islam? Pluralism, as you probably know, is not without any

ideology; it is part of a language founded and sustained in critical scholarship which, in turn, functions as an extension of areligious, even
anti-religious, Western scholarship. (Western scholarship, although not
physically limited to the West, I need to remind you, is but an extension of a whole culture which has clear hegemonic interests over the
so-called under-developed world.) Isn't it correct to say that you guys
have really sold out hook(er?), line and sinker to neo-colonialism –
particularly of the cultural type?

Tolerance is perhaps OK. Pluralism, however, goes beyond this: it
talks about valuing differences and being enriched by them. Spell out
for us how *shirk* [polytheism] enriches Islam, what we have to learn
from ancestor veneration in African Traditional Religion, what
Hinduism and its multiple gods have to teach us. How is your postmodernity, with its absence of boundaries, overlapping gods, and
million ideas really different from *shirk*? Hope you do not think that
you have a monopoly over hermeneutics. Allow me quote a biblical
scholar, Francis Schussler Fiorenza in conclusion:

> To take into account the historical, cultural and political condi-
> tions about the demise of biblical authority is to view the
> scriptures historically but to view ahistorically both ourselves and
> our views on scriptures. Descriptions about the demise of biblical
> authority are as much autobiographical statements as they are
> objective descriptions. ('The Crisis of Scriptural Authority,
> Interpretation and Reception')

Has it occurred to you that perhaps it is you, your like and the postmodernity that breeds you that require scrutiny and rethinking rather
than Islam?

Yours etc.,

Farid

Dear Farid,

That name one is an interesting one. 'Faried' is the Afrikaans and, in the South African context, also the working-class, version of the spelling. 'Farid' is the more correct transliteration of the Arabic, but also, in my context, a somewhat more sophisticated spelling. I think that my shift to 'Farid' reflects my one movement into the world of scholarship and, yes, also away from my working-class background. This is part of the tension which many progressive thinkers and activists undergo as they move on (ahead? up?) in life. I am afraid that I have not managed too well to integrate my commitment to the marginalized with my own being and lifestyle.

After a recent public accusation that I was playing to the Jewish and Christian gallery, a friend, Muhammed Gulbar, said: 'I'm sure that you're pretty used to this kind of thing and even indifferent to it.' No, I am not indifferent to criticism; on the contrary, I am quite sensitive despite my image of strength and arrogance. I read what people write in response to my work and I take their concerns on board when the opportunity arises. I do not always have the time or the inclination to respond to all criticism in the form that the critic may desire. In the same manner that I leave my audience free to respond or not and in the way that they choose, I should not be compelled to respond in any particular manner. I do, however, try to avoid any kind of discourse that is seemingly going to generate more heat than clarity, and when I smell that people have dug in and are spoiling for a fight with a good bit of drama then I tend to walk away.

Anyway, on to more substantial issues. First, where does the Qur'an and Hadith fit into my thinking? Of course, I would argue that the text is invariably and inevitably used as pre-text, that is, always used to justify a prior opinion and that this has always been the case in all religious communities, even in serious academic texts wherein the author does not mention a single word about him or herself and his or her context. The problem is with the negative air that surrounds notions of prior opinion and the need to question this. Is prior opinion always baseless? Is it the same as *hawa* (whims and fancy)? Is prior opinion always unethical? This is an old argument in the world of classical Islam; the Mu'tazilites argued that reason can also be a basis for theology and law and that the text always has to be consistent with reason.

If I see a banana peel lying on the road, then I do not need a hadith to tell me that I should remove it. It is, however, nice to find that there is, in fact a hadith that speaks about the virtue of removing it and there is nothing wrong about 'using' that hadith to encourage people to remove obstacles from the road to prevent harm to others.

I can say all the 'correct' things about where the Qur'an and Hadith fit into my thinking, which would make the more conservative Muslim happy. The reality is that even for them, that would be more a statement of where they believe these fit in rather than where they actually fit in. Each Muslim tendency, ranging from the most orthodox to the most progressive, really employs a very limited selection of qur'anic texts and hadith in its thinking and programmes. They do not consciously discard the rest; it's just that somewhere along the very unarticulated line they find greater appeal in some, although at the level of faith, certainly in the case of the Qur'an, they hold on to the whole.

Perhaps it would have been more helpful had you asked where Allah and the Prophet or his *sunnah* fit into my thinking. I tried to deal with the transcendent nature of Allah and of the supremacy of that trancendence over all else. I also think that in looking at Hadith we should be careful that we try to discern a pattern of prophetic ethics and behaviour rather than a set of rules for everything. The latter is a minefield of confusion, distortion and gems. The former, only gems.

It is, of course, true that in some ways, we do fly in the face of tradition. However, we need to bear in mind that tradition is really the common wisdom of the time combined with the dominant perception of that community's heritage. Memory and perception, though, are notoriously selective and upon closer scrutiny we end up with a very nebulous and fluid tradition. Remember how, in 1892, the Muslims of Cape Town rose up against the government to protest against the allocation of distant burial grounds and inoculation against smallpox? In the case of the burial grounds, they believed it compulsory to physically carry the deceased to the graveyard and in the case of inoculation, they believed that one should not interfere with the will of God. Now we all use a hearse, painting it green to tie us to tradition, and inoculation has become part of preparation for the haj. (Talking about hearses, in England the Muslims use the long black ones, yes, the same ones the Christians use and, yes, the driver wears black and doffs a top hat!

And the hearse waits right outside the mosque. It's enough to make a South African Muslim corpse sit up and rush back to his family!)

The other thing about tradition is its ever-present shadows. Throughout Muslim tradition there have been the people who raise difficult questions, who tread where most dread to, who fear the stagnation in the closet more than the pain of the storms and wind and the joys of the sunshine. Abu Dharr al-Ghiffari (May Allah be pleased with him), that lone-ranger Companion who banged on doors soon after the death of the Prophet, asking them to give up all their superfluous wealth, is as much a part of our tradition as 'Uthman (May Allah be pleased with him), the Caliph who attempted to silence him. Many factors have coalesced to ensure that 'Uthman emerged as mainstream and Abu Dharr as 'deviant'. (Well, at least to the Sunni mind; the Shi'ites have it reversed. Or do we?) Look at the history of any society and its traditions, in any age, and for every 'Uthman there will be an Abu Dharr – and they are all a part of its traditions.

At a socio-historical level, mortals can judge who were the 'subverters' and whether those aspects of tradition which people like us subvert were in need in subversion. We are, after all, living on a continent where many of yesterday's terrorists are today's liberators. At an eschatological level, let Allah be the judge. The difficulty for the dominant voices today is that those from the shadows are often more articulate and able to engage with modernity and postmodernity. On the other hand, those who believe that they form the substance of tradition, rather than its shadow, are no longer able to have the monopoly over shaping tradition. When the one may control the *mimbar* (pulpit) the other will have the Internet and the TV. While the TV may today be denounced as *haram* (prohibited), we know that yesterday they also denounced loudspeakers for transmitting the *adhan* (call to prayer) as *haram*. Soon they will embrace the devil's box as well.

The challenge – one that I am, admittedly, hopeless at – to those who want to live in the open is to do so without the arrogance of know-alls and the self-righteousness of those who see only backwardness in their own.

Is there something unique about Islam that makes me hold on to it and makes me desire it as a faith for others to follow?

Yes, there is. There a is childhood prayer that still comes easily to me and which I utter in genuine joy from time to time. 'I am well pleased with Allah as my Lord, with Islam as my *din* [faith/

religion/path] and with Muhammad as a Prophet and Messenger.' I
would be hard pressed to define exactly what it is in Islam that makes
me hold on, but I do know that it is not only the social activism from
which I derive so much inspiration. Why, when I sit alone in a restau-
rant in Brazil and am about to enjoy a piece of cake do I immediately
call the waiter when I detect a peculiar taste? I find out that it contains
alcohol and ask that it be removed. There is no one to see me. And so
I hold on for deeply personal and inexplicable reasons, admittedly with
varying degrees of tenacity. Islam is unique for me and has served me
well. *Alhamdulillah*. I have no desire and have never had any desire for
another path.

I am not sure if I would want to offer normative Islam as the path for
the milkman or the priest around the corner but I do imagine that it
would suit a few other people and, yes, I could offer it to them for consideration. I would, however, want to offer islam, in the literal sense of
submission to the will of Allah, to all and sundry. At the same time, I
will resist the temptation to work out the nitty gritty of how each one
should respond to that call to islam which, I believe, resides deep
inside everyone.

At the bottom of all of the questions raised above is the question of
where to draw the line. I find this an infinitely difficult one. I get asked
all the time, and I ask it of myself and of others all the time. The
assumption that one can draw lines and that these will actually have any
impact on our theology or law is problematic. We have this notion that
sometime ago the doors of *ijtihad* (creative juristic thinking) were
closed. (When, on what date, at what time and by whom?) There is no
definable moment where any one person – even the most conservative
– stops thinking, other than unconsciousness of death. Human beings
will always be confronted with new dilemmas and challenges based on
new knowledge and deeper awareness. You know, removing one's
shoes, accepted today as an intrinsic part of our prayer preparations,
was never practised by the Prophet. How does one fast from dawn to
dusk when you end up at a place where the sun does not set for six
months? Are you a traveller, and therefore entitled to reduce your
prayer units or to abstain from fasting, when a very comfortable first-
class plane journey transports you in a trice thousands of miles away?

Is the haunting question of drawing lines not rooted in our desperation
for safety and security rather than in any sensible appreciation of the

inherently dynamic nature of the human condition? One of the great thinkers in the Muslim world today, Ebrahim Moosa, always answers 'Allah, Allah is the limit' when I ask him this question. I am not entirely convinced that this is the best answer. Perhaps his sense of certainty about Allah is greater than mine, perhaps he is less afraid of tumbling off this whatever it is that all of us 'rethinkers' are on. However, for the moment I, too have to make do with that as a response.

And Allah knows better.

Yours sincerely,

Farid

NOTES

INTRODUCTION

1. In previous writing I have always referred to these people as 'fund-amentalists'. The following quotation, has, however, convinced me otherwise: 'I do not believe that this term [fundamentalist] is appropriate for them at all. They absolutely do not abide by the fundamentals. Instead they dogmatically adhere to the secondary commandments and outdated forms, and sacrifice the principles and fundamentals to the pettiest of their own interests' (Rajavi, *Islam and Women's Equality*, p. 22).

2. This is a note for my brother, Shaik Tahir Sitoto, who in his review of the manuscript noted: 'Sounds too cliché loaded.' It may well be. However, the Call of Islam's pioneering, regular and insistent inclusion of the term 'non-sexist' at a time when it was not cliché loaded means that was our own vision long before it became a cliché in the liberation movement.

3. The Tablighi Jama'ah is a revivalist movement founded in India by a Deobandi scholar, Mawlana Muhammad Ilyas, in the early part of this century. The world of Islam's only truly international move-ment, the group avoids all forms of overtly political discourse and follows a uniformly rigid and literalist interpretation of the *sunnah*, the deeds and sayings of the Prophet Muhammad. Found all over the world, the movement enjoys enormous popularity among Muslims of Indian, particularly those of Gujerati, descent.

ONE

1. The problematic around the use of the male personal pronoun for Allah is dealt with in Chapter 5, albeit briefly.

2. I make a conscious distinction between 'muslim' and 'Muslim'. The former is used in the literal sense of someone who or something that submits to the will of Allah (islam), while the latter denotes someone who belongs to or is identified with the socio-religious community of Islam irrespective of the extent of his or her faithfulness.

3. I am aware of the clumsiness of using language in this manner. I prefer to sacrifice linguistic smoothness for inclusivity.

4. This section first appeared as an article in *Worldview*, the magazine of the Muslim Students Association at the University of Cape Town, 4 (4), August 1985.

5. The reference to sheets of plastic over our heads is to the apartheid regime's practice of waiting until the cold winter to evict illegal black squatters in the cities. They were expected to remain in their 'independent' homelands. The reference to mixing sand with flour comes from accounts by social workers who worked in the most impoverished areas during the apartheid years. They spoke about how parents added sand to their children's food, in a desperate attempt to fill their stomachs.

6. Muslims believe that before the flight to Medina, the Prophet Muhammad experienced a Night Journey, or the Ascent. While asleep next to Ka'bah, he was awoken by the Angel Gabriel who took him through the sky to Jerusalem (the *mi'raj*) where, alongside the prophets Abraham, Moses, Jesus and others, he prayed at the site of the Temple of Solomon. The Prophet Muhammad then ascended through the seven heavens to the Divine Presence (the *isra*) where the daily prayers were made obligatory. While the majority of the orthodox believe that this event was a physical one, others have offered contrary opinions.

TWO

1. It is a common Muslim belief, based on a text from the Qur'an (Q. 7:172) that at some point before the physical creation, Allah gathered the souls of all of humankind and asked *'Alastu bi rab-bikum?'* (Am I not your Lord?), to which the souls unanimously responded *'Bala!'* (Yes, indeed!).

2. The widespread practice of this group, though, is actually to dis-
    regard the personal realities and economic conditions of people
    when they volunteer to go 'in the path of Allah'. This has led to
    several ruined marriages, the loss of jobs, and so on.

THREE

1. The apartheid regime initially did not allow interracial mixing at
    any level of sport. Subsequently, it permitted the mixing of national
    teams but not at club or provincial level. Any exception to this,
    including Black teams wanting to utilize White sports facilities,
    required permission from the government. This policy was referred
    to as 'multi-racial' sports. In contrast to this, the vast majority of
    South Africans opted for 'non-racialism' in sports. By this they
    meant a refusal to accept race as a criteria at any level and a boy-
    cott of all White venues, rather than asking for permission to
    use them.

FIVE

1. These questions are dealt with in my book *Qur'an, Liberation and
    Pluralism* (Oxford: Oneworld, 1997).
2. The 'Islamic Movement' is the generic term used by a number of
    diverse religio-political groups throughout the world to describe
    themselves and their ideological affinity to each other. These range
    from the Muslim Brotherhood in Egypt, to the Jama'at-I-Islami in
    Pakistan and are usually described by others as fundamentalist.
    Among them there is much debate as to which group qualifies for
    inclusion.
3. In the northern provinces the debate is sadly still about women
    having access to mosques.
4. The New Apostolic Church offered a venue for this man and all
    other parents who identified with him to start a private Whites-only
    school on its premises.
5. In many parts of Europe it is quite common for Christians to allow
    Muslims the use of their buildings, especially churches. A while
    ago I attended a meditative (*dhikr*) gathering being conducted by a

group of Sufis in a church in Bonn. To my knowledge, it has never been an issue among Muslims in Germany whether such use is permissible or not.

SIX

1. Husain ibn 'Ali (d. 680) was the grandson of the Prophet. He led an insurrection against Yazid ibn Mu'awiyah, the disputed ruler of the Muslims. This insurrection culminated in the death of Husain and the massacre of his supporters at the Battle of Karbala, an event that signals the formal birth of Shi'ism.
2. The Barelvis are an Indo-Pak tendency in Islam who focus on love for the Prophet (Peace be upon him) as a means of salvation. They believe that the Prophet is alive and condone a number of folk religious practices such as celebrating the death anniversary of saints. The Deobandis may be described as the Calvinists of Islam. Rejecting any popular expression of Islam and what they regard as heretical accretions (*bid'ah*), they focus on adhering to what they regard as the correct beliefs and Prophetic practice (*sunnah*) as the means of attaining salvation.
3. The texts are examined in considerable detail in my book *Qur'an, Liberation and Pluralism* (Oxford: Oneworld, 1997).
4. This is a reference to the now abandoned slogan of the Pan-Africanist Congress of Azania (South Africa). It has been modified by People Against Gangsterism and Drugs (Pagad) to read 'One [drug] Merchant, One Bullet!'

SEVEN

1. Here I am specifically referring to those groups that are so constituted by choice, conviction or genetic or biological accident. I am not talking about the state affirming those particular social classes that have been disadvantaged by more than three hundred years of colonialism and patriarchy.
2. The exact circumstances around the death of Staggie are unclear and no one has been held liable for it. Furthermore, recent evidence suggest that undercover agents of the police may have had a hand in circumstances leading to the killing.

3. The Truth and Reconciliation Commission, headed by Archbishop Desmond Tutu, was created during the constitutional negotiations leading to the present democratic dispensation. It is intended to uncover the truth of human rights abuses during the apartheid era and has the power to provide full amnesty to perpetrators who prove a political motive and offer full disclosure of their crimes.

SELECT BIBLIOGRAPHY

Al-Din Attar, Farid. 1966. *Muslim Saints and Mystics*. London: Routledge & Kegan Paul Ltd

Al-Talib, Hisham. 1992. *Training Guide for Islamic Workers*. Herndon: International Institute of Islamic Thought

Bashier, Zakaria. 1978. *The Meccan Crucible*. London: FOSIS

Bonhoeffer, Dietrich. 1959. *The Cost of Discipleship*. London: SCM Press

Esack, Farid. 1997. *Qur'an, Liberation and Pluralism: An Islamic Perspective of Interreligious Solidarity against Oppression*. Oxford: Oneworld Publications

Fiorenza, Francis Schussler. 1990. 'The Crisis of Scriptural Authority, Interpretation and Reception'. *Reception 2* (2), 15–26

Frankl, Victor. 1963. *Man's Search for Meaning*, trans. Ilse Lasch. Boston, Mass.: Beacon Press

Fromm, Eric. *Escape from Freedom*. 1941. New York: Holt, Rinehart & Winston

Fynn. 1977. *Mister God, This Is Anna*. London: Collins

Harris, Thomas A. 1969. *I'm OK, You're OK*. New York: Harper & Row

Holland, Muhtar. 1975. *The Duties of Brotherhood in Islam*. Leicester: The Islamic Foundation

Justice in Transition. 1994. South African Truth and Reconciliation Commission

Kandhlawi, Mohammad Zakariyyah. 1994. *Stories of the Sahabah*. New Delhi: Idara Ishaat e Diniyat

Khan, Muhammad Z. 1975. *Gardens of the Righteous: Riyadh as-Salihin of Imam Nawawi*. London: Curzon Press

Kritzinger, Klippies. 1991. *Believers in the Future*. Proceedings of the National Interfaith Conference on Religion–State Relations,

2–4 December, 1990. Salt River: World Conference of Religion and Peace

Kubler-Ross, Elizabeth. 1995. *On Death and Dying*. London: Routledge

Lapierre, Dominique. 1986. *The City of Joy*. London: Arrow Books

Life Line Trainees' Manual. 1980. Cape Town: Life Line

Mernissi, Fatima. 1994. *The Harem Within: Tales of a Moroccan Childhood*. London: Bantam Books

Powell, John. 1975. *Why Am I Afraid to Tell You Who I Am?* London: Fontana

Rajavi, Maryam. 1995. *Islam and Women's Equality*. Paris: Foreign Affairs Committee of the National Council of Resistance of Iran.

Shah, Idries. 1972. *The Magic Monastery*. London: Cape

Sherrard, Phillip. 1976. 'Modern Science and the Dehumanization of Man'. *Studies in Comparative Religion* 10 (2), 74–92

Tagore, Rabindranath.1912. *Gitanjali*. Calcutta: n.p.

Tracy, David, 1987. *Plurality and Ambiguity*. New York: Harper & Row

INDEX